# Take-Home Leveled Readers

Below-level

# Science

PEARSON

Scott Foresman

Editorial Offices: Glenview, Illinois • Parsippany, New Jersey • New York, New York
Sales Ofices: Needham, Massachusetts • Duluth, Georgia • Glenview, Illinois
Coppell, Texas • Sacramento, California • Mesa, Arizona

sfsuccessnet.com

ISBN: 0-328-19727-0



2 3 4 5 6 7 8 9 10 V004 13 12 11 10 09 08 07 06 05

# Table of Contents

# To the Teacher

Scott Foresman provides three Leveled Readers for every chapter of *Scott Foresman Science*, Grades 1–6: a *Below-Level Leveled Reader*, an *On-Level Leveled Reader*, and an *Advanced Leveled Reader*.

All three readers teach the same science concepts, same vocabulary, address the same target reading skill and contain the same graphic organizer as the corresponding student edition chapter, just at three different reading levels—providing access to important science content for all students. The On-level and Advanced readers also use additional examples to enrich the chapter and extend ideas

This book contains reproducible copies of the Below-Level Leveled Readers for Grade 4. These are designed for you to reproduce and send home with your students as appropriate. Encourage students to share these books with parents or family members in order to practice reading skills and reinforce science content.

Online versions of these and other readers are also available through the Scott Foresman Leveled Reader Database.

# Classifying Plants and Animals

by Camille La Vouché



| Genre | Comprehension Skill | Text Features | Science Content |
|---|---|---|---|
| Nonfiction | Compare and Contrast | • Labels<br>• Captions<br>• Charts<br>• Glossary | Classifying Plants and Animals |

**Scott Foresman Science 4.1**

## What did you learn?

**1.** What parts does a plant cell have that an animal cell does not have?

**2.** What are six kingdoms used for classification?

**3.** How does an animal get its scientific name?

**4.** **Writing** in Science  Animals have adaptations to help them survive in their environment. Describe on your own paper adaptations that some animals have to protect themselves from predators. Use examples from the book to support your answer.

**5.** **Compare and Contrast** How are vascular and nonvascular plants the same? How are they different?


**Illustration:** 5 Robert Ulrich

**Photographs:** Every effort has been made to secure permission and provide appropriate credit for photographic material. The publisher deeply regrets any omission and pledges to correct errors called to its attention in subsequent editions. Unless otherwise acknowledged, all photographs are the property of Scott Foresman, a division of Pearson Education. Photo locators denoted as follows: Top (T), Center (C), Bottom (B), Left (L), Right (R) Background (Bkgd)

Opener: ©Zig Leszczynski/Animals Animals/Earth Scenes; Title Page: ©John Conrad/Corbis; 4 (CL) ©Carolina Biological/Visuals Unlimited, (BL) ©SIU/Visuals Unlimited, (BR) ©Alfred Pasieka/Photo Researchers, Inc.; 6 (CR) ©Stephen Dalton/NHPA Limited, (BR) Getty Images; 7 (TL) ©T. Beveridge/ Visuals Unlimited, (TC) ©L. Stannard/Photo Researchers, Inc., (TR) ©Eric Grave/Phototake, (BL) Getty Images, (BC) ©Craig Tuttle/Corbis, (BR) ©Ken Cole/Animals Animals/Earth Scenes; 8 (CL) Getty Images, (BL) ©Kevin Schafer/Corbis; 9 (TL) Getty Images, (TL) ©Ken Cole/Animals Animals/Earth Scenes, (TC) ©John Conrad/Corbis, (TR, TC, B) ©DK Images, (TC) ©Ray Richardson/Animals Animals/Earth Scenes, (TL) ©Kevin Schafer/Corbis; 10 (L) Sue Atkinson/©DK Images, (BL) ©John Durham/Photo Researchers, Inc.; 11 (TL) Karl Shone/©DK Images, (BL) ©DK Images, (CL) Lee W. Wilcox; 12 (CR) Getty Images, (BR) ©DK Images; 13 ©Wolfgang Kaehler/Corbis; 14 (CL) Getty Images, (CL) ©Jane Burton/DK Images, (CL, BL) ©DK Images, (BL) ©Ray Richardson/Animals Animals/Earth Scenes; 15 (CL, BR) ©DK Images; 16 (CL, BC) ©DK Images, (TR) ©Jim Tuten/Animals Animals/Earth Scenes; 17 (T, BL) ©DK Images; 18 (CL) ©DK Images, (BL) ©Andrew Syred/Photo Researchers, Inc., (BC) Jerry Young/©DK Images, (BR) ©F. J. Jackson/Robert Harding Picture Library Ltd., (CR) Dave King/©DK Images; 19 (CL, BR, BL) ©Dwight R. Kuhn, (CR) ©Chase Swift/Corbis; 20 ©DK Images; 21 (CL) ©Ray Richardson/Animals Animals/ Earth Scenes, (BR) ©DK Images; 22 (BR) ©Ralph A. Clevenger/Corbis, (TR) ©Ray Richardson/Animals Animals/Earth Scenes; 23 ©Anup Shah/Nature Picture Library.

ISBN: 0-328-13859-2

**Glossary**

| | |
|---|---|
| **cell** | the smallest unit of a living thing that can carry out all life functions |
| **chloroplast** | the part of a plant cell that traps energy from the Sun |
| **cytoplasm** | the gel-like substance in a cell that has what the cell needs to do its job |
| **genus** | a group of closely related living things |
| **invertebrates** | animals without backbones |
| **nucleus** | the control center of a cell |
| **species** | a group of similar organisms that can mate and produce offspring |
| **vertebrates** | animals with backbones |

# Classifying Plants and Animals

**by Camille La Vouché**

# What are the building blocks of life?

## What Cells Are

A **cell** is the smallest unit of a living thing. A cell can carry out life functions. All living things are made of cells. Some are made of one cell. Plants and animals have many cells. Cells are the building blocks of life.

Cells have jobs. Cells can help a living thing use energy, grow, and reproduce. Some cells keep a living thing healthy. Cells can develop only from other cells.

You can use microscopes to see cells. A microscope makes objects look bigger than they are. Scientists look at cells through a microscope. Then they learn many things about cells.

A microscope helps scientists see the details of a cell.

## How Animals Learn

Some behavior must be learned. Young animals learn by watching their parents or other adults.

## Parents Teach Offspring

Young animals can learn to hunt by watching their parents. A young lion practices pouncing on prey by pouncing on its mother's tail.

## Offspring Teach Parents

Some adult animals learn from their young. A young monkey taught adult monkeys how to wash sand off their food.

## Learned and Inherited

Some behaviors are inherited and learned. The white-crowned sparrow is born knowing how to sing. But it must learn the song its species sings.

## Animal Instincts

Instincts are behaviors that animals inherit from parents. Instincts help animals meet their needs. Ducklings have the instinct to follow their mother. This is how they get food and protection.

## Migration

Food can be hard to find in places where the winter is cold. Migration is traveling to find food or a place to reproduce.

Migration can be difficult. Some amphibians may have to cross busy roads when they migrate. Some animals must travel long distances to escape the cold winter.

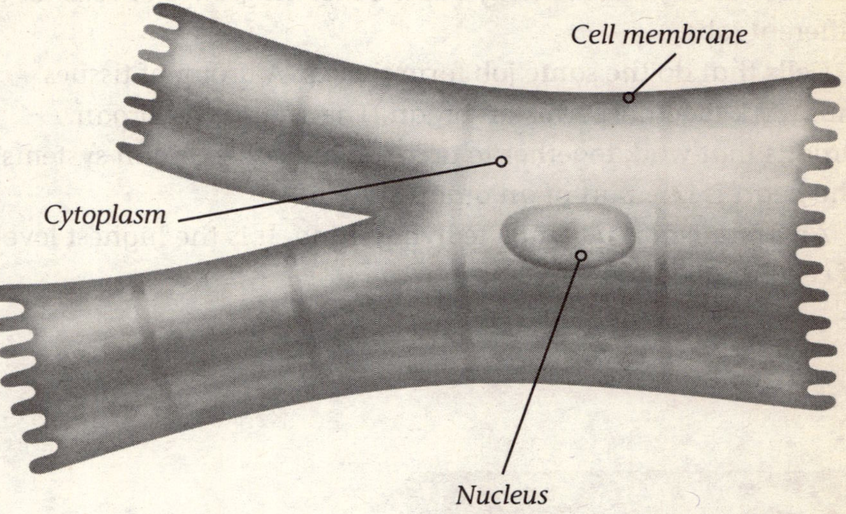

Canada geese migrating

## Hibernation and Inactivity

Some animals become inactive during very cold weather. This inactivity is called hibernation. It is an instinct. Some hibernating animals save energy by moving very little. Others do not move at all.

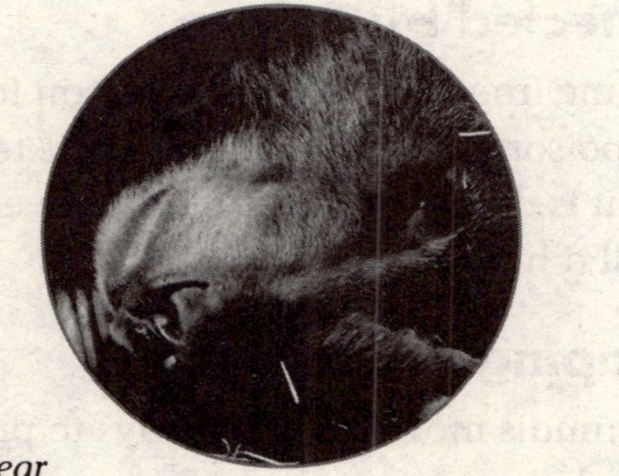

Bear hibernating



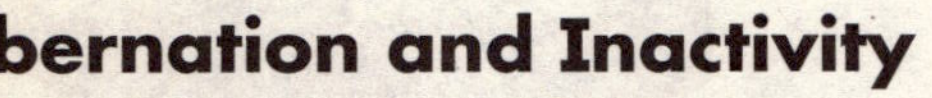


The size and shape of a cell are related to the cell's job.

## The Parts of a Cell

Animals such as eagles and elephants do not look alike. They are made of cells. These cells have parts that are alike. Each part of a cell has a job.

Plant cells and animal cells have a nucleus, cytoplasm, and a cell membrane. The **nucleus** tells the cell what to do. **Cytoplasm** is a gel-like material. It has what the cell needs to do its job. The cell membrane is the border of the cell. It separates the cell from what is outside of it.

# Cells Working Together

Cells are organized into groups. Different groups of cells do different jobs.

Cells that do the same job form tissues. A group of tissues that work together forms an organ. The heart is an organ. Organs that work together to do a job are called organ systems. The heart is one part of an organ system.

An organism is a complete living thing. It is the highest level of cell organization.

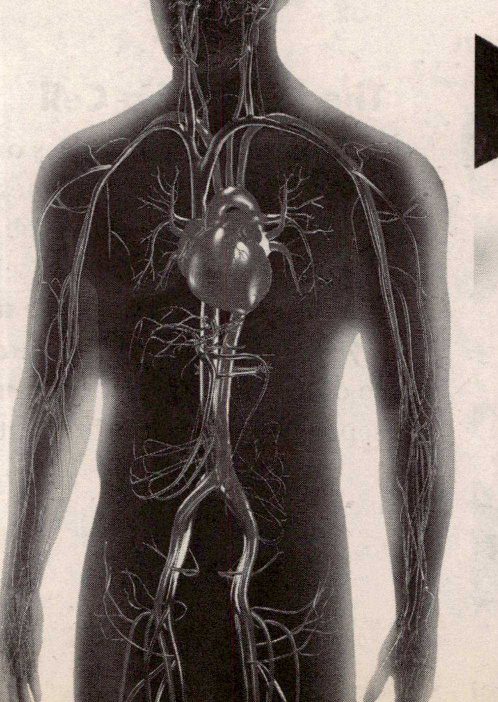

A group of one kind of cell is a tissue. Each kind of tissue does a certain job.

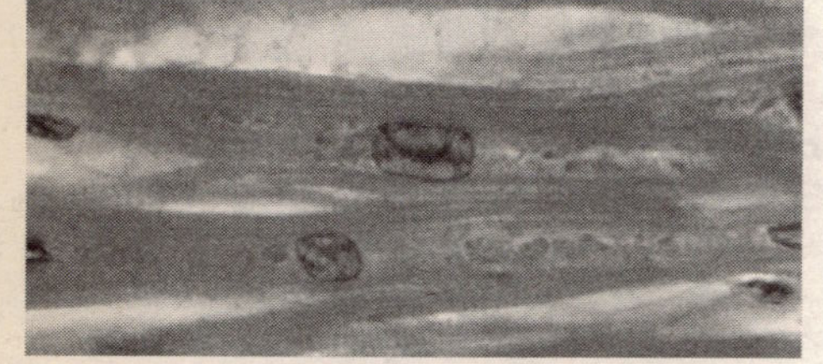

A group of tissues that work together is an organ. The heart is one organ in an animal.

Many organs work together in an organ system. The heart, blood, and blood vessels are some parts of one system.

# Adaptations that Protect Animals

An animal's color can help it blend into its surroundings. This helps it hide from predators. A bright color can mean an animal is poisonous. Some animals have quills or hard shells for protection.

## Blending In

Colors, shapes, and patterns can hide an animal. The rock ptarmigan has dark feathers in the summer. In the winter it has white feathers. It blends with the snow.

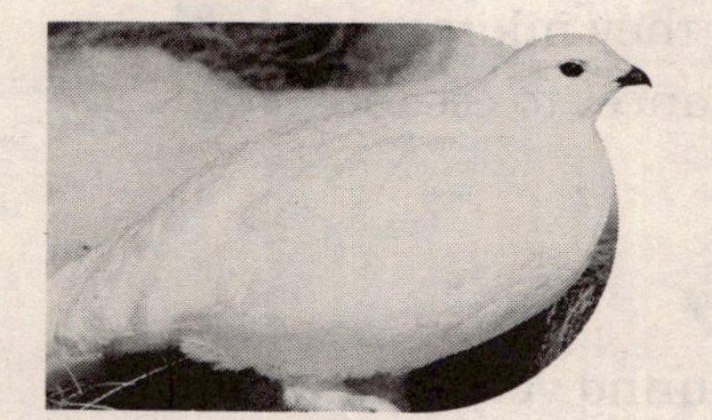

Rock ptarmigan in winter

Rock ptarmigan in summer

## Protected by Poison

Some frogs and toads use poison for protection. The poison-dart frog's bright colors tell predators that it is dangerous. It can produce enough poison to kill a human!

## Escaping Predators

Animals move in many ways to protect themselves. Birds' wings help them fly away from predators. Fish have fins that help them swim away. Some animals can run for a long time.

# How do animals adapt?

## How Animals Get What They Need

Young animals inherit traits, or physical features, from their parents. A physical feature or behavior that helps an animal survive and reproduce is an adaptation. All animals need food, water, oxygen, and shelter. Animals that adapt well have a better chance to survive and reproduce.

## Birds' Adaptations

Birds have feathers to help them fly. The shape of birds' beaks helps them get food. Ducks have webbed feet to help them swim.

## Other Adaptations

Polar bears have thick coats of fur to keep them warm. They have sharp teeth and claws to catch and hold food.

Plant cells have parts that animal cells do not have. Plant cells have chloroplasts. A **chloroplast** traps energy from the Sun. This energy helps the plant make its own food.

Each plant cell has a cell wall. The cell wall is a layer outside the cell membrane. It supports the plant cell. It also protects the plant cell.

### A Plant Cell

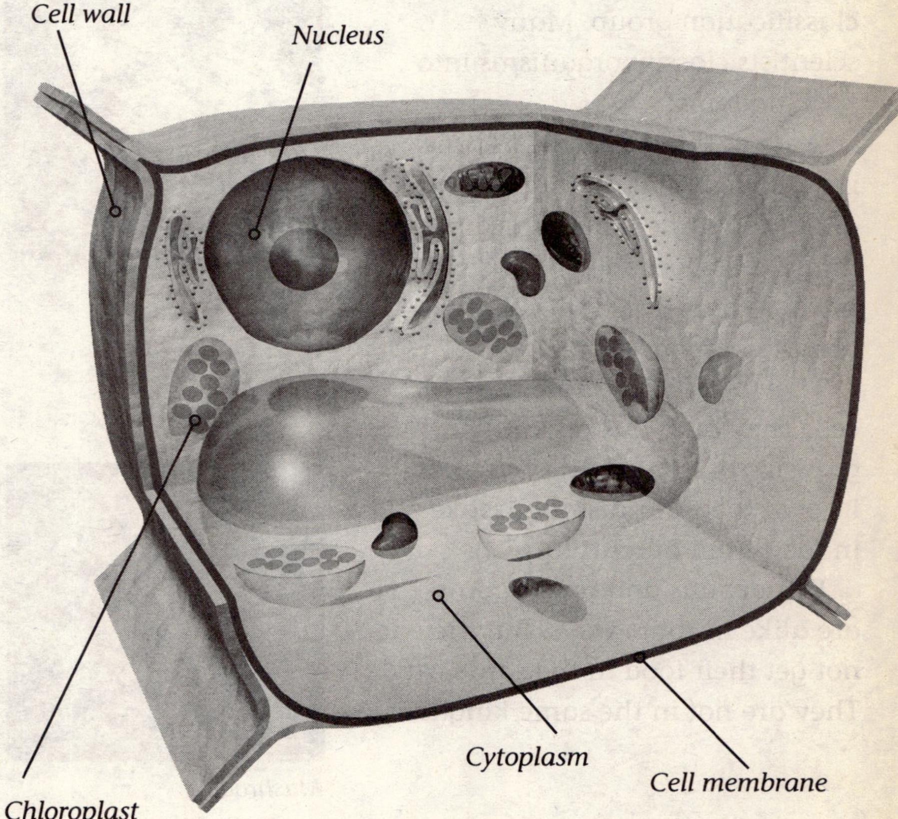

# How are living things grouped?

## Classification Systems

Scientists sort living things into groups. Organisms in the same group have things in common.

## Kingdoms

A kingdom is the largest classification group. Many scientists classify organisms into six kingdoms.

Answer these questions to see if a dandelion and a mushroom are in the same kingdom. How many cells does the organism have? Where does it live? How does it get food?

They both have more than one cell. They both live on land and grow in soil. A dandelion makes its own food. A mushroom takes in food from other things.

Dandelions and mushrooms are alike in some ways. But they do not get their food in the same way. They are not in the same kingdom.

*Dandelions*

*Mushrooms*

## Mollusks

A snail is a mollusk. It has a muscular structure called a foot. The foot oozes a slimy liquid. This helps the snail move. Some mollusks, such as oysters, do not move far. Some are good swimmers.

The largest invertebrate is the giant squid. It can be 15 meters, or 50 feet, long.

## The Life Cycle of the Brown Snail

Mother snails dig nests to lay eggs. They can lay 85 eggs in a nest. The eggs hatch in two to four weeks. A newly-hatched snail has to get its own food. First, it will eat its own eggshell. It will then eat other eggs. Snails live for about ten years.

1. The brown garden snail lays its eggs.

2. The eggs hatch in two to four weeks.

3. Newly hatched snails must find food to grow.

4. Adult snails reproduce and the life cycle begins again.

# Kingdoms of Living Things

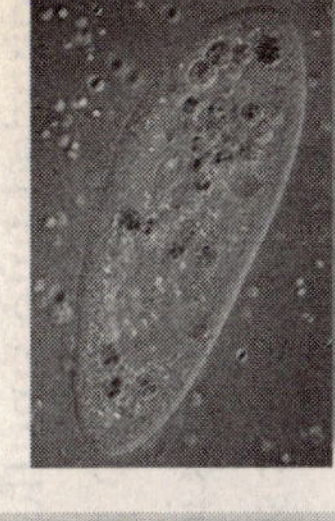

**Protists**
Most protists have one cell. They have a nucleus and other cell parts. Some get food. Others make their own. Algae and paramecia are protists.

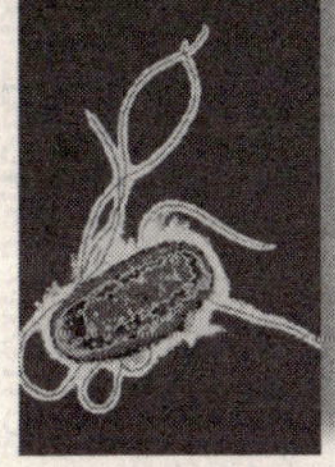

**True Bacteria**
True bacteria have one cell. They have no separate nucleus. They live in water or on land. Some get food. Others make their own food.

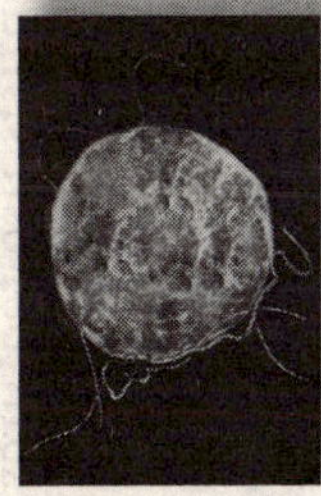

**Ancient Bacteria**
Ancient bacteria are made of one cell. They have no separate nucleus. They live in water or on land. They make their own food.

**Animals**
Animals have many cells. The cells make up tissues, organs, and organ systems. Animals live in water or on land. They eat plants and other animals.

**Plants**
Plants have many cells. Each cell has a nucleus and other parts. The cells form tissues and organs. Plants live on land or in water. They use sunlight to make food. Dandelions are plants.

**Fungi**
Fungi have many cells. Each cell has a nucleus and other parts. Fungi absorb food from other living or nonliving things. They live on land. Mushrooms are fungi.



---

## Invertebrates

Animals with no backbones are called **invertebrates.** Jellyfish, worms, spiders, snails, and clams are invertebrates. They have soft bodies.

## Arthropods and More

Arthropods are animals with jointed legs. They are the largest group of invertebrates. Their legs and bodies are in sections. Insects, spiders, and crabs are arthropods. They have a hard, lightweight outer skin called an exoskeleton.

## Spiders

Spiders are arthropods. They have eight legs. They have two main body parts. They can spin silk. Most spiders use this silk to make webs. Webs trap their prey.

**Scientists have identified more than one million species of invertebrates.**

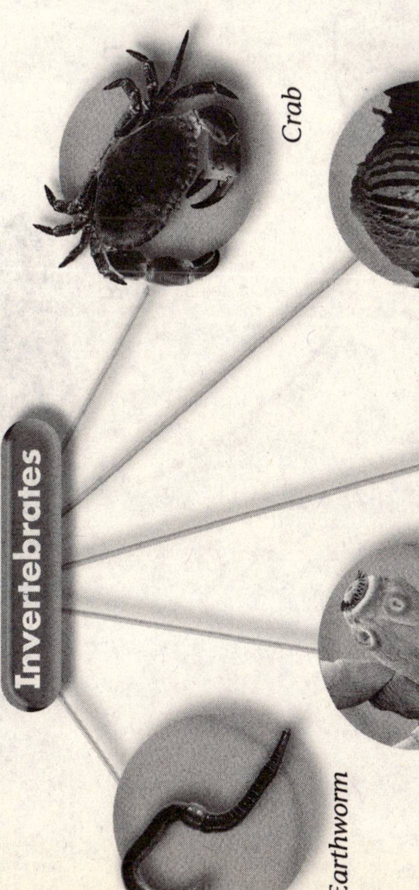

## Getting More Specific

Kingdoms are made up of smaller groups. Each group is then divided into smaller and smaller groups. Scientists use features of an organism to put it into groups.

Genus and species are the two smallest groups. They make up an organism's scientific name. A **genus** is a group of closely related plants or animals. A **species** is a group of similar organisms that can mate and produce offspring. The species name usually comes from a feature, such as the color of the organism or where it lives.

## Members of the Cat Family

Most scientific names are Latin words. An animal's scientific name is the same all over the world. The house cat and the black-footed cat are both in the *Felis* genus. But they are different species. The house cat's species is *domesticus*, or "of the house." The black-footed cat's species is *nigripes*, or "black feet."

The scientific name of this house cat is *Felis domesticus*.

The scientific name of this black-footed cat is *Felis nigripes*.

The python grows and reproduces. It can live as long as 25 years.

Soon the mother leaves, and the young python must care for itself.

# Life Cycle of a Reptile

The Burmese python is a long, thick snake. It can be six meters (about twenty feet) long. It is not poisonous. It uses heat sensors on its upper lip to find food. It has a strong sense of smell. A python squeezes its prey and swallows it whole. The Burmese python can swallow animals whose bodies are larger than its own head.

A female python can lay as many as 100 eggs.

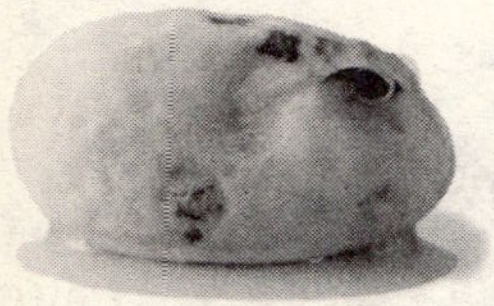

The mother python wraps herself around her eggs to keep them warm.

The young python hatches in about six to eight weeks.

## The Animal Kingdom

Kingdom

Division

Class

Order

Family

Genus

Species

# How are plants classified?

## How Plants Transport Water And Nutrients

Bamboo is very tall. How do the cells at the top of this tall plant get water and nutrients from the soil? The plant has tubelike structures. The tubes bring water and nutrients to every part of the plant. Plants that have these tubes are called vascular plants. Grass, dandelions, and trees are vascular plants.

Vascular tissue also supports the plant's stems and leaves. The plant is able to grow larger.

Tubelike structures

The tissues of this bamboo slice can only be seen with a microscope.



## Reptiles

Reptiles are one group of vertebrates. They live in water and on land. Alligators, crocodiles, snakes, lizards, and turtles are reptiles. Reptiles have lungs for breathing. Their dry skin has scales or plates all over.

Alligators and crocodiles look alike. But they are different. The long teeth in an alligator's bottom jaw cannot be seen when its mouth is shut. A crocodile's teeth can be seen when its mouth is shut.

The python has a very long backbone.

# How are animals classified?

## Animals with Backbones

The animal kingdom is made up of two groups. Animals that have backbones are in one group. They are called **vertebrates.** There are five kinds of vertebrates.

### Vertebrates

| | |
|---|---|
| **Fish**  | Fish usually have scales. They live only in water. Fish get oxygen mostly w th gills. Fish are cold-blooded. Most lay eggs. |
| **Amphibians**  | Amphibians are covered with skin. They can live on land and in the water. To breathe, they use lungs or gills or both. They are cold-blooded. Amphibians hatch from eggs. |
| **Reptiles**  | Reptiles have scales. Most reptiles live on land. Some can live in water. They use lungs to breathe. Reptiles are cold-blooded. They usually lay eggs. |
| **Birds**  | Birds have feathers. They usually live on land. Many birds spend much time in water. Birds use lungs to breathe. They are warm-blooded. All birds lay eggs. |
| **Mammals**  | Mammals have hair or fur. Mos- live on land. A few live in water. They breathe with lungs. Mammals are warm-blooded; they make their own heat. Most mammals have live births. |





## More Down-to-Earth Plants

Plants that do not have tubelike structures are nonvascular plants. They cannot grow very tall. They do not have real roots, stems, or leaves. Water and nutrients move from one cell to the next cell.

### Mosses

Mosses are the largest group of nonvascular plants. They make their own food. Some can live in low temperatures.

### Hornworts

Hornworts do not have true stems or leaves. They tend to live in warm places.

### Liverworts

Liverworts grow on moist rocks or soil by streams. Some have a spicy smell. Some look like flat leaves. Some have the shape of a liver.

## How Plants Make New Plants

Scientists also classify plants by how they reproduce, or make new plants. Some plants reproduce using seeds. Other plants reproduce using spores.

## Flowers and Seeds

Many plants with flowers or cones make seeds. A seed has a young plant and food inside of it. Most seeds come from flowering plants. Seeds can have different shapes and sizes. A cactus, a fruit tree, and a poppy are flowering plants.

The pod of a soybean holds two or three seeds or beans.

## Cones and Seeds

Conifers are plants that make seeds without flowers. Conifers can grow cones. Some cones make pollen. Some cones make seeds. Evergreen plants are conifers. They do not lose their leaves, or needles, during the year.

A pine cone holds the seeds and pollen of a conifer.

## Spores

Ferns and mosses are plants that do not make seeds. They make tiny cells. The tiny cells become new plants. These cells are called spores. A spore might become a new plant if it falls into a shady, moist place. It will get nutrients there.

Spore cases look like brown dots or streaks under a fern's leaves. The spore cases hold hundreds of spores.

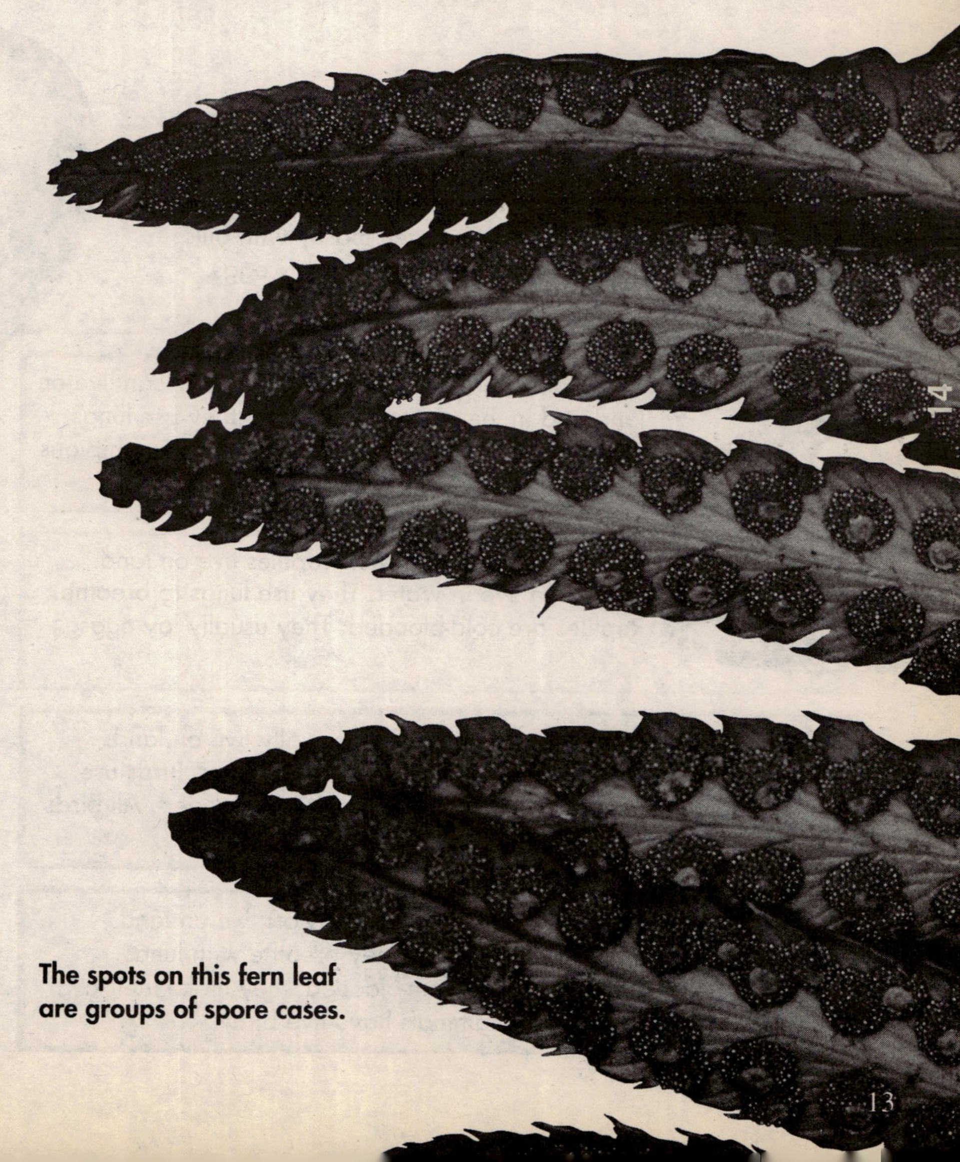

The spots on this fern leaf are groups of spore cases.

Science Science

# Energy from Plants

by James Anderson



| Genre | Comprehension Skill | Text Features | Science Content |
| --- | --- | --- | --- |
| Nonfiction | Draw Conclusions | • Captions<br>• Labels<br>• Text Boxes<br>• Glossary | Plants |

Scott Foresman Science 4.2

PEARSON
Scott Foresman

scottforesman.com

DK

ISBN 0-328-13862-2

90000

9 780328 138623

# Vocabulary

chlorophyll

dormant

fertilization

ovary

photosynthesis

pistil

sepal

stamen

## What did you learn?

1. What are some things a plant needs to survive?

2. What is chlorophyll? What does it do for a plant?

3. Why are roots important for a plant?

4. **Writing** in Science  Flowers have four main parts that are used in reproduction. Describe on your own paper what these parts are and what role they have in reproduction. Include details from the book to support your answer.

5. **Draw Conclusions** If you see a plant beginning to grow, what can you conclude about its environment?

**Illustration:** 4 Robert Ulrich
**Photographs:** Every effort has been made to secure permission and provide appropriate credit for photographic material. The publisher deeply regrets any omission and pledges to correct errors called to its attention in subsequent editions. Unless otherwise acknowledged, all photographs are the property of Scott Foresman, a division of Pearson Education. Photo locators denoted as follows: Top (T), Center (C), Bottom (B), Left (L), Right (R) Background (Bkgd)
Opener: (CR) ©Richard LaVal/Animals Animals/Earth Scenes, (CL) Getty Images, (Bkgd) PhotoLibrary; Title Page: ©DK Images; 2 ©George D. Lepp/Corbis; 4 (R) ©DK Images, (BR) ©TH Foto-Werbung/Photo Researchers, Inc.; 7 ©DK Images; 8 (BL) Brand X Pictures, (R) ©DK Images; 9 (C) ©Carolina Biological/ Visuals Unlimited, (R) ©DK Images; 10 (B, CL) ©Royalty-Free/Corbis; 12 ©Merlin Tuttle/BCI/Photo Researchers, Inc.; 15 ©John Kaprielian/Photo Researchers, Inc.; 16 (CL, C, CR) ©DK Images; 17 (TL, CR) ©DK Images; 18 (B) ©DK Images, (L) Stephen Oliver/©DK Images; 19 ©Merlin Tuttle/BCI/Photo Researchers, Inc.; 20 ©Ed Reschke/Peter Arnold, Inc.; 21 ©Dwight R. Kuhn; 22 (L, BR) ©DK Images, (BC) Brand X Pictures; 23 (BL, R) ©DK Images.

ISBN: 0-328-13862-2

# Energy from Plants

## by James Anderson

## Glossary

**chlorophyll** the material that makes plants green and takes in energy from the Sun to make food

**dormant** in a state of rest

**fertilization** the process in which a sperm cell and an egg cell come together

**ovary** the part of the pistil of a plant that produces egg cells

**photosynthesis** the process in which plants use sunlight, carbon dioxide, and water to make food for themselves

**pistil** the female part of the plant

**sepal** a small green leaf below the petals that covers and protects a flower

**stamen** the male part of a plant that produces pollen

# What are plants' characteristics?

## Plant Cells

How are a giant redwood tree in California and a small dandelion alike? They are both living things. They both have many cells. They are both in the plant kingdom.

The redwood tree and the dandelion are also different. The redwood tree grows about 90 meters tall. The dandelion comes a little above your ankle.

## Grafting

An apple grower may have an apple tree that grows good apples but has weak roots. Another apple tree may have strong roots but bad apples. The apple grower can join together branches from each tree. This is called grafting. Grafting will work only if the tubes that carry food, water, and nutrients in the plant match up. Then new tubes will grow.

Plants have many different parts that work together as a system. Throughout their lives, they are always growing and changing.

Hyacinth

Potato plant

## New Plants From Plant Parts

Some plants grow from leaves, roots, or stems. These plants are usually just like the parent plant.

A tulip starts as a bulb. A bulb is an underground stem. It is made of thick layers of leaves that store food. The leaves grow up out of the soil. They turn green and make food.

Smaller plants can grow right on the leaves of a parent plant. The piggyback plant is one such plant. A potato may have sprouts growing on its buds. These sprouts can become new potato plants.

## New Plants from Stems

Some plants have stems called runners. Runners grow along the ground. Roots grow from some spots on the runners, and leaves develop. These leaves are new plants. Strawberries have runners.

Look at a piece of a redwood tree and a piece of a dandelion under a microscope. They have similar parts that are similar sizes. These parts are cells. Plants are made of cells. Plant cells are grouped into tissues. Tissues that work together form organs.

Plants have many parts. Some parts take in water and materials from soil. Other parts use energy from the Sun to turn water and materials into food. Other parts move food to cells throughout the plant.

*Crown Imperial lily*

*Amaryllis*

*Strawberry*

## How Plants Make Food

Plants need sunlight and water to live, grow, and reproduce. They need carbon dioxide from the air. They also need mineral nutrients from the soil.

## Photosynthesis

Plants make their own food. The food is sugar. **Photosynthesis** is the process of making this sugar. For photosynthesis, plants need carbon dioxide from the air. They need water from the soil.

There are tubes in the stem of the plant. Water and nutrients move through the tubes from the roots to the leaves. Plants use energy from the Sun to change these materials into food.

## A Two-Step Cycle

Some plants with spores reproduce in two steps. First, the plant produces a spore. The spore can germinate. It grows into a plant with both male and female cells. The male and female cell combine. This is the second step. This produces a fertilized egg that grows into a plant.

Spore cases hold spores. These cases can burst. This releases many spores into the air. The spores may land near the parent plant. They may drift far away. The spores will stay dormant until the conditions are right. Then the spores can begin to grow into new plants.

## Starting to Grow

A seed may not grow as soon as it falls to the ground. The environment must be right for the seed to grow. A seed needs water, oxygen, and the right temperature.

A seed holds a young plant. Food in the seed gives the plant the energy it needs to begin growing. If a seed does not have everything it needs, it rests, or stays **dormant**, and does not grow. It can stay dormant for a long time.

## Spores

Some plants do not grow from seeds. They grow from spores. A spore is made of only one cell. You can only see it with a microscope. It stores very little food. A spore must have the right environment to grow. A spore needs wet ground and constant moisture. Then it can become a new plant.







Oxygen and water are left when photosynthesis is complete. They move in and out of plant leaves through tiny holes in the bottom of the leaves.

The tubes also move sugar to parts of the plant that need food. Roots, stems, and leaves store extra sugar.

## Chloroplasts

Photosynthesis happens in the chloroplasts of the cells in leaves. Chloroplasts have **chlorophyll.** This makes them green. Chlorophyll takes in energy from the Sun. Plants use this energy to turn water, carbon dioxide, and mineral nutrients into sugar, oxygen, and other food material.

### Cross Section of a Leaf

# What are the parts of plants?

## The Roles of Leaves and Stems

Groups of cells do certain jobs. Some cells make food. Some carry nutrients through the plant. Cells that do the same job make tissues. Wood is a tissue. Tissues work together to make organs. Roots, stems, and leaves are all organs. Most plants including the redwood tree and the dandelion have these parts.

### Leaves

Leaves make food for a plant. Leaves can be different shapes and sizes. The different sizes and shapes help plants live in different environments. A pine tree has thin, sharp needles. This keeps them from losing too much water. A banana plant can have leaves that are wider than a kitchen table!

Leaves may be different shapes and sizes. But they all produce food for the plant.

Most leaves are flat on top to catch as much sunlight as possible. The leaves use the energy of sunlight to make food.

## Wind as a Helper

Dandelion puffs are made of small white threads. These threads catch in the wind and fly far away. Cottonweed puffs and milkweed plants also have these threads.

Maple trees have wing-shaped fruits. They twirl through the air. Tumbleweeds blow across the land in the southwestern part of the United States. Seeds fall off the plant.

## Water as a Helper

Some seeds are carried by water. Coconuts are the fruits of one kind of palm tree. They can float on water to new places. There the seed may become a tree.

Seeds can move in many ways. Yet most seeds do not grow into new plants.

Animals can help move seeds from one place to another.

## Seeds on the Move

Suppose all the cherries on a cherry tree fell to the ground. Many of the seeds would start to grow. Some seeds would grow better if they were farther away from the parent tree. Then they could get more water, nutrients, and sunlight. Many plants have adaptations that allow their seeds to be moved.

## Animal Helpers

Some animals eat fruits with seeds. The seeds in the animals' droppings are then left at new places. Some fruits have tiny hooks that attach to animals' fur. The fruits fall off the animals. The seeds are moved to new places. Some animals bury seeds and nuts for the winter. These seeds and nuts may grow where they are buried.

## Stems

A tree trunk is similar to the stalk of a grass plant. Both are stems. Stems have two important jobs. They move food, water, and minerals between the roots and the leaves. They also hold the plant up so its leaves can get sunlight.

A tree trunk is a hard stem. It grows thick and strong. It can support a large plant. Bark is made of a layer of dead cells. Bark protects the plant.

Some stems are soft. They bend easily. Daisies and dandelions have soft stems. These stems are often green. They carry out photosynthesis.

## The Roles of the Roots

Roots hold a plant in the ground. Roots take in mineral nutrients and water from the soil. Roots do not make food. They have no chlorophyll. Some roots can store food. This food is used when the plant cannot produce enough food through photosynthesis.

## Fibrous Roots

Roots need water and nutrients. Roots grow away from the stem. The roots of some plants spread in many directions. They form a fibrous root system. These roots can take in water and mineral nutrients from a large area. Trees and most grasses have fibrous roots.

*Onions*

*Daisies*

**Fibrous roots do not grow thick or deep. They spread out to find what the plant needs.**

**The seedling grows into an adult plant. The plant inherits the color of the flowers from its parents.**

**The plant might flower and make seeds for many years. Eventually, the plant will die. Its life cycle will be complete.**

**When a flower is pollinated it produces fertilized eggs. These eggs develop into seeds. The new seeds germinate. The cycle begins again.**

A seed may not grow as soon as it falls to the ground. A seed will only sprout when its environment is the right temperature. The seed also needs the right amount of oxygen and water in order to start to grow. If it does grow, the roots will grow into the ground. This is because of gravity. The new stem will grow upward. It grows toward the sunlight.

# What is the life cycle of a plant?

## Life Cycle of a Flowering Plant

Different plants live for different periods of time. A tomato plant may only live for a few months. A bristlecone pine tree can live for more than 4,000 years! A plant's life cycle includes every change a plant goes through during its life.

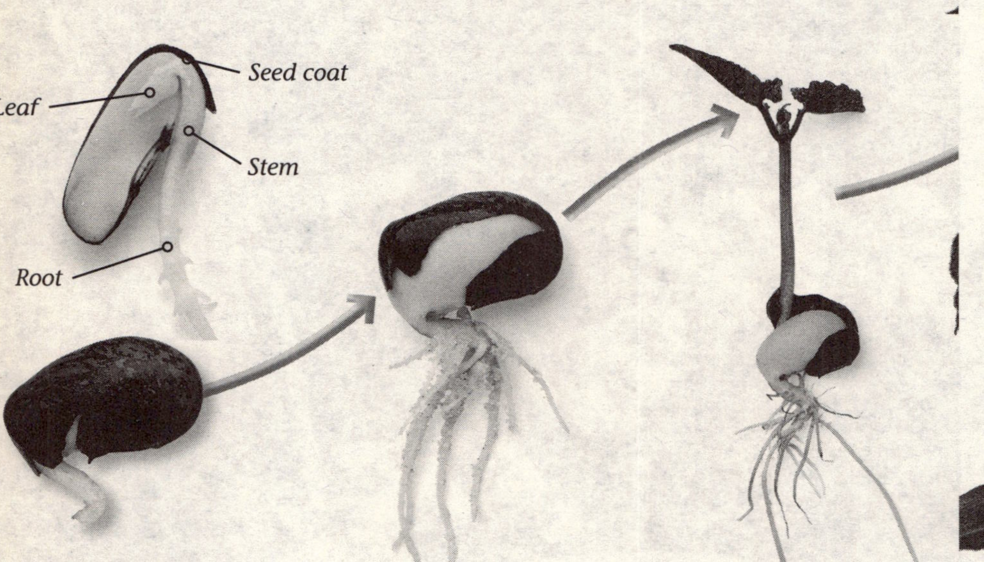


When a seed begins to grow, or germinate, it takes in water. It swells. The seed coat opens.

The young plant inside the seed uses stored food to grow. The first root and the first stem push through the seed coat.

The leaves grow. They make food for the plant through photosynthesis. The stem and roots grow. More leaves form.



## Taproots

Plants such as dandelions, turnips, and carrots have a large main root called a taproot. A taproot grows straight down. It takes in water and nutrients from the soil. The root becomes thicker when it stores food. Smaller roots grow from the side of a taproot.

A root has tiny hairs sticking out around it. These root hairs allow the root to take in more mineral nutrients and water.

**Tiny root hairs take in water and mineral nutrients.**

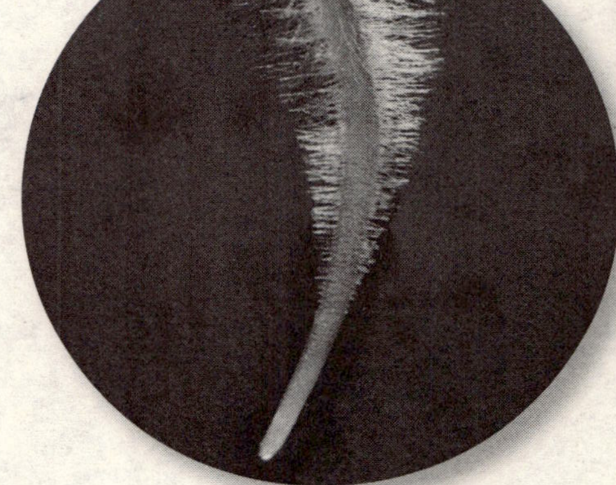

Radish

## Plants Without Roots

Some plants are able to get what they need without roots. They are called air plants. They take in moisture from the air. They take in nutrients from dust in the air. Spanish moss is an air plant.

# How do plants reproduce?

## Parts of Flowers

Scientists classify plants in many ways. One way is by how they make new plants, or reproduce. Plants that reproduce are put into two groups. Plants that make seeds are in one group. This group contains flowering plants and conifers.

Most flowers have four main parts. The easiest part to see is the petal. Petals can be colorful. They protect the seed-making parts. They attract living things such as bees, birds, and butterflies.

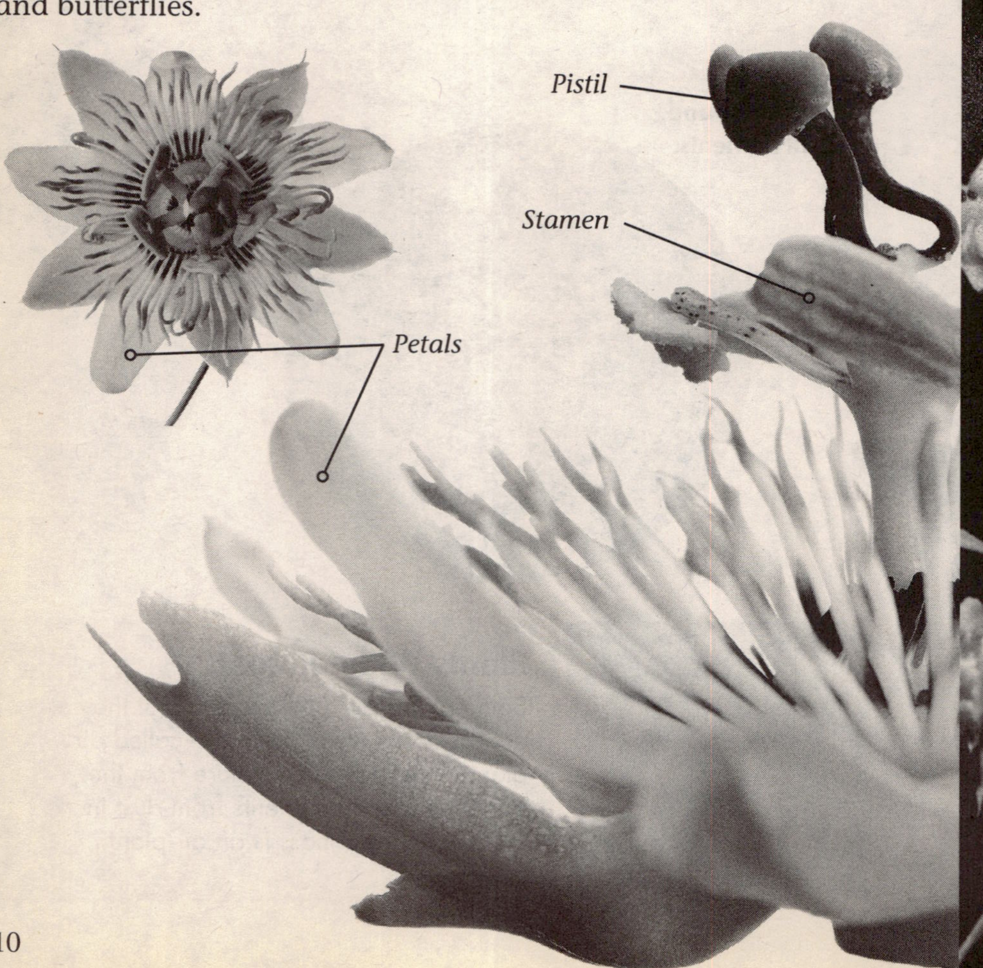


The wind pollinates grasses and most trees. The wind moves the pollen from stamens to pistils. Plants that use wind for pollination do not attract animals. They do not have bright colors or sweet scents. They make a lot of pollen for the wind to carry. This way, at least a few grains of pollen will land on another flower.

## Fertilization

A flower changes after fertilization. The petals and stamens dry up and fall off. The plant does not need them. Inside the ovary, the fertilized egg becomes a seed. The ovary gets bigger. It may become a fruit. This fruit protects the seed or seeds. Some fruits are moist and fleshy, such as apples or grapes. Some are dry and hard, such as a peanut shell. When the fruit is ripe, the seeds can form new plants.

**One ragweed plant can release more than one million grains of pollen into the air.**





Small green leaves grow below the petals. Each leaf is called a **sepal.** The sepals cover and protect the flower bud. The sepals are pushed apart as the flower bud opens.

At the center of the flower are small, knoblike parts. These parts make up the **pistil.** The pistil is the female part of the plant. It makes egg cells.

Smaller stalks are around the pistil. Each stalk is a **stamen.** The stamens are the male parts of the plant. They have structures called anthers at their tips. Anthers make tiny grains of pollen. The sperm in the pollen combines with the egg cells in the pistil to make seeds.

### Incomplete Flowers

Some flowers do not have the four main parts. The corn plant has two kinds of flowers. One is a male flower with stamens but no pistils. The other is a female flower that has pistils but no stamens.

## Pollen on the Move

A seed forms when pollen gets from a stamen to a pistil. Animals can help move pollen.

Nectar is a sweet liquid that flowers make. This is food for bees, birds, butterflies, and bats. They are drawn to the nectar by the scent of a flower and the color of its petals.

While the animal eats, pollen on the stamens rubs onto its body. That pollen may then rub onto the pistil of the next flower the animal visits. So the pollen moves from one plant to another. This is called pollination.

When pollen lands on a pistil, a thin tube grows from the pollen down to the thick bottom part of the pistil. This bottom part is called the **ovary.** Egg cells are in the ovary. The sperm cells in the pollen move down the pollen tube into the ovary. A sperm cell and an egg cell come together. This is **fertilization.**

29

# Ecosystems

by Helen N. George

| Genre | Comprehension Skill | Text Features | Science Content |
|---|---|---|---|
| Nonfiction | Sequence | • Captions<br>• Call Outs<br>• Text Boxes<br>• Glossary | Ecosystems |

**Scott Foresman Science 4.3**

# Vocabulary

carnivores

community

decomposers

ecosystem

herbivores

niche

omnivores

population

## What did you learn?

1. What are some living things in an ecosystem? What are some nonliving things?

2. What is the major source of energy for life on Earth?

3. Why are decomposers important in an ecosystem?

4. **Writing** in Science  Food webs are made of several food chains. Look at the food web on pages 18 and 19. Describe on your paper how the energy moves through a food web. Use examples from the book to support your answer.

5. **Sequence** Describe the steps involved in the process of decay.

**Illustration:** Title Page, 4 Bob Kayganich
**Photographs:** Every effort has been made to secure permission and provide appropriate credit for photographic material. The publisher deeply regrets any omission and pledges to correct errors called to its attention in subsequent editions. Unless otherwise acknowledged, all photographs are the property of Scott Foresman, a division of Pearson Education. Photo locators denoted as follows: Top (T), Center (C), Bottom (B), Left (L), Right (R) Background (Bkgd)
Opener: ©Breck P. Kent/Animals Animals/Earth Scenes; 2 ©Andrew Brown/Ecoscene/Corbis; 4 ©Andrew Brown/Ecoscene/Corbis; 5 (TR) ©Michael Townsend/Getty Images, (CR) ©Steve Terrill/Corbis, (CR) ©David Muench/Corbis, (BR) ©David Keaton/Corbis; 7 (BR) ©Konrad Wothe/Minden Pictures, (B) ©George H. H. Huey/Corbis; 8 ©George H. H. Huey/Corbis; 9 (BR) ©D. Robert & Lorri Franz/Corbis, (CL) ©Tim Fitzharris/Minden Pictures; 10 (C) ©John Cancalosi/Nature Picture Library, (L) ©Buddy Mays/Corbis; 11 ©Jeff Foott/Nature Picture Library; 12 Getty Images; 13 ©Sally A. Morgan/Corbis; 14 (TR) ©Stephen J. Krasemann/DRK Photo, (BR, C) ©Kennan Ward/Corbis, (L) ©Michael Llewellyn/Getty Images; 15 (TC) Getty Images, (CL) ©Steve Kaufman/Corbis, (BL) ©Kevin Schafer/Corbis, (BR) ©Michael & Patricia Fogden/Corbis; 16 ©Randy Wells/Getty Images; 17 ©Roland Birke/Peter Arnold, Inc.; 18 (CL) ©Roland Birke/Peter Arnold, Inc., (TR) ©DK Images, (CR) © Royalty-Free/Corbis, (BC) British Antarctic Survey/SPL/Photo Researchers, Inc.; 19 (TL) © Royalty-Free/Corbis, (BC) ©George D. Lepp/Corbis, (TR) ©Joe McDonald/Corbis; 21 ©Raymond Gehman/Corbis; 23 ©Breck P. Kent/Animals Animals/Earth Scenes.

ISBN: 0-328-13865-7

Copyright © Pearson Education, Inc.

All Rights Reserved. Printed in the United States of America. The blackline masters in this publication are designed for use with appropriate equipment to reproduce copies for classroom use only. Scott Foresman grants permission to classroom teachers to reproduce from these masters.

2 3 4 5 6 7 8 9 10 V004 13 12 11 10 09 08 07 06 05

# Glossary

**carnivores**   consumers that get energy from eating animals

**community**   different populations that work together in an ecosystem

**decomposers**   organisms that break down dead organisms

**ecosystem**   all the living and nonliving things in an environment and how they interact

**herbivores**   consumers that get energy from eating plants

**niche**   the special role or job of an organism in its habitat

**omnivores**   consumers that get energy from eating both animals and plants

**population**   all the organisms of one species in an ecosystem



# Ecosystems

## by Helen N. George

# What are the parts of ecosystems?

## What a System Is

A system has parts. These parts work together to do a job. A system can have living and nonliving parts. Every part of a system is important. The system will not work as well if any part is damaged or missing.

A bicycle is a simple system. The frame, handlebars, and the rider all work together.

Most ecosystems need inputs. Inputs are things coming into the system. They also need outputs. Outputs are things leaving the system. The activity of the rider is an input of a bicycle system. The dust from the tires is one output.

Living things need energy. One way that energy moves from one organism to another is through a food chain. Food chains always begin with energy from the Sun. Sometimes several food chains overlap and form a food web.

Living things also need matter. They need minerals, oxygen, and carbon dioxide. Matter flows through a food web in the same way that energy does. In any ecosystem, decay is needed. Decay returns minerals and nutrients to the soil.

Ecosystems have many living and nonliving parts. The parts work together. All the organisms in an ecosystem have needs. Organisms must adapt to survive in their ecosystem. A cactus, for example, has adapted to the dry desert. Many populations of organisms work together to make up a community. Every organism has a niche, or job, within its habitat.

## Ecosystems

An **ecosystem** is all of the living and nonliving things in an environment. It also is how they interact. An ecosystem can be as large as a desert. It can be as small as a rotting cactus.

The living things in an ecosystem are animals, plants, fungi, protists, and bacteria. The nonliving things in an ecosystem are air, water, soil, sunlight, climate, and landforms. The living and nonliving parts work together.

## Kinds of Ecosystems

The needs of an organism must be met in its environment. Some plants and animals will survive in the environment better than others will. Some will not survive at all. Soil and climate affect which plants and animals will do well in an area. Desert plants and animals have adaptations to help them live in a dry environment. The giant saguaro cactus can fill up with water. It can store this water until the next rainfall.

**Desert**
A desert is the driest ecosystem. Plants and animals adapt to live with little water. Some desert organisms are roadrunners, coyotes, shrubs, and cactuses.

Oxygen helps organisms break down food. Organisms get energy from food. They put carbon dioxide into the air or water.

Plants take in carbon dioxide from the air or water. They also put oxygen back into the air.

Carbon dioxide is part of the decay process. It is put into the air when decomposers break down dead organisms.

**Tundra**
A tundra is cold and dry. The ground under the surface is frozen all year long. Some grasses can grow. Trees cannot grow. Caribou and arctic foxes do well during the spring and summer.

**Forest**
Forests get more rain than grasslands do. Forests have many animals, trees, and wildflowers. Some forest animals are squirrels, raccoons, deer, and foxes.

**Tropical Rain Forest**
A rain forest is always wet. There are many species of plants and animals in the rain forest. Colorful birds live there. Beautiful flowers live there.

**Grasslands**
Grasslands are covered with tall grasses. They have moderate rainfall. Bison, prairie chickens, and grasshoppers are found in North American grasslands.

# Decay in Ecosystems

All living things will die and rot, or decay. Ecosystems need decay. Without decay, wastes and dead organisms would build up and get in the way of living organisms.

Decay begins when scavengers eat parts of dead organisms. Decomposers such as bacteria and fungi break down the dead organisms. This returns nutrients and minerals to the ecosystem.

# Rate of Decay

An organism decays more slowly in colder temperatures. It decays faster in warmer temperatures.

Oxygen also speeds decay. Some bacteria and fungi need oxygen to grow and live. That is why you keep food covered. Moisture also affects decay. Moisture makes many decomposers grow better and work faster.

Nonliving objects decay much more slowly than objects that used to be alive. Decomposers will break down a dead insect faster than a pebble.

# Organisms and Their Environment

A **population** is one species of organisms that live in a part of an ecosystem. Prairie dogs make up one animal population in a desert. Barrel cactuses make up a plant population in the desert. The size of a population depends on how much water, food, and space there is.

Different populations can live together in the same area. They make up a **community.** All the organisms found in a desert ecosystem are a community.

A habitat is where an organism lives within an ecosystem. The habitat of the Gambel's quail is near shrubs in the Sonoran desert. It can hide from predators there. Everything an organism needs to survive is found in its habitat.

*Sandhill crane*

*Osprey*

*Great blue heron*

The sandhill crane is an omnivore. It eats many different things. It eats seeds, berries, invertebrates, reptiles, and fish. The great blue heron eats mollusks and amphibians. It stabs its prey with its beak and swallows it whole. The osprey is a carnivore. It eats mostly fish. Sometimes it eats snakes and amphibians.

Look at this swamp food web. Follow the arrows to see how energy flows to and from all the different organisms.

## How Matter Flows Through A Food Web

A food chain shows how matter and energy flow through an ecosystem. Producers and consumers can be part of more than one food chain. The overlapping food chains are a food web.

Single-celled algae take in sunlight and matter from their environment. Zooplankton feed on algae. Freshwater snails also feed on algae. These snails are consumers. They are prey of the great blue heron. The blue-spotted sunfish lives near beds of algae. It eats zooplankton and other small invertebrates.

## Special Roles

Every organism has a job to do in its habitat. This is its **niche.** A niche includes the food the organism eats, how it gets its food, and which other species use the organism for food.

Every population in a habitat has a different niche. Hummingbirds and roadrunners share a desert habitat. They have different niches. The Lucifer hummingbird eats small insects, spiders, and nectar from plants. It hides from its enemies, such as the roadrunner, by sitting on tall plants. The roadrunner's niche is to hunt scorpions, lizards, and snakes. It runs away from enemies, such as the coyote.

# How does energy flow in ecosystems?

## Energy in Plants and Animals

The main energy source for life on Earth is the Sun. During photosynthesis, green plants change energy from the Sun into chemical energy. This chemical energy keeps the plant alive. Plants are called producers. They make, or produce, their own food.

Many organisms cannot make their own food. They must eat other organisms. Consumers are organisms that eat other living things. **Herbivores** are consumers that get energy by eating plants. **Carnivores** are consumers that eat animals. **Omnivores** eat both plants and animals. Consumers that eat dead plants and animals are scavengers. Some scavengers are carnivores.

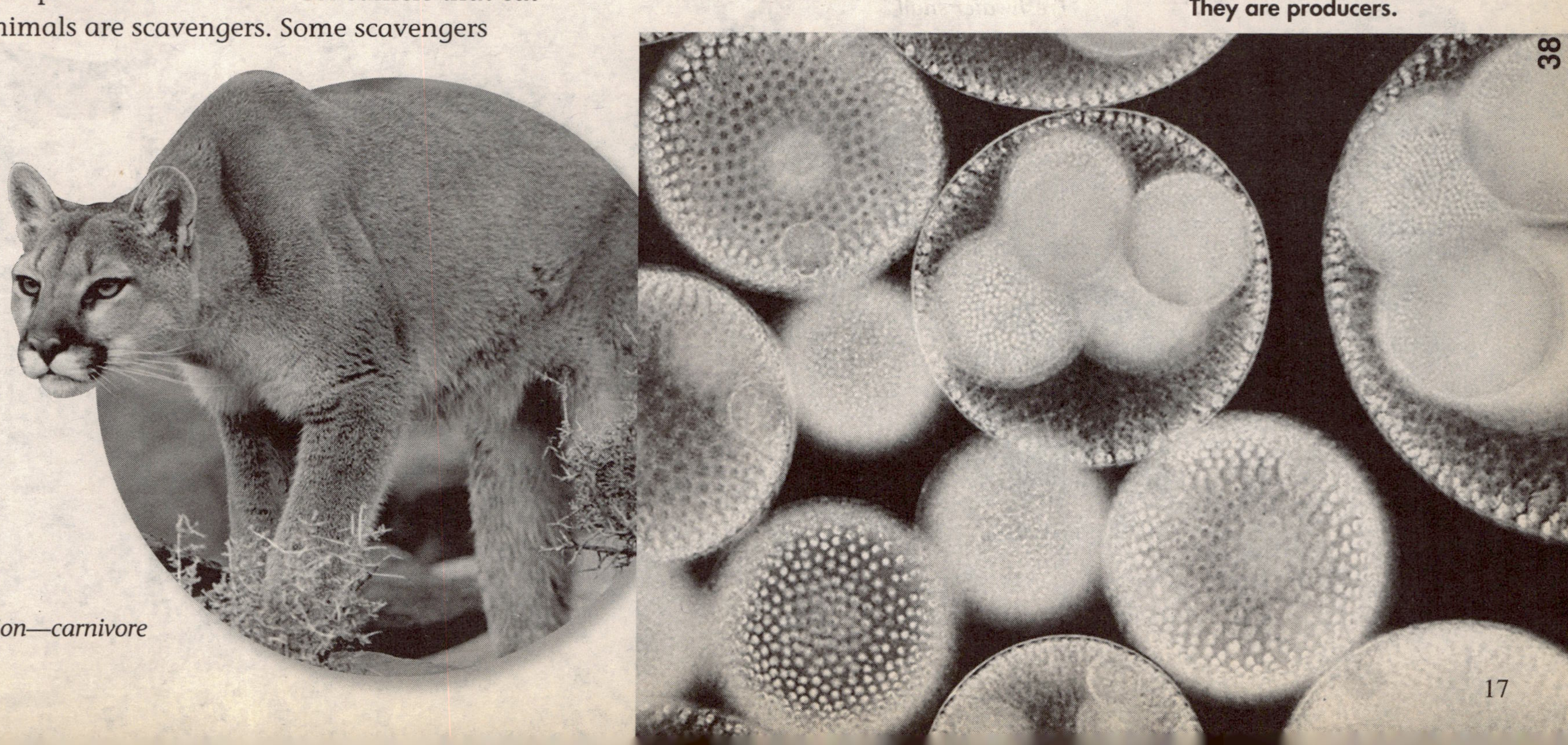

*Mountain lion—carnivore*

One large producer in the Okefenokee Swamp is the bald cypress tree. This tree has needlelike leaves. The bottom of the bald cypress tree is very wide. Parts that grow from the roots and stick out of the water look like "knees." Some bald cypress trees grow more than 30 meters (100 feet) tall.

Single-celled algae are small producers in the Okefenokee Swamp. These plantlike protists carry out photosynthesis. This makes them producers.

Matter and energy move through an ecosystem. Plants take in nutrients from the soil. They also take in gases from the air. Herbivores eat plants to get the matter and energy they need. The matter and energy pass to carnivores that eat the herbivores.

**Algae have only one cell. They are producers.**





38

# How does matter flow in ecosystems?

## Water Ecosystems

Almost three-fourths of the surface of Earth is covered with water. Many organisms live in water ecosystems. Some organisms live in the salt water of ocean ecosystems. Other organisms live in fresh water.

Wetlands are another kind of water ecosystem. In wetlands, water is covering the soil or is near the top of the soil. Swamps are wetlands that are wet all year. The Okefenokee Swamp in southern Georgia and northern Florida has many producers.

Okefenokee Swamp

Organisms may have different adaptations to help them survive in their niche. Some carnivores, such as mountain lions, have claws to help them catch their prey. Mountain lions also have sharp teeth for eating the prey. Herbivores such as deer do not need to catch their food. They have teeth for tearing leaves off plants. Some herbivores have stomachs with four parts to help them digest their food. Scavengers, such as turkey vultures, tear meat with their sharp beaks.

*Bighorn sheep—herbivore*

*Coati—omnivore*

# A Food Chain

The energy that producers store moves through a food chain. This happens when organisms eat and are eaten.

Food chains start with energy from the Sun. The energy moves to producers. Energy moves through a food chain. It flows from the "eaten" to the "eater." Arrows show how the energy is moving.

In a desert ecosystem, the coyote and the mountain lion compete for black-tailed jackrabbits and Gambel's quails. They eat collared peccaries too.

Look at this food web. Did you notice that roadrunners eat rattlesnakes? A roadrunner can run 25 kilometers per hour. It is one of the few animals that can catch a rattlesnake.

A food web can change any time the size of a population changes. Hunting, storms, pollution, and disease can also change a food web.

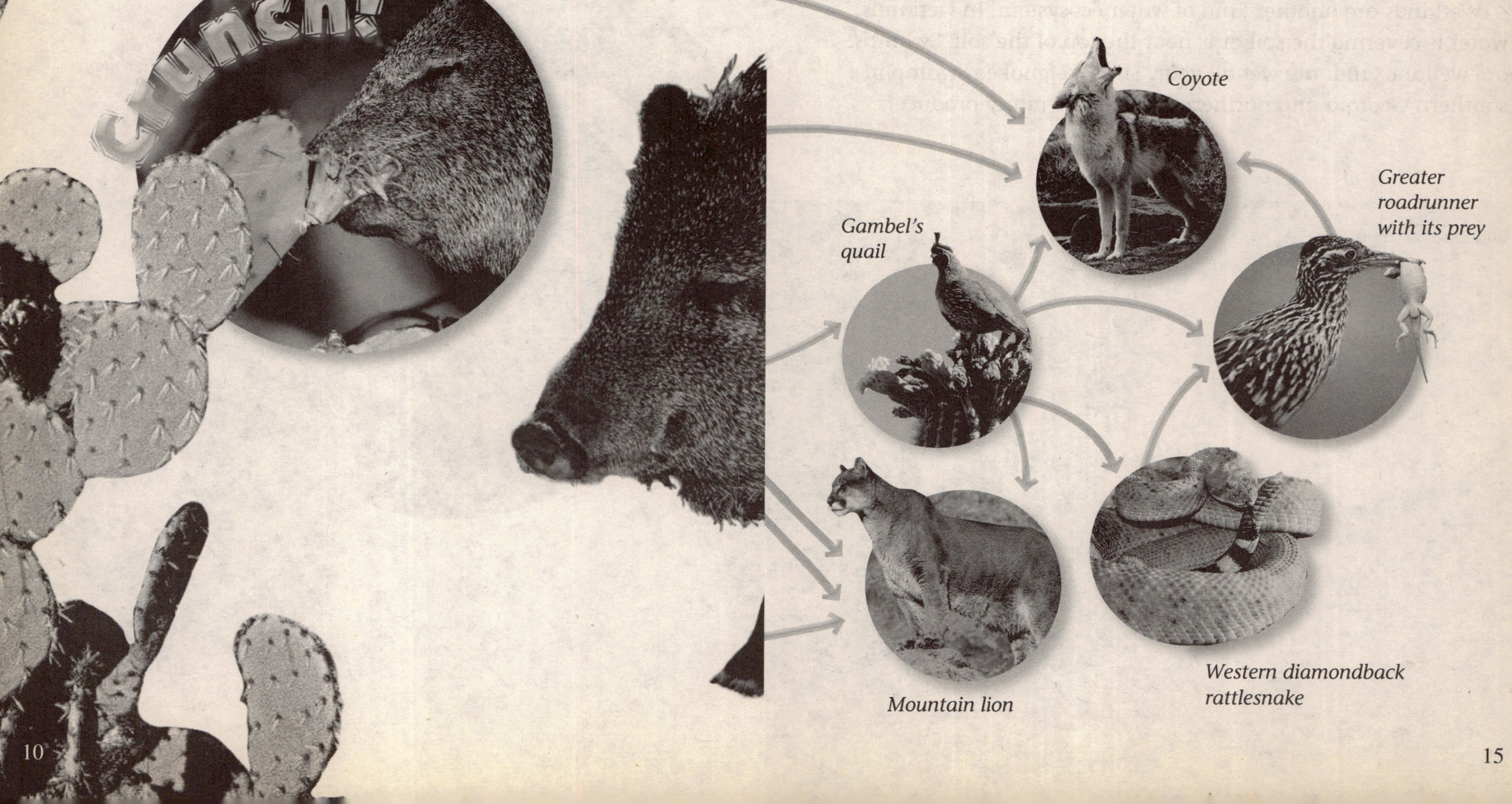

## A Food Web

One food source can be part of several food chains. A food web is a system of overlapping food chains. Energy moves in many directions in a food web.

Producers and consumers may be eaten by many different organisms. Predators often eat more than one kind of prey.

A desert ecosystem has food chains. In one food chain the prickly pear cactus is a producer. It takes in energy from the Sun. An omnivore such as the collared peccary eats the prickly pear cactus. The collared peccary takes in energy that was stored in the cactus. A predator such as the coyote hunts the collared peccary. Then the coyote takes in energy from the collared peccary, which got energy from the cactus.

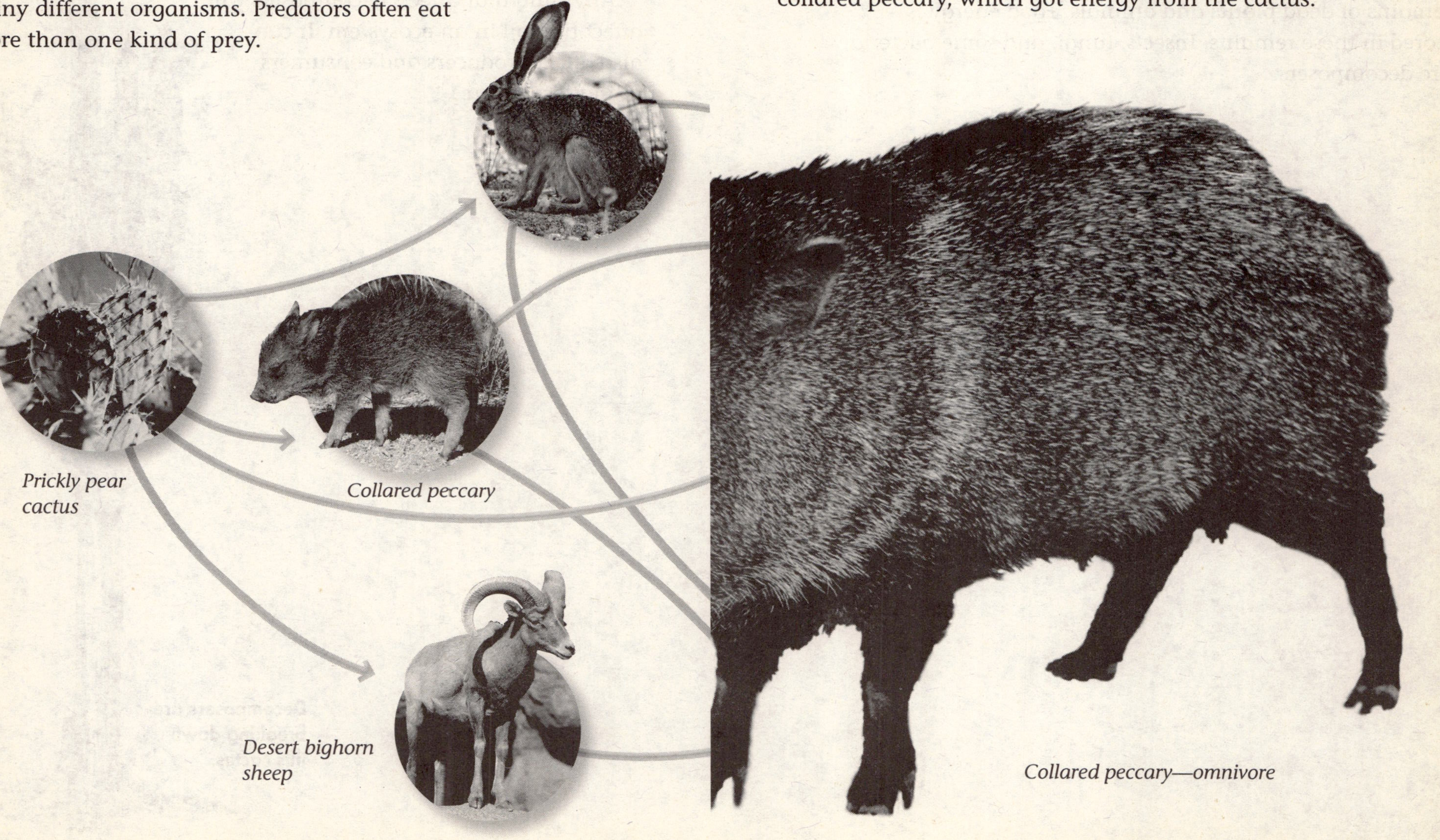

*Black-tailed jackrabbit*

*Prickly pear cactus*

*Collared peccary*

*Desert bighorn sheep*

*Collared peccary—omnivore*

## Small Things That Make a Big Difference

What if an ecosystem had only producers and consumers? One day the nutrients in the soil would be used up. The plants would die. Then there would be nothing for the herbivores to eat. Nutrients and minerals must be put back.

**Decomposers** are organisms that eat the waste and remains of dead plants and animals. Food energy is stored in these remains. Insects, fungi, and some bacteria are decomposers.

Mushrooms are fungi. They are decomposers.

Decomposers break down the plant and animal remains into minerals and nutrients. These minerals and nutrients go back into the water, air, and soil. Living plants take them in. Animals take in these minerals and nutrients when they eat the plants.

Anything that affects decomposers will affect the soil in an ecosystem. It can also affect producers and consumers in that ecosystem.

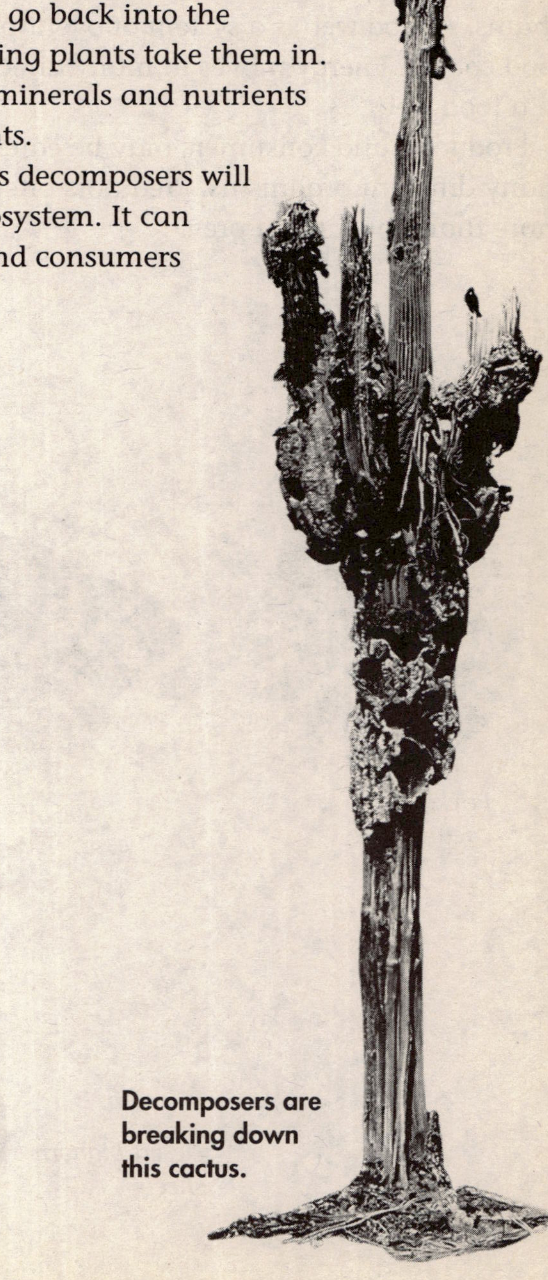

Decomposers are breaking down this cactus.

# Changes in Ecosystems

by Sharon Franklin

| Genre | Comprehension Skill | Text Features | Science Content |
| --- | --- | --- | --- |
| Nonfiction | Cause and Effect | • Labels<br>• Captions<br>• Call Outs<br>• Glossary | Ecosystem Changes |

**Scott Foresman Science 4.4**

## What did you learn?

1. What are some things that organisms may compete for?

2. Explain the relationship between parasites and hosts.

3. What are some positive and negative effects of a forest fire?

4. **Writing** in Science   Strip mining can damage ecosystems. On your own paper, describe some of this damage. Include details from the book to support your answer.

5. **Cause and Effect** What effect can people have on the environment?

**Illustration** 10, 11 Peter Bollinger 23 Bob Kayganich
**Photographs:** Every effort has been made to secure permission and provide appropriate credit for photographic material. The publisher deeply regrets any omission and pledges to correct errors called to its attention in subsequent editions. Unless otherwise acknowledged, all photographs are the property of Scott Foresman, a division of Pearson Education. Photo locators denoted as follows: Top (T), Center (C), Bottom (B), Left (L), Right (R) Background (Bkgd)
Opener:(Bkgd) ©E. R. Degginger/Color-Pic, Inc., (TR) ©Michael Fogden/Animals Animals/Earth Scenes
Title Page: ©DK Images 2 ©Orion Press/Corbis 4 ©David Muench/Corbis, (CC) Getty Images, (BR) Hans Neleman/Getty Images 5 (CL) ©Art Wolfe/Getty Images, (TL, CR) ©DK Images, (CC) ©Lynda Richardson/Corbis, (TR) ©Gary W. Carter/Corbis 6 © Royalty-Free/Corbis 7 ©Ron Austing; Frank Lane Picture Agency/Corbis 8 ©David Muench/Corbis 9 ©Jon Sparks/Corbis 12 ©Sullivan & Rogers/Bruce Coleman Inc. 13 ©DK Images 14 ©DK Images 15 ©Peter Scoones/SPL/Photo Researchers, Inc. 16 ©Martin B. Withers; Frank Lane Picture Agency/Corbis 17 (T, B) ©Marty Cordano/DRK Photo 18 ©Getty Images 19 ©Bettmann/Corbis 21 ©Adrian Lyon/Getty Images 22 (TR) ©Vince Streano/Corbis, (CR) ©Bruce Hands/Getty Images 23 (TL) Getty Images, (TR) ©Ed Reschke/Peter Arnold, Inc., (BL) ©Doug Sokell/Visuals Unlimited, (BR) ©Myrleen Ferguson Cate/PhotoEdit

ISBN: 0-328-13868-1

Copyright © Pearson Education, Inc.

# Changes in Ecosystems

## by Sharon Franklin

**Glossary**

| | |
|---|---|
| **competition** | the struggle among organisms to get what they need to live and reproduce |
| **endangered** | in danger of becoming extinct because so few members of the species are left |
| **extinct** | no longer existing; usually referring to a species |
| **hazardous waste** | materials that are harmful to people, to other organisms, and to the environment |
| **host** | an organism that provides food or shelter to another living thing |
| **parasite** | an organism that harms the host it lives on or in |
| **succession** | a slow change over time from one community of organisms to another |

# How are ecosystems balanced?

## Needs of Living Things

A chipmunk comes out of its forest burrow. It runs up to a mushroom. The mushroom is just one source of food for the chipmunk. This is one of the many ways plants and animals interact in a balanced ecosystem.

The Great Smoky Mountains are home to more than ten thousand kinds of plants and animals. The Eastern American chipmunk is just one.

## Preserving the Environment

Our nation is full of beautiful natural areas. Visitors look down into the Grand Canyon's vast depths. Others watch millions of gallons of water rush over Niagara Falls.

One way to keep special places safe is to develop national parks. People can visit national parks and enjoy these beautiful areas.

Organisms interact within an ecosystem. Some relationships help both organisms, while some relationships help only one organism. Some relationships may even harm one organism. Environmental changes can happen quickly or slowly. People can cause a great deal of change within an environment. It is important that we help keep the balance of all ecosystems.

## Land Reclamation

Federal laws now make mining companies replace the rock and soil they remove. They must replant the area with native trees and grasses. This is known as reclaiming.

Coal mining began in some states in the 1840s. Damage to the land was not fixed for more than 100 years. In the 1970s new laws were passed. They changed how mining could be done. One law requires coal companies to study an ecosystem before mining. They must have a plan on how they will reclaim the land.

California has reclaimed several mining areas. A gravel pit in Sacramento County is once again a water environment. Other mined areas now grow alfalfa, corn, and strawberries.

The chipmunk needs food, air, water, and shelter in order to live. It gets food and air from the forest plants. It gets water from puddles and streams. Forest trees make a safe place to dig a burrow in the ground. The burrow keeps the chipmunk warm. It also keeps the chipmunk safe from predators such as hawks and foxes.

Plants and animals depend on their environment. They need food, air, water, and shelter to be healthy and grow. Good soil and the right weather are also important. Plants and animals can only live in places that meet their needs. The Great Smoky Mountains meet all the Eastern American chipmunk's needs.

The Eastern American chipmunk is one of many species found in the Great Smoky Mountains.

## A Balancing Act

An ecosystem is similar to a seesaw. Animals are on one side. Food, space, and shelter are on the other side. In a healthy ecosystem, the seesaw is balanced. If too many animals are added, there will not be enough food or shelter for all of them. The seesaw will not be balanced.

Plants also need a balanced ecosystem. Plants need water, sunlight, the right soil, and enough space. What happens if you plant seeds too close together? Many seeds will not have enough space to grow.

## Stripping Away the Land

Many valuable substances are under the surface of Earth. Coal is one example. Strip mining is a way to get coal out of the ground. Big machines dig up and clear away the top layers of soil. The digging leaves huge pits. No trees, rocks, or plants are left to hold the dirt. Over time the land begins to erode. The dirt and rocks wash into nearby rivers and ponds. Ecosystems surrounding these areas are greatly affected.

It is important to restore the land so animals can return or so the land can be used to grow crops.

## Land Pollution

Did you know that every person throws away about two kilograms, or almost four and a half pounds, of garbage every day? Most trash is dumped in landfills. Then it is covered with soil. Garbage, litter, and other materials can cause pollution.

Another kind of land pollution is caused by **hazardous waste.** Hazardous waste harms humans and other organisms. Some hazardous waste is poison. It can cause diseases. Other waste can start fires. It can react in dangerous ways with other materials. Until recently, most hazardous waste was put into containers that were buried in the ground. Some containers leaked. The waste went into the ground and damaged the environment.





Plants and animals work together to keep an ecosystem in balance. For example, rabbits eat grass. Less grass means more space for other plants to grow. But red foxes eat rabbits. Then there are fewer rabbits to eat the grass. Therefore, more plants grow. The plants produce more air and water that all animals need.

Ecosystems have changes all the time. Living things are born. They live, die, and decompose. The water in ponds can dry up. But rain returns water to the ponds. Animals take in oxygen from the air. Plants put oxygen back into the ecosystem. All these changes help keep ecosystems in balance.

# How do organisms interact?

## Change in Ecosystems

When an ecosystem's resources change, the number of living things changes. When chipmunks have enough to eat, their population can increase. More chipmunks will use more resources. At some point, there will not be enough food, water, and space for all of the chipmunks. Some will die. Others may move to a new place. With fewer chipmunks, there will again be enough resources. The chipmunk population will increase.

## Competing

When different organisms in an ecosystem need the same limited resources, **competition** occurs. Organisms have adaptations that can help them live and grow successfully.

## Polluted Water

Wastes and chemicals can also pollute rivers, lakes, and oceans. Some wastes are dumped right into the water through sewer systems. Chemicals are used on land to grow plants or kill insects. Rain washes the chemicals into lakes and rivers. The chemicals can kill the plants and animals that live there.

Chemicals and other kinds of pollution in rivers and streams can flow into the oceans. Oil spills and leaks sometimes happen during the drilling and shipping of oil. This pollutes the ocean. Ocean plants, fish, and birds are coated with oil. The birds often drown.

**The Cuyahoga River was heavily polluted with oil, logs, and other wastes. In 1952 it caught fire. This led to the Clean Water Act, which makes it illegal to pollute water.**

# How do people disturb the balance?

## People and the Environment

Like other organisms, we depend on our environment for food, water, and shelter. But unlike other organisms, we can change our environment in various ways to meet our needs. We cut down trees for lumber. We clear land to plant crops. We build roads through forests. Each change can upset the balance of the ecosystem.

Sometimes we put wastes into the environment that upset the ecosystem. Harmful gases, dust, dirt, and other wastes pollute the air and water. Cars and factories put harmful chemicals into the air. These chemicals can harm people. They can damage plants. They may cause animals to lose food or shelter.

Many organisms compete for living space. Plants compete for light and water. Birds compete for the same places to build nests. Other animals, such as foxes and owls, compete for the same food.

## Sharing Resources

Some animals find ways to avoid competing. Hawks and owls both hunt the same animals. But hawks hunt during the day. Owls hunt at night.

Some animals live in groups. Wolves hunt deer together. The deer form tight groups to help keep the herd safe. This makes it harder for a wolf to attack any one deer.

## Helping Each Other

Two organisms may live closely together. Sometimes this helps both organisms. Sometimes this helps only one organism. Animals, plants, fungi, protists, and bacteria can have these helpful relationships.

Lichens are fungi and algae that live together. The algae give the fungi nutrients and water. The fungi shelter the algae from the Sun.

## Living Side by Side

Oak trees give shelter to moss. The moss neither helps nor harms the oak tree.

Animals can also have this kind of relationship. Silverfish may travel with army ants. The insects eat the food the army ants leave behind. They neither help nor harm the army ants.

Lichens can grow on rocks.

## Natural Disasters

In 1993, very heavy rain caused the Mississippi and Missouri Rivers to overflow. Some areas of land were flooded for almost seven months. The waters left large areas of land covered with sand and mud.

The flooding killed many trees and grasses. Birds lost nesting places and had fewer babies. However, some fish populations increased. The water gave the fish new areas in which to feed and reproduce.

Fires can destroy entire forests. But they also can help new plants to grow.

## Rapid Changes

A hurricane's strong winds rip up trees. Heavy rains and giant waves flood coastal towns. One lightning strike can set an entire forest on fire.

Other natural events, such as earthquakes and volcanic eruptions, can also change an environment in an instant. These changes can mean that some species must find a new home because the resources they need are gone.

Sometimes natural events can help keep the environment in balance. Forest fires burn dead and dying plants, making room for new plants to grow. The Table Mountain pine tree has cones that open in the heat of a fire. Then new pine trees can grow.

## Causing Harm

Sometimes one organism is helped while another is harmed. The organism that is helped is a **parasite.** A parasite lives on or in another organism. The organism that is harmed is the **host.** The host is a source of food for the parasite.

Balsam woolly adelgids are insects that are parasites. They feed on Fraser fir trees. When these parasite insects feed, they harm the trees.

# How do environments change?

## The Process of Change

What is now a forest area may have been a lake thousands of years ago. But over many years the lake may have dried up. The area became a marsh. Marsh grasses and bushes grew. Then the environment changed more. Trees began to grow. Today the area is a forest. The slow change from one community of organisms to another is **succession.**

Fossils can tell us about life on Earth long ago. Fossils help us understand past environmental changes. Scientists may find marine animal fossils in dry climates. This tells scientists that a big change happened. It tells them that shallow seas once covered what is now a dry area.

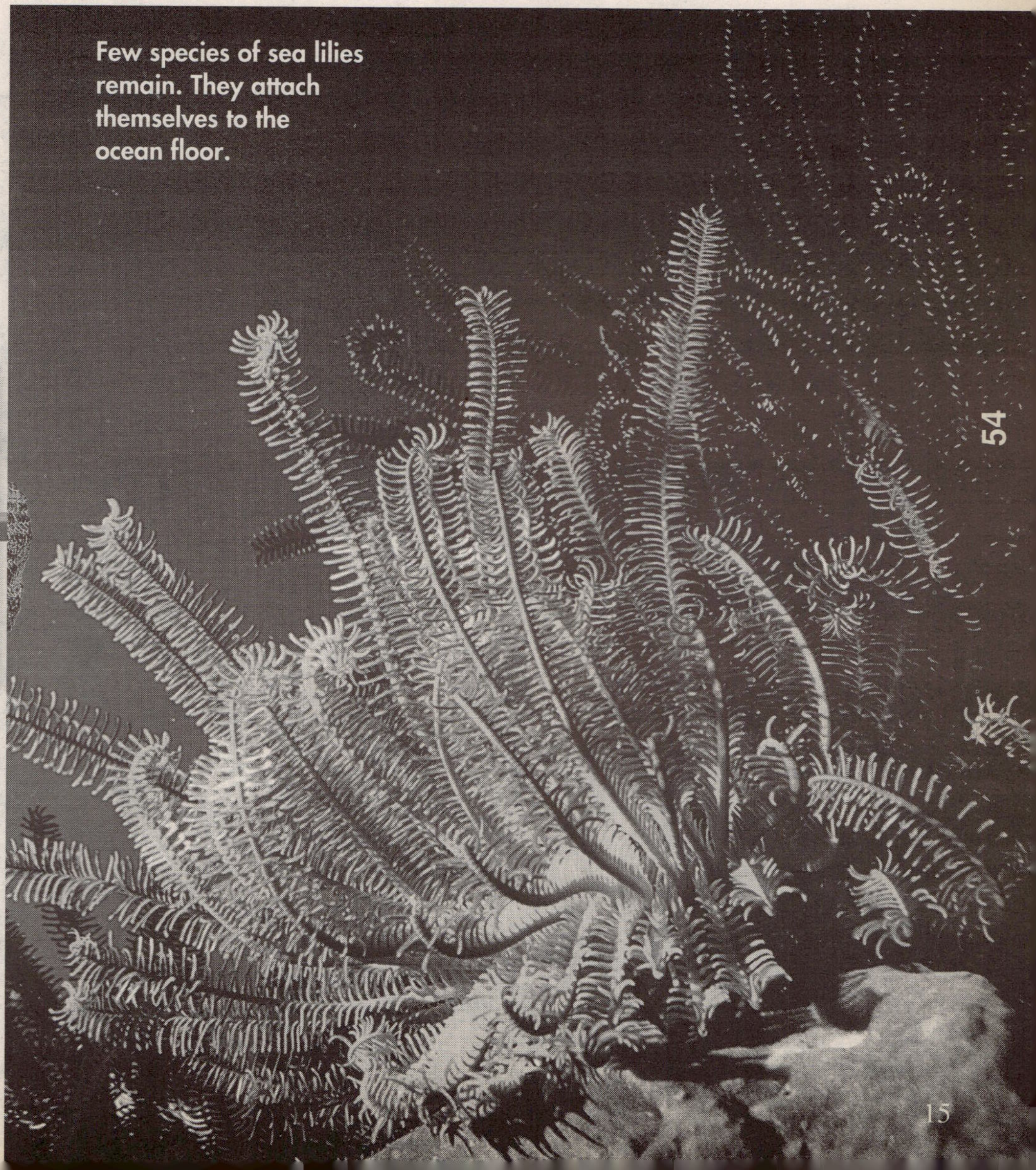

Very few living things are in a newly formed lake. Rivers will carry soil into the lake. Algae, bacteria, and spores from fungi may be in the soil.

These organisms add nutrients to the lake. Now small plants can grow. Herbivores will move into the ecosystem.

Few species of sea lilies remain. They attach themselves to the ocean floor.

## Species Then and Now

How do we know how species have changed over time? To find out, scientists study fossils. They compare fossils from long ago with organisms that are alive today.

Woolly mammoths became extinct long ago. Some were frozen solid in ice. Scientists have learned about them from their fossils. Scientists compare them with elephants of today. Both animals have large tusks and long noses. Their skeletons are very similar. The woolly mammoth and modern-day elephants are so alike that scientists group them in the same family.

Many sea lilies have been preserved as fossils.

## One Step at a Time

Succession usually takes place in stages. For example, bare land might first change to grassland. Next, shrubs may begin to grow. Then, over time, the shrub land may become forest. Areas continue to grow and change until there is a balance. For a time there are few changes.

Average temperature, winds, and rainfall over many years make up an area's climate. Changes in climate slowly affect ecosystems. Parts of North America were covered in snow and ice more than fifteen thousand years ago. No trees, grasses, or flowering plants could grow in the cold climate. But slowly the climate grew warmer. Then plants could grow, and animals could live there. Over time the forests we see today were formed.

Many animals and plants now live and interact in this community. Slowly the lake fills with soil, leaves, and decomposing organisms. The lake becomes a marsh.

Eventually the marsh fills and dries up. Trees begin to grow. The marsh is changing into a forest.

## 12

# Changing Species

In the 1800s and early 1900s, many passenger pigeons flew over the Great Smoky Mountains. But by 1915 not one passenger pigeon was left. The species had become **extinct**, or died out. Why do living things become extinct?

Sometimes species will not survive if the environment changes. In the past, volcanoes, climate changes, and meteors caused animals to become extinct. Today, most animals become extinct for two reasons. Their homes are destroyed, and they have no place to live. Other animals are hunted until they are extinct. A species usually cannot survive once its number drops below a certain level.

Passenger
pigeon

Some species have such small populations that they are in danger of becoming extinct. They are called **endangered** species. Species that may soon be endangered are called threatened species. Endangered and threatened species may leave their environments. They may try to find another place to live.

Some species are saved from becoming extinct. In 1970 the peregrine falcon was endangered. Many people worked together to help save this species. By 1999, its population had grown so that it was no longer endangered.

Peregrine
falcon

## 13

Science Science

# Systems of the Human Body

### by Abby Roberts



| Genre | Comprehension Skill | Text Features | Science Content |
| --- | --- | --- | --- |
| Nonfiction | Draw Conclusions | • Labels<br>• Captions<br>• Text Boxes<br>• Glossary | Body Systems |

**Scott Foresman Science 4.5**

PEARSON
Scott Foresman
scottforesman.com

DK

ISBN 0-328-13871-1

9 780328 138715  90000

## Vocabulary

immune system

infectious disease

involuntary muscles

neuron

pathogens

vaccine

voluntary muscles

## What did you learn?

**1.** What is one mineral that bones need? Why do bones need this mineral?

**2.** What are the important parts of the central nervous system?

**3.** What do white blood cells do?

**4.** **Writing** in Science  The human body needs oxygen to survive. On your own paper, write to explain how oxygen enters and moves through the body. Use details from the book to support your answer.

**5.** **Draw Conclusions** Your ribs are bones. They protect your body's organ systems. Which systems do they protect? Why is it important to protect these systems?

**Illustration:** Title Page, 5, 7, 9, 13, 15, 17, 19 Big Sesh Studios
**Photographs:** Every effort has been made to secure permission and provide appropriate credit for photographic material. The publisher deeply regrets any omission and pledges to correct errors called to its attention in subsequent editions. Unless otherwise acknowledged, all photographs are the property of Scott Foresman, a division of Pearson Education. Photo locators denoted as follows: Top (T), Center (C), Bottom (B), Left (L), Right (R) Background (Bkgd)
Opener: ©Dr. Dennis Kunkel/Visuals Unlimited; 2 (CR) ©Dr. Donald Fawcett/Visuals Unlimited, (Bkgd) ©Dr. Richard Kessel & Dr. Randy Kardon/Tissues and Organs/Visuals Unlimited, 3 ©Prof. P. Motta/Univ. "La Sapienza"/Photo Researchers, Inc.; 4 (TL) ©Science Photo Library/Photo Researchers, Inc., (BL) ©CNRI/Photo Researchers, Inc.; 6 (CL) ©Innerspace Imaging/Photo Researchers, Inc., (BL) ©SPL/Photo Researchers, Inc., (BL) ©Dr. Donald Fawcett/Visuals Unlimited; 10 Getty Images; 11 ©Scott Camazine/ Photo Researchers, Inc.; 17 ©Alfred Pasieka/Photo Researchers, Inc.; 18 ©Prof. P. Motta/Dept. of Anatomy/University "La Sapienza", Rome/Photo Researchers, Inc.; 19 ©Susumu Nishinaga/Photo Researchers, Inc., 20 ©Quest/Photo Researchers, Inc.; 21 (B) ©Dr. Kari Lounatmaa/Photo Researchers, Inc.; 21 ©Dr. David M. Phillips/Visuals Unlimited 22 (TL, CC, CL, BL) ©Bettmann/Corbis; 23 (TL, TR) ©Dr. Donald Fawcett & E. Shelton/Visuals Unlimited

ISBN: 0-328-13871-1

# Systems of the Human Body

**by Abby Roberts**

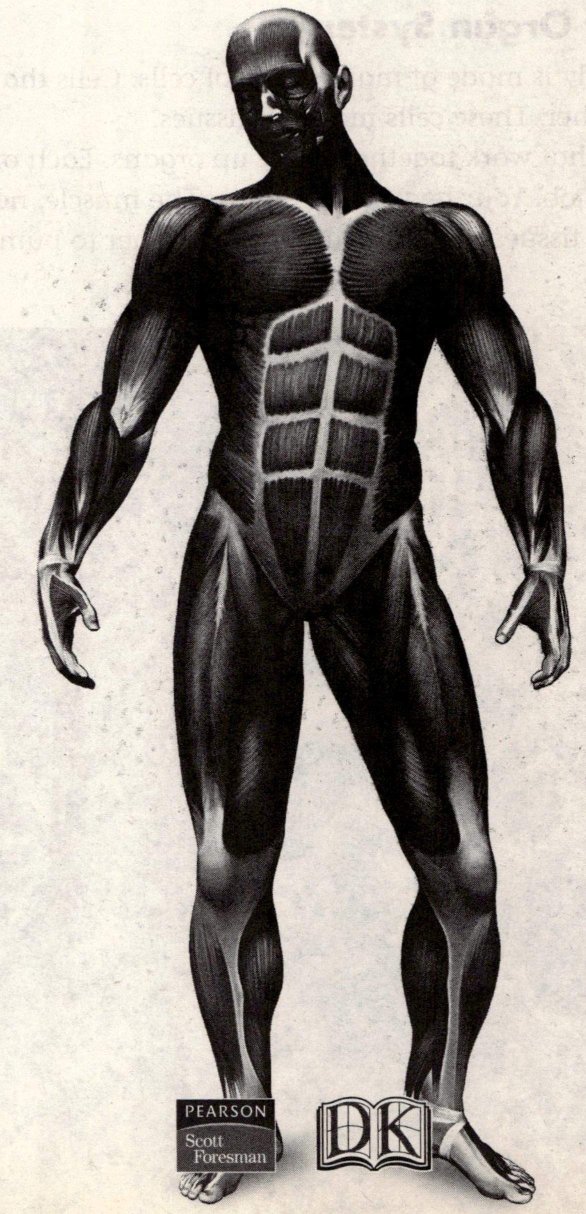

**Glossary**

**immune system** — the system that helps protect you against pathogens

**infectious disease** — an illness that is caused by pathogens

**involuntary muscles** — muscles that do their jobs without you having to think about it

**neuron** — one of the cells forming the brain, spinal cord, and nerves; nerve cell

**pathogens** — organisms that cause disease

**vaccine** — a medicine that protects you from a disease

**voluntary muscles** — muscles that you can choose to move

# What are the skeletal and muscular systems?

## Parts of Organ Systems

Your body is made of many kinds of cells. Cells that are alike work together. These cells make up tissues.

Tissues that work together make up organs. Each organ does a different job. Your heart is an organ. The muscle, nerve, and connective tissues in your heart work together to pump blood.

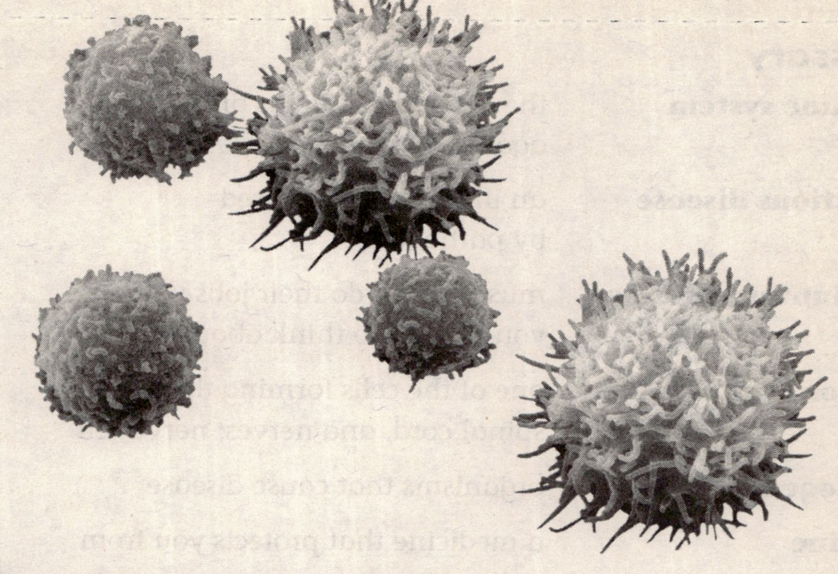

## Attacking the Invaders

The **immune system** helps protect you against pathogens. Blood cells and other tissues make up your immune system.

White blood cells make antibodies to stop pathogens. An antibody is a chemical. It keeps pathogens from infecting other cells. Your immune system uses antibodies that you already have to fight infection.

## Preventing the Disease

A **vaccine** is a kind of medicine that protects you from a disease. It can make you immune to a disease. The vaccine helps make special antibodies to kill the pathogens.

All the systems of your body work together. Your skeletal and muscular systems help you move. Your digestive, circulatory, and respiratory systems bring your cells what they need. Your nervous system controls your body. Your immune system protects you from sickness.

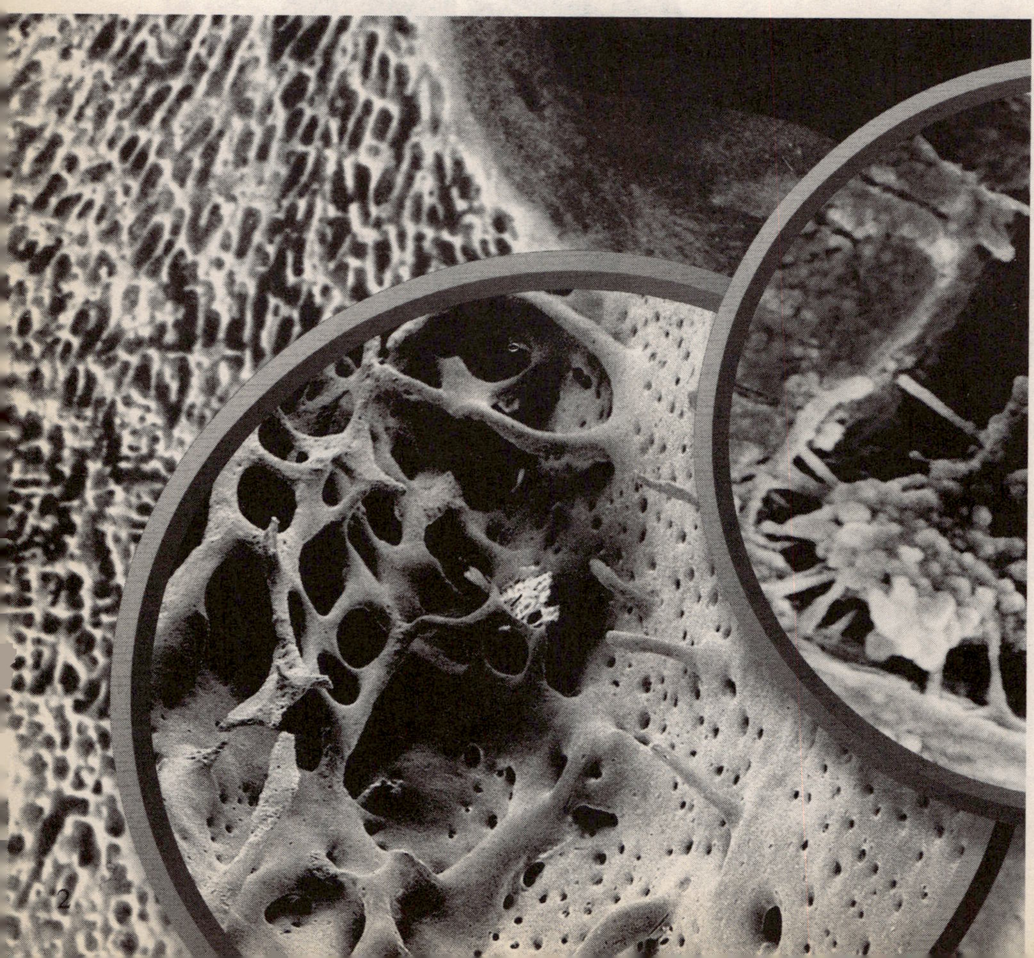

## How Your Body Fights Infections

Many years ago, people began to learn about infectious diseases. They learned why people got sick. They also learned how to protect people from getting sick.

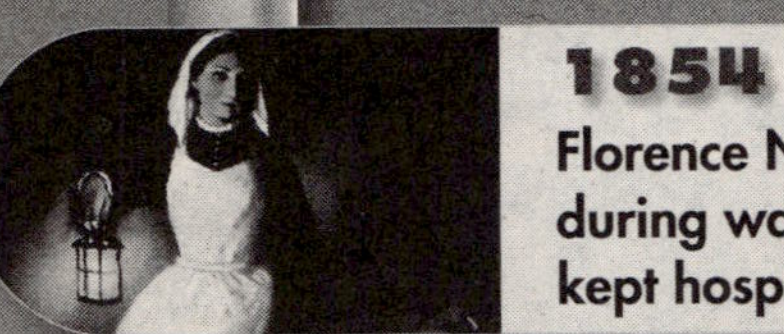

A group of organs that work together is an organ system. The heart and blood vessels are part of the circulatory system. All parts of an organ system are important. Damage to any organ in the system will affect the other organs in the system.

The different organ systems in your body work together. What happens when you go inline skating? Your skeletal and muscle systems help you stand and move. Your nervous system controls your movement. Your muscles get energy from your respiratory and circulatory systems.

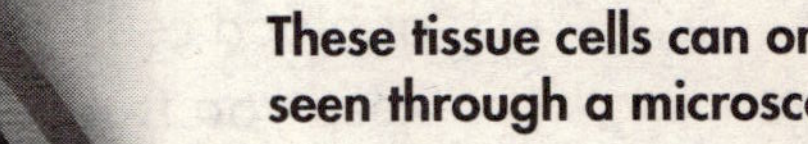
These tissue cells can only be seen through a microscope.

**Types of Joints**
Your shoulders and hips have ball-and-socket joints. A bowl-shaped area of a bone holds the end of another bone in place. This joint allows your leg to move in a circle.

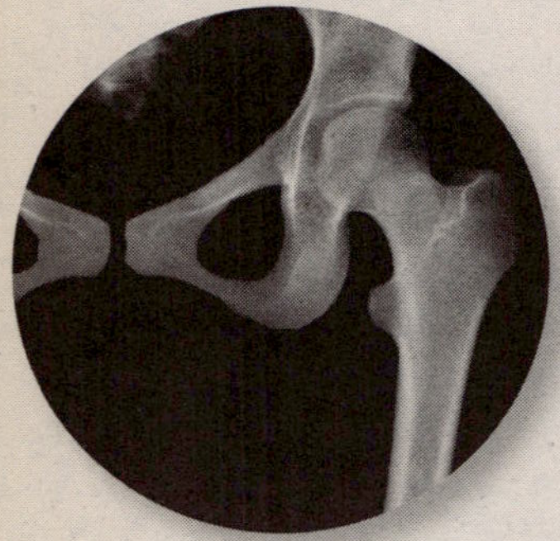

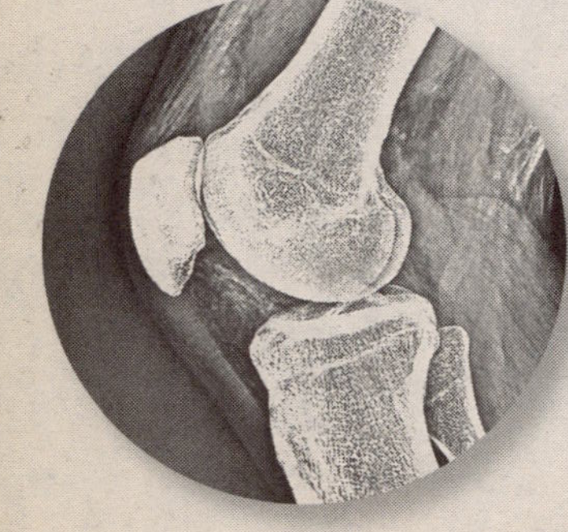

Your knees and elbows have hinge joints. These joints help you move your bones back and forth. Hinge joints allow you to bend or straighten your legs.

## The Skeletal System

Your skeleton is made mostly of bone tissue. Your skeleton holds up your body. It also protects your organs. Your ribs are bones that protect your heart. Your skeleton helps you move. Your muscles are attached to your bones.

## Building Strong Bones

Bones need minerals. Calcium is a mineral that helps make new bone tissue. It keeps bones strong. Calcium also helps other tissues work well.

Many bones make different kinds of blood cells. Some blood cells help keep you from getting sick. Others help bleeding stop when you are cut.

Bones are attached to each other at the joints. Tissues are around joints. Tissues protect them. Tissues also keep bones together.

## Staying Healthy

Some harmful microorganisms move though the air. You should cover your mouth and nose when you cough or sneeze. Then you won't send microorganisms through the air to someone else.

If you touch an object that has microorganisms living on it, and then you put your hands near your mouth, you can get sick. That's why it is important to wash your hands before you eat. Also, make sure that objects such as towels, dishes, and glasses are clean before you use them.

Strep throat is an infection caused by bacteria. These bacteria make a poison that infect the throat and the surrounding tissues.

Food may contain harmful bacteria that make people sick. Many cases of food poisoning are caused by bacteria called *E. coli*.

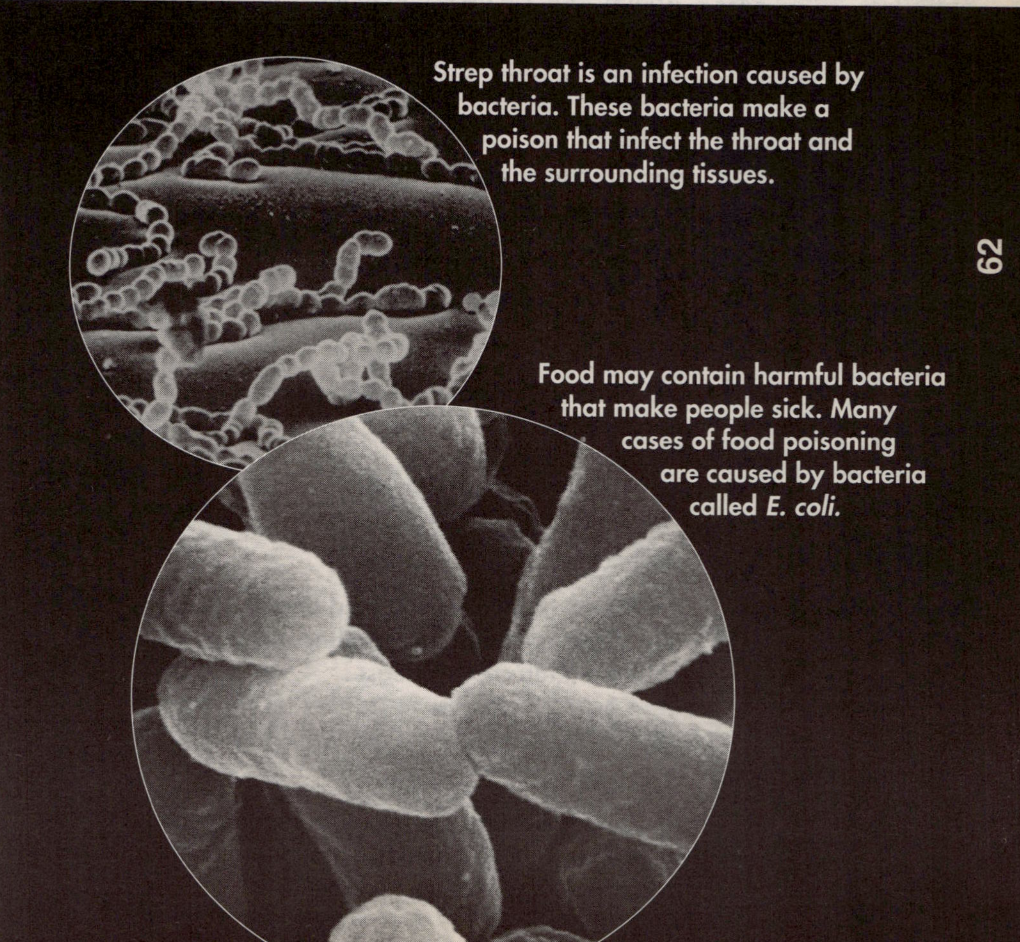

## Bacteria and Viruses

Organisms that cause disease are called **pathogens.** If pathogens get into your body, more of them will grow. They will form an infection in your body, making you sick.

An illness that is caused by pathogens is called an **infectious disease.** An infectious disease spreads from one organism to another. If you have pathogens in your body, you can get an infectious disease. Then you may give it to someone else.

Two kinds of pathogens are bacteria and viruses. Viruses are tiny; they are much smaller than bacteria. They use cells in your body to make more viruses. Different viruses attack different cells. For example, some attack the cells in your nose, mouth, and throat. Then you get a cold.

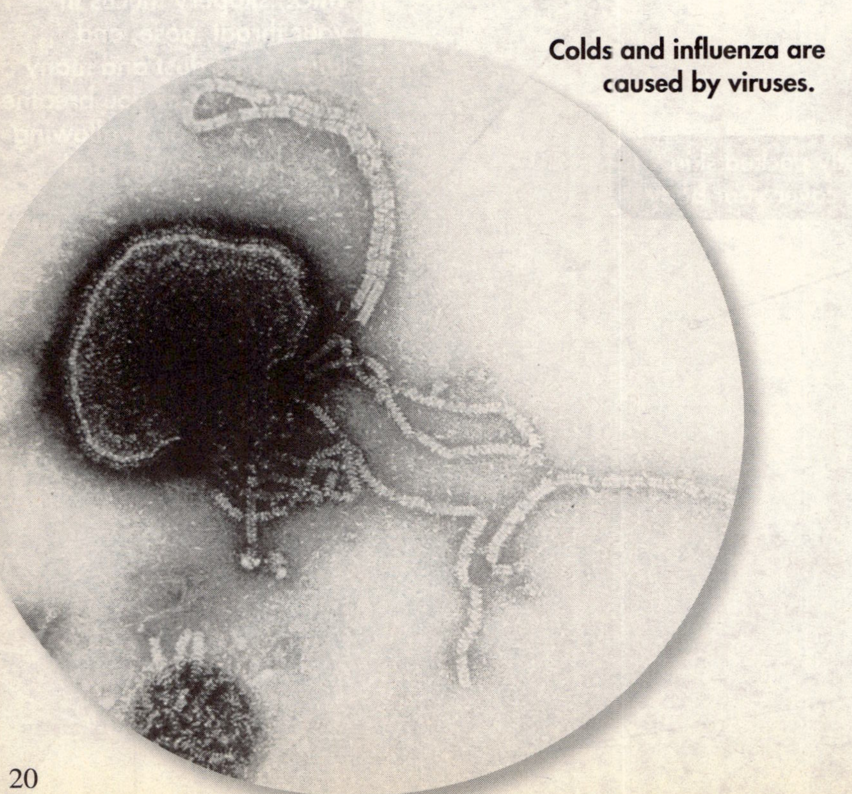

Colds and influenza are caused by viruses.





## The Human Skeleton

There are 206 bones in an adult skeleton. Bones are different shapes and sizes. The shape of a bone has to do with its job.

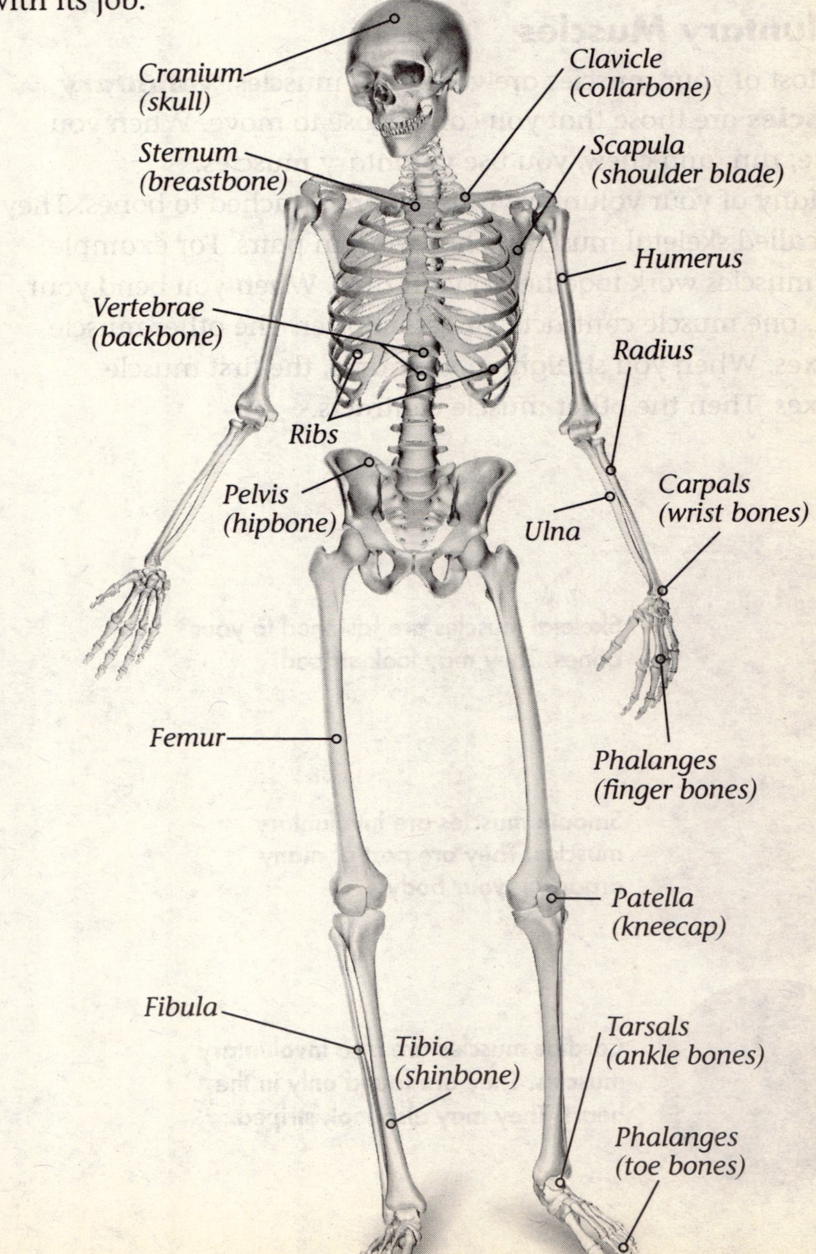

## The Muscular System

Muscles help the bones in your body move. Muscles help you breathe, swallow, walk, and smile.

## Voluntary Muscles

Most of your muscles are voluntary muscles. **Voluntary muscles** are those that you can choose to move. When you smile, run, and chew, you use voluntary muscles.

Many of your voluntary muscles are attached to bones. They are called skeletal muscles. They work in pairs. For example, two muscles work together in your arm. When you bend your arm, one muscle contracts, or gets shorter. The other muscle relaxes. When you straighten your arm, the first muscle relaxes. Then the other muscle contracts.

Skeletal muscles are fastened to your bones. They may look striped.

Smooth muscles are involuntary muscles. They are part of many organs in your body.

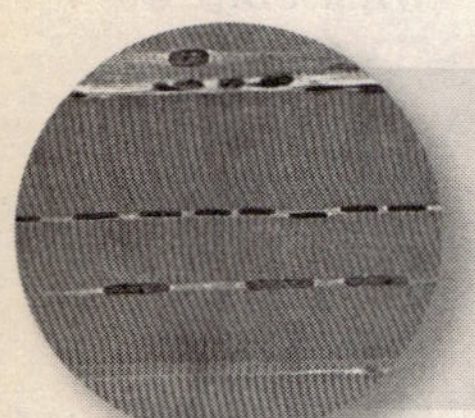

Cardiac muscles are also involuntary muscles. They are found only in the heart. They may also look striped.

## Your Body's Defenses

Some microorganisms are harmful. Your body has cells, tissues, and organs that work to protect you.

Your skin protects you. For example, there are acids in your sweat. These acids kill many harmful microorganisms that might make you sick.

The tears in your eyes and the saliva in your mouth also protect you. Tears wash away harmful microorganisms in your eyes. Saliva catches microorganisms in your mouth and washes them away.

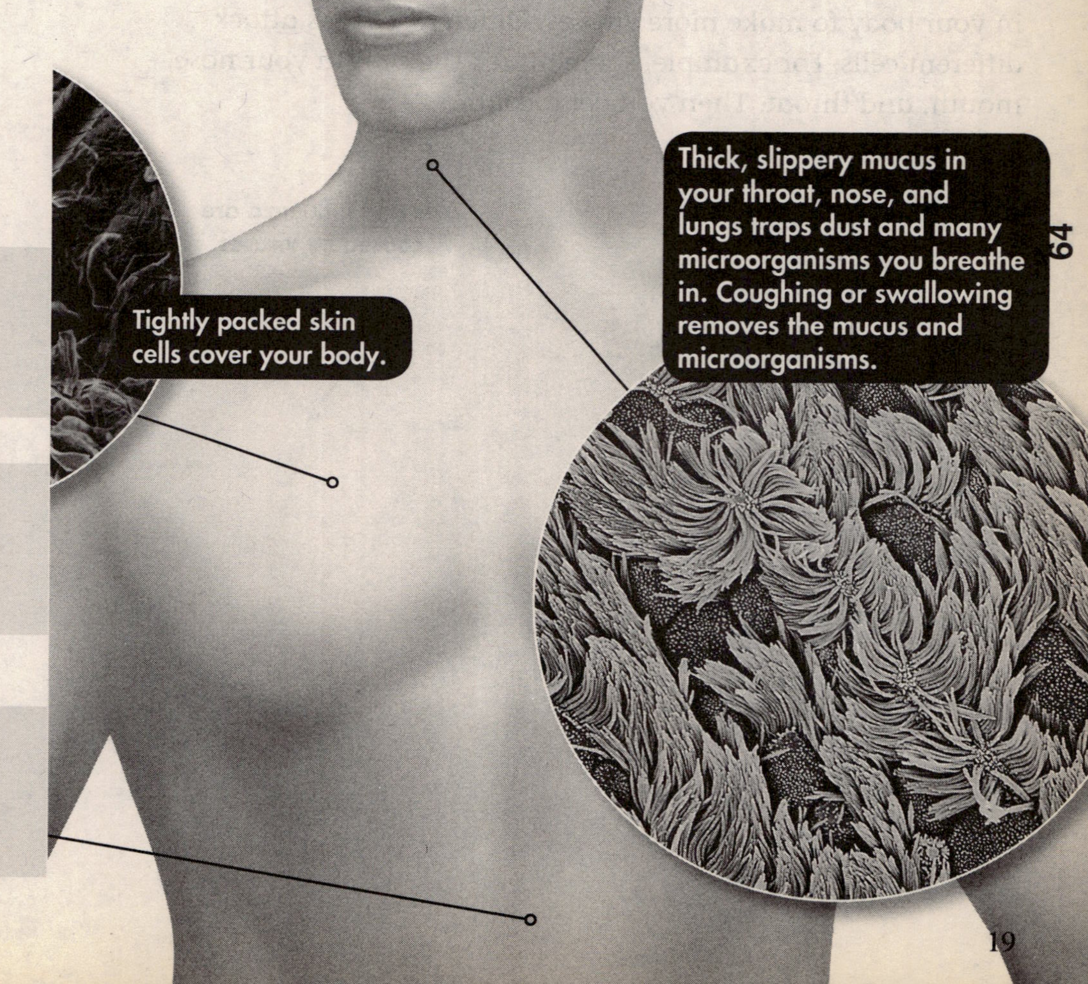

# How does the body defend itself?

## Microorganisms in Your Body

When you get a cut, you clean it. Then you cover it with a bandage. That way, the cut will not get infected. It can get infected if organisms that cause disease get into the cut. Most of these organisms are so small that you need a microscope to see them. They are called microorganisms.

Some microorganisms live in your body all the time. They are not harmful. Some are on your skin and others are in your mouth.







## Involuntary Muscles

Other muscles are called **involuntary muscles.** Involuntary muscles work whether you tell them to or not. Involuntary muscles help you breathe. They help keep blood moving in your body.

**Your body has more than 600 different skeletal muscles.**

# What are the respiratory and circulatory systems?

## The Respiratory System

Human beings need oxygen to stay alive. Oxygen is a gas in the air. When you breathe, air enters your nose and mouth. It moves into your throat, or pharynx. Then air travels into a tube called the windpipe, or the trachea. The trachea splits into two smaller tubes called bronchial tubes. Air goes through the bronchial tubes into your lungs.

In your lungs, bronchial tubes split into many tiny tubes. Each tiny tube leads to an air sac. Tiny blood vessels are around each air sac. Oxygen moves from the air in each sac into these blood vessels. Then the blood carries oxygen to all the cells in your body.

The brain is a moist, spongy organ made up of billions of nerve cells.

## The Brain

Your brain is an organ. It is made up of billions of nerve cells. The layers of tissue that cover and protect the spinal cord also cover and protect the brain. The skull, as well as a watery liquid inside it, also help keep the brain safe.

## Neurons

A **neuron,** or a nerve cell, is the basic unit of the nervous system. A nerve is made of a bunch of neurons. Many bunches of neurons make up the spinal cord. Neurons carry information. They send signals to and from the brain.

Every neuron has a cell body and a nucleus. The cell body has two kinds of parts sticking out of it. One kind carries signals toward the neuron. The other kind carries signals away.

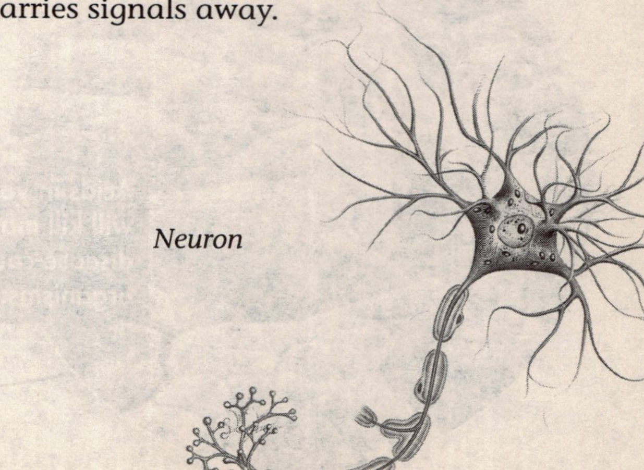

*Neuron*

# The Central Nervous System

Your body has a control center. It is the central nervous system. The brain and spinal cord are the important parts of this system.

The central nervous system brings messages from one organ to another. It controls your breathing, your heartbeat, and the movement of your muscles.

The central nervous system gets information from organs such as your eyes, ears, nose, and tongue. Suppose you hear a friend yell "Catch!" You see the ball. Your brain tells your muscles to reach for it. This happens because of your central nervous system.

## The Spinal Cord

Your spinal cord joins your brain to the rest of your body. Layers of tissue cover and protect it. Your brain decides what your body should do. Then it sends messages through your spinal cord. Sometimes your spinal cord reacts before you even think about what to do. For example, you don't think about blinking your eyes. You just do it!

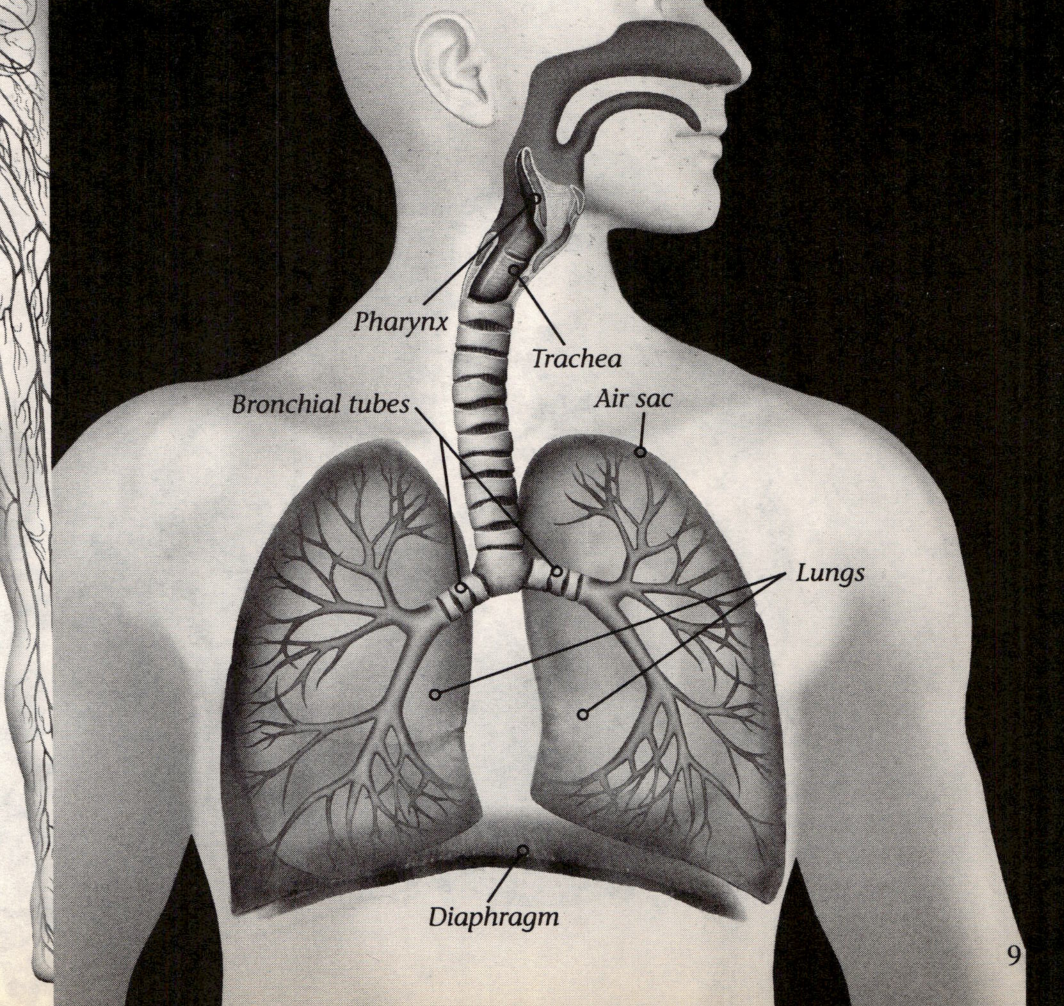


# Take a Breath!

The cells in your body use oxygen. They give off the gas carbon dioxide. As you breathe out, the carbon dioxide leaves your body.

The lungs are organs. They help move gases in and out of your body. Lungs do not have muscles. A muscle called the diaphragm is just below your lungs. The diaphragm has the shape of a dome. When your diaphragm tightens, it pulls air into your lungs. When it relaxes, the air is pushed out.

## How Pumps and Passages Work Together

The respiratory and circulatory systems work together. They bring oxygen into your body. They take carbon dioxide out of your body.

You breathe in oxygen using your respiratory system. The oxygen goes into the air sacs in your lungs. From there it passes into your blood.

Your heart is one part of your circulatory system. The drawing is a model of a human heart.

Your teeth and saliva break down food.

Next, you swallow the food. It goes down a tube. The tube is your esophagus. Muscles push the food into your stomach.

Your stomach has smooth muscles that grind up the food. The food mixes with juices in your stomach. It turns into thick liquid. The liquid goes into a very long tube called the small intestine. More juices are mixed in.

The juices in the small intestine break the food into important nutrients. These nutrients move into the blood vessels. Blood carries the nutrients to the cells in the body.

Some parts of food are not broken down. These parts move into the large intestine. They are turned into waste. Waste from food leaves the body.

# What are the digestive and nervous systems?

## The Digestive System

Is pizza one of your favorite foods? Pizza, or any food that you eat, must be broken down into nutrients. Your digestive system does this job. It digests, or breaks down, all the food that you eat.

Digestion starts when you take a bite of food. The food moves through the organs of the digestive system. These organs break the food down into important nutrients. The nutrients pass into the blood vessels. Blood carries them to your body's cells.

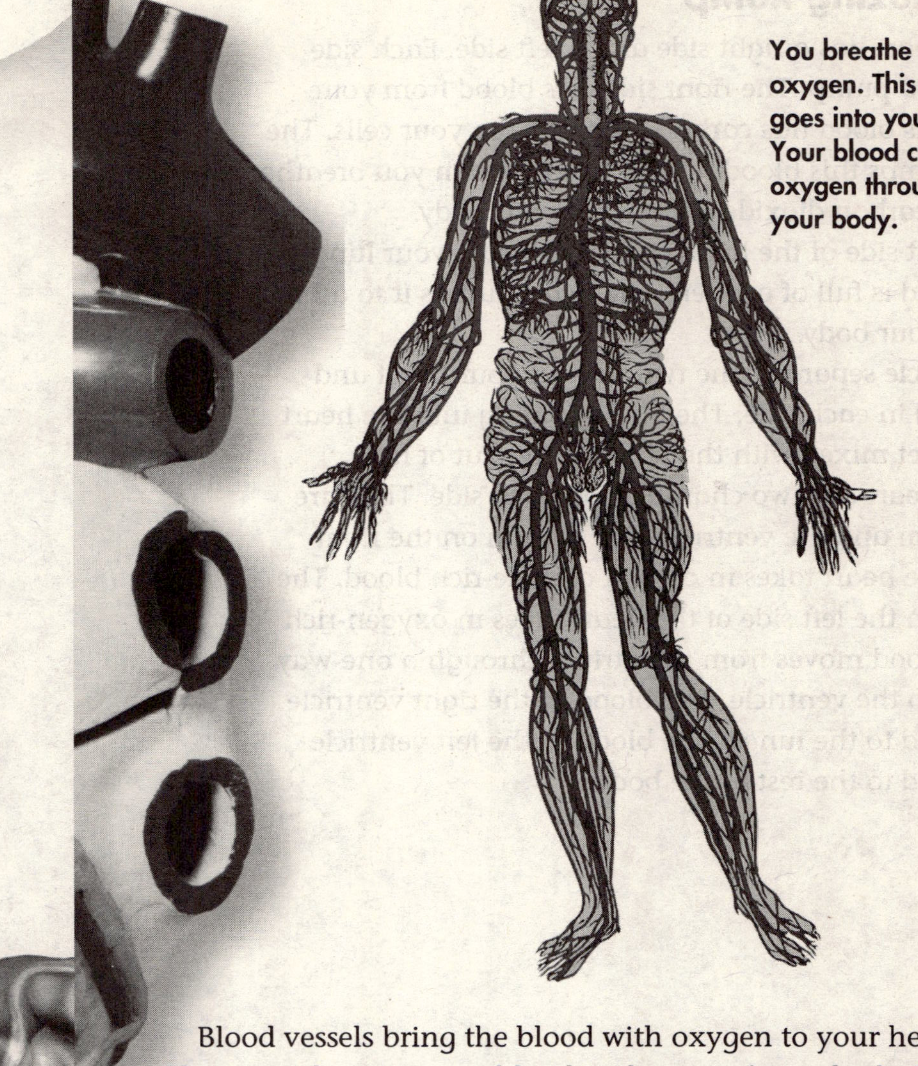



Blood vessels bring the blood with oxygen to your heart. Then your heart pumps blood to the rest of your body. The blood brings oxygen to the cells of your body.

Your circulatory system moves blood through your body. The parts of this system are your heart, blood vessels, and blood.

# An Amazing Pump

The heart has a right side and a left side. Each side works as a pump. The right side gets blood from your body. This blood has carbon dioxide from your cells. The heart pumps this blood to your lungs. When you breathe out, the carbon dioxide goes out of your body.

The left side of the heart gets blood from your lungs. This blood is full of oxygen. The heart pumps it to all the cells in your body.

A muscle separates the two sides of your heart and the blood in each side. The blood coming into the heart doesn't get mixed with the blood going out of it.

Your heart has two chambers on each side. They are the atrium and the ventricle. The atrium on the right side of the heart takes in carbon dioxide-rich blood. The atrium on the left side of the heart takes in oxygen-rich blood. Blood moves from the atrium through a one-way valve into the ventricle. The blood in the right ventricle is pumped to the lungs. The blood in the left ventricle is pumped to the rest of the body.

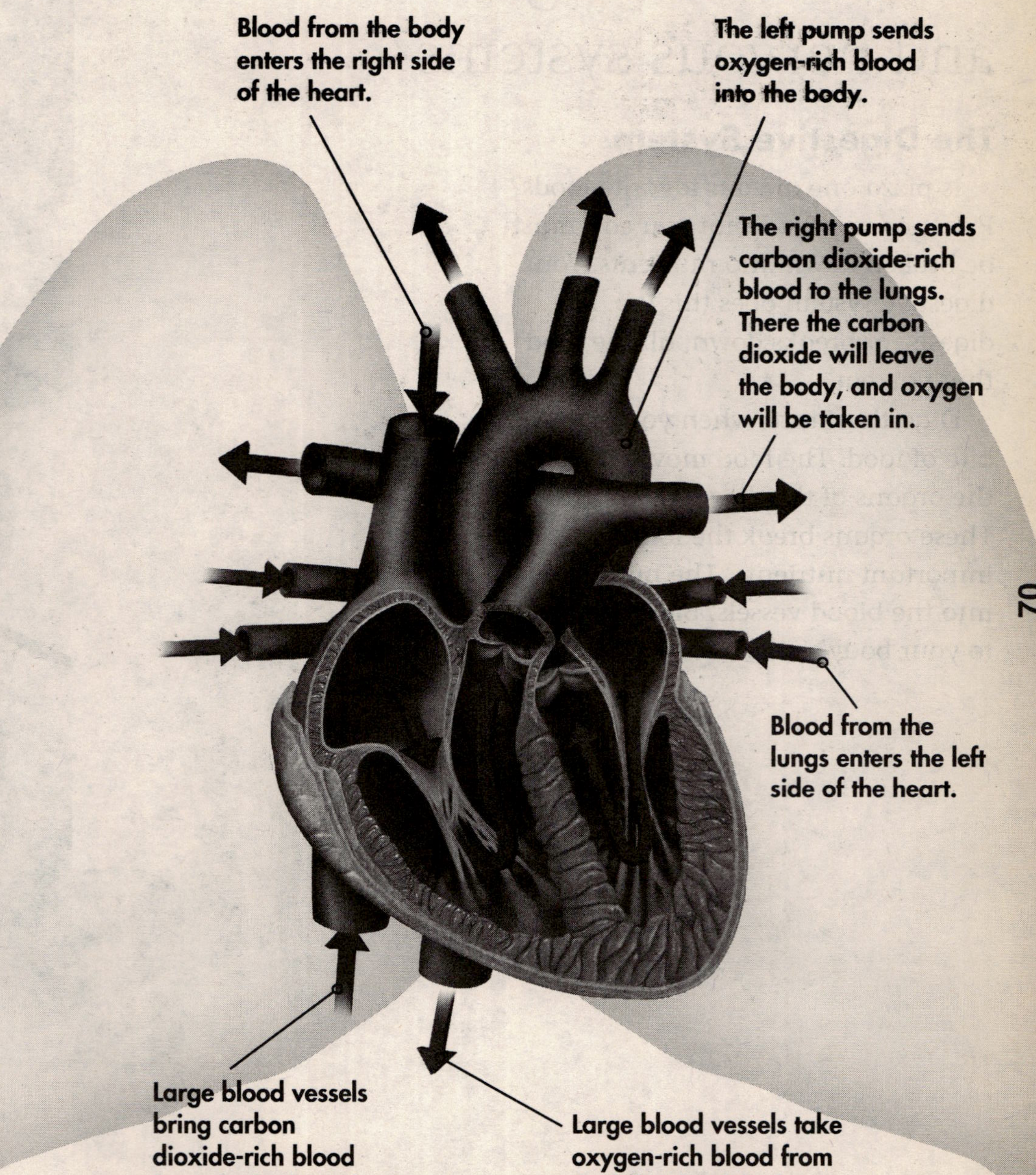

# Water Cycle and Weather

### by Harrison James

| Genre | Comprehension Skill | Text Features | Science Content |
| --- | --- | --- | --- |
| Nonfiction | Cause and Effect | • Captions<br>• Labels<br>• Text Boxes<br>• Glossary | Weather and Water Cycle |

**Scott Foresman Science 4.6**

PEARSON
Scott Foresman

DK

ISBN 0-328-13874-6

9 780328 138746

90000

scottforesman.com

71

**Vocabulary**

anemometer

barometer

condensation

evaporation

front

humidity

meteorologist

precipitation

wind vane

## What did you learn?

1. Why can't you drink salt water?

2. How do scientists classify clouds?

3. What are some tools used to measure weather? What does each tool measure?

4. **Writing** in Science  Water is recycled through the water cycle. Describe on your own paper how the water cycle works. Include details from the book to support your answer.

5. **Cause and Effect** What causes a cold front? What effects does a cold front have on weather?

**Illustrations:** 14 Bob Kayganich
**Photographs:** Every effort has been made to secure permission and provide appropriate credit for photographic material. The publisher deeply regrets any omission and pledges to correct errors called to its attention in subsequent editions. Unless otherwise acknowledged, all photographs are the property of Scott Foresman, a division of Pearson Education. Photo locators denoted as follows: Top (T), Center (C), Bottom (B), Left (L), Right (R) Background (Bkgd)
Opener: ©Steve Wilkings/Corbis, Title Page: ©DK Images; 2 ©Earth Satellite Corporation/Photo Researchers, Inc.; 4 ©Tom Van Sant/Corbis; 6 ©Charles O'Rear/Corbis; 8 (TR, CR) ©DK Images; 9 ©Darwin Wiggett; 12 ©DK Images; 13 ©DK Images; 16 (BL) ©Leonard Lessin/Peter Arnold, Inc., (R) ©David Lees/Corbis; 17 (BL) ©Getty Images, (TR) Stephen Oliver/©DK Images, (BR) ©DK Images; 20 ©DK Images; 23 (Bkgd) ©British Antarctic Survey/Photo Researchers, Inc.

ISBN: 0-328-13874-6

# Water Cycle and Weather

## by Harrison James

**Glossary**

| | |
|---|---|
| **anemometer** | a tool that measures wind speed |
| **barometer** | a tool that measures air pressure |
| **condensation** | water vapor changing into liquid |
| **evaporation** | liquid water changing into water vapor |
| **front** | the area where two air masses meet |
| **humidity** | the amount of water vapor in the air |
| **meteorologist** | a scientist who studies weather conditions |
| **precipitation** | water in any form that falls to Earth |
| **wind vane** | a tool that shows wind direction |

# Where is Earth's water?

## Earth—The Water Planet

Water is found all over Earth. Bodies of water can be used to get from one place to another. Nearly $\frac{3}{4}$ of the surface of Earth is covered with water. Millions of organisms live in water. These organisms get their food from water. People can use these organisms for food.

Water can be a liquid, solid, or gas. At 0°C, water freezes into ice, which is a solid. Ice melts into liquid water at this temperature. At 100°C, water becomes water vapor, which is a gas.

## In the Future

Burning fossil fuels adds carbon dioxide and other pollutants to the atmosphere. There are "greenhouse gases" in our atmosphere. Some of these are water vapor and carbon dioxide. In the right amount, greenhouse gases help keep Earth warm. Too many greenhouse gases increase the temperature of Earth. Climates may change if Earth's temperature rises even a few degrees. Part of the polar ice cap could melt. This could add water to oceans. This could lead to flooding.

Scientists and world leaders are looking for ways to replace fossil fuels with cleaner energy. Using cleaner energy in smaller amounts will be better for Earth. These efforts show how important it is to protect Earth.

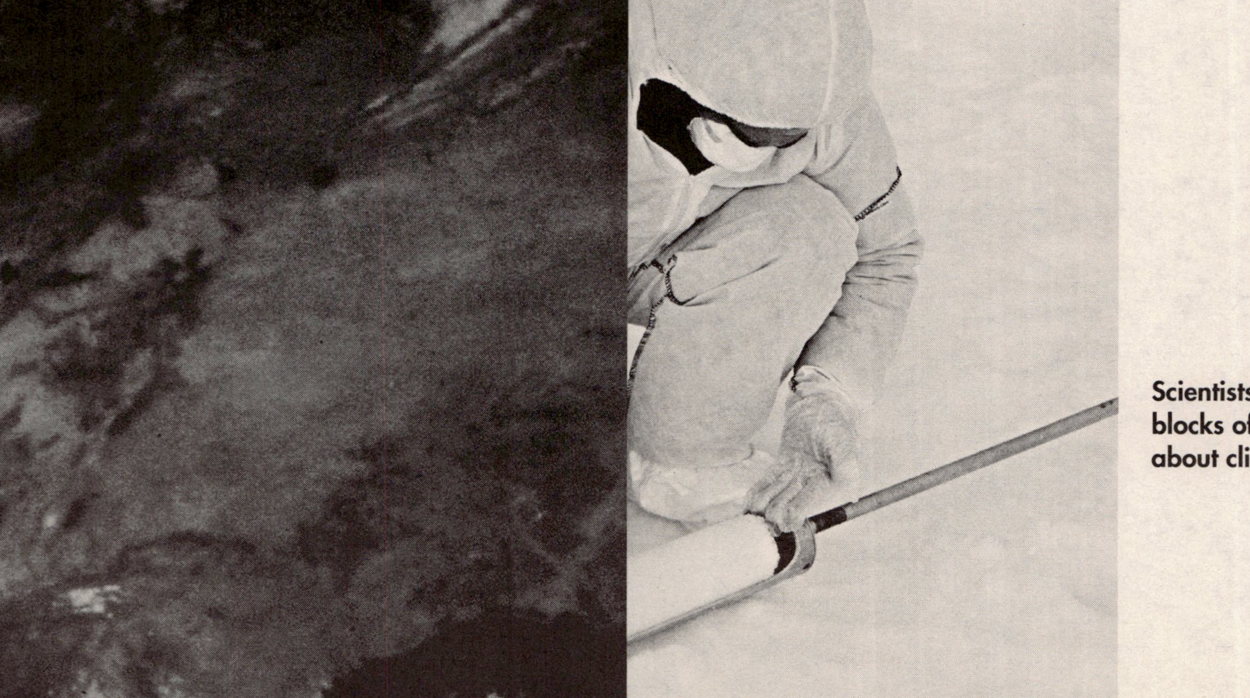

Scientists can study blocks of ice to learn about climates.

## At Present

Earth's climate has experienced cycles in the last two and a half million years. A warm period is followed by a cold period. Then another warm period takes over. We are in a warm period now. The last cold period ended about ten thousand years ago. Earth's climate and temperature change slowly during these cycles. Some scientists worry that people are causing Earth's temperature to change more quickly than it would on its own. They are concerned that these man-made changes are harmful.

Some water near Earth's surface is water vapor. This is mostly water that is found in the atmosphere. But the oceans and seas make up more than $\frac{97}{100}$ of the water found on Earth. Almost all of the rest is frozen in glaciers and polar ice caps. Lakes and rivers make up less than $\frac{1}{100}$ of the water on Earth.

All the oceans of the world are connected. They make up one huge body of salty water. The ocean is divided into sections. Each section is given a name. Look at the chart to see the name and the size of each section.

| Approximate Areas of the Oceans of the World | | | | | |
|---|---|---|---|---|---|
| Ocean | Pacific | Atlantic | Indian | Southern | Arctic |
| Area (km²) | 165 million | 82 million | 73 million | 20 million | 14 million |

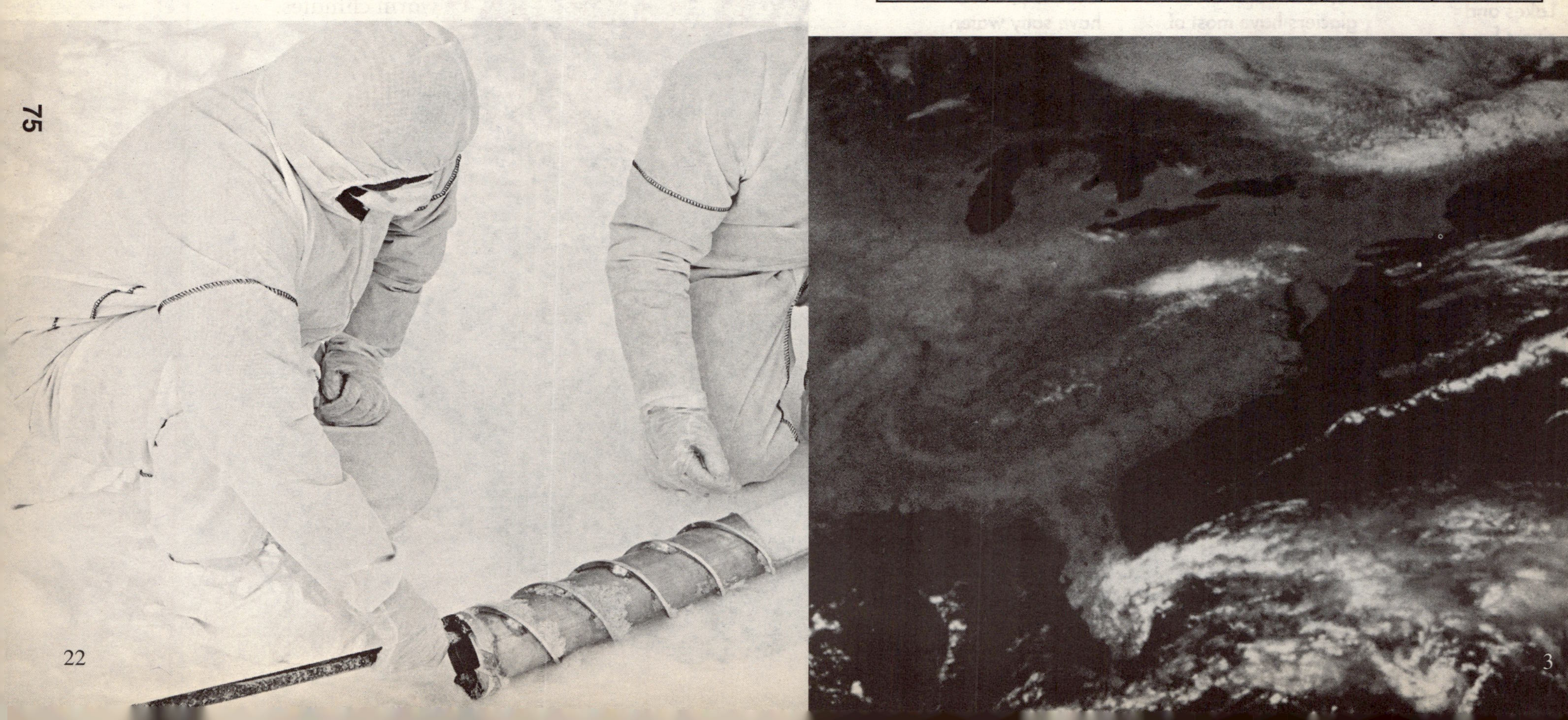

## Salty Water

Ocean water tastes different from our drinking water. Ocean water is very salty. In fact, it is so salty that it is not good to drink. The human body cannot use water that is as salty as the ocean.

Water is made of hydrogen and oxygen. Rivers have dissolved salt and minerals in them. They carry these dissolved materials to the ocean. Ocean water is water mixed with many dissolved solids. Much of the salt in ocean water comes from these dissolved solids. Most of the salt in the ocean is the same salt you use on food. In fact, most of our table salt comes from the ocean.





Tree rings can tell scientists about the climate when the tree was growing. You can see rings in a cut tree trunk. Each ring in a tree trunk shows the growth that took place in one year. A wide ring means there were good growing conditions that year.

Earth's crust can also give scientists information about past climates. Scientists can estimate when each layer of the crust was formed. Coal found in the crust means that layer formed during a warm climate. Coal forms from bodies of organisms that lived long ago in warm climates.

## How Weather and Climate Have Changed

About four billion years ago, Earth cooled and the atmosphere formed. The climate of Earth has changed many times since then. It has had very cold periods and warm periods. During the last cold period, thick sheets of ice spread from the North and South Poles. They covered almost one-third of Earth's surface.

Scientists learn about Earth's climate in many ways. They can drill into glaciers. The ice they remove tells them about the climate when the ice froze. They may find air bubbles in ice from the last cold period. This tells scientists what air was like when it was trapped.

## Differences in Saltiness

Not all water at the surface of the ocean has the same amount of salt. In warm, dry places, water from the ocean quickly moves into the air as water vapor. Salt does not move into the air. The ocean water that's left is even saltier.

The ocean water around the North and South Poles is less salty. Water does not become water vapor as quickly in cold places as it does in warm places. There is also less salt in areas where a lot of fresh water mixes with ocean water. The fresh water can come from rivers, melting ice, and heavy rain.

Most water on Earth is salty ocean water. Some fresh water is in lakes, rivers, and streams. Much of Earth's fresh water is frozen in glaciers and polar ice caps. It cannot be used for drinking.

## Earth's Water

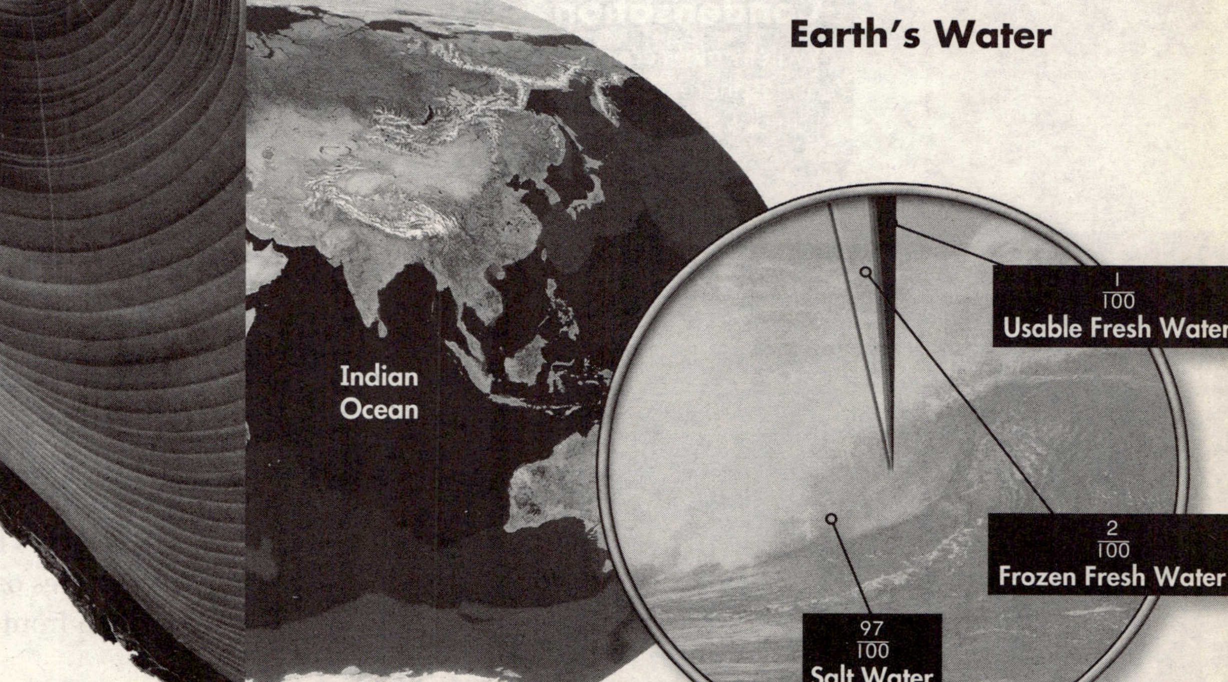

# How do water and air affect weather?

## How Water Is Recycled

Water moves from the surface of Earth into the atmosphere and back again. This is the water cycle. After it rains, some water will flow into lakes, rivers, or the ocean. The rest will go into the air. The particles that make up water are always moving. Heat from the Sun makes them move faster. The particles become a gas called water vapor. **Evaporation** is liquid water changing into water vapor.

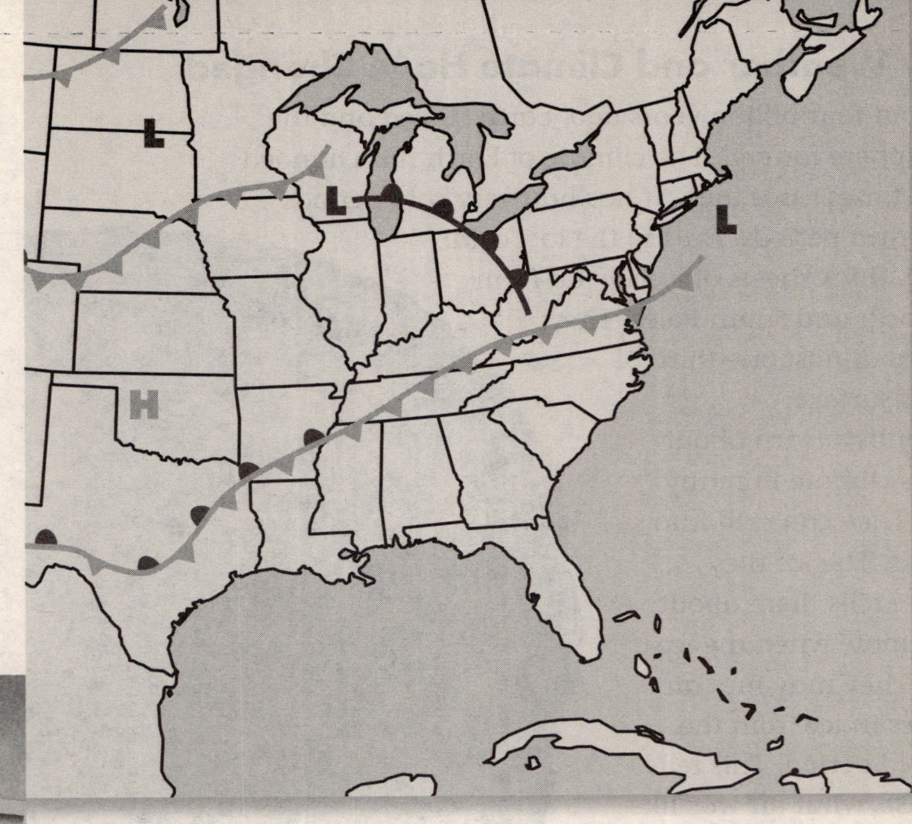


## Tracking Weather

Measurements and information from weather radar and satellites are put into maps and charts. Meteorologists use this to predict weather. Charts can record daily weather conditions.

## Reading Weather Maps

A weather map uses symbols to show fronts and weather conditions. A legend, or key, explains what everything means. The letters H and L show areas of high and low pressure. Triangles on lines mean cold fronts. Half circles mean warm fronts.

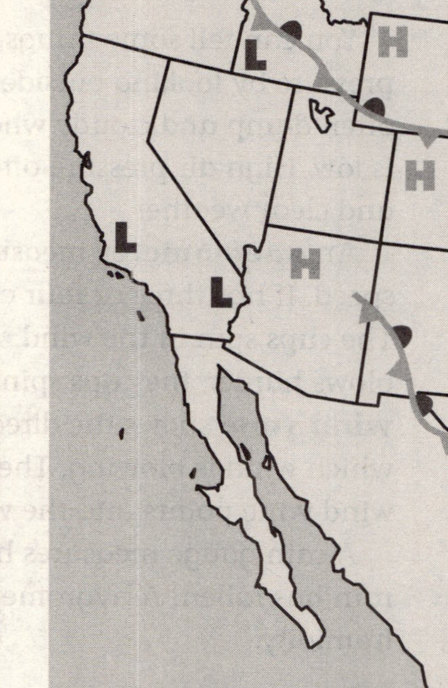




## Predicting Weather

Weather in the same place is usually similar from year to year. Summer days are warmer than winter days. Figuring out the weather from day to day is not as easy.

Meteorologists measure temperature, precipitation, air pressure, and wind. They find fronts and areas of high and low pressure. They use this information to make a forecast. A forecast tells what the weather will probably be for the next few days.

Weather radar gives information that is used to make computer models. Radar pictures show how the atmosphere is changing. Meteorologists can find out where rain has fallen. This information also helps them make forecasts.



Water vapor turns to liquid when the temperature is low. **Condensation** is water vapor becoming liquid when it cools.

Clouds are made of tiny drops of water or crystals of ice. These drops and crystals join together until they are so heavy that gravity pulls them downward to Earth's surface. **Precipitation** is water in any form that falls to Earth.

Temperature, the movement of air, and the amount of water vapor in the air affect the water cycle. Land features, such as mountains, also have an effect. Clouds form when wind blows moist air up one side of a mountain. More precipitation will fall on that side of the mountain. Water moves through the water cycle. The total amount of water on Earth does not change.

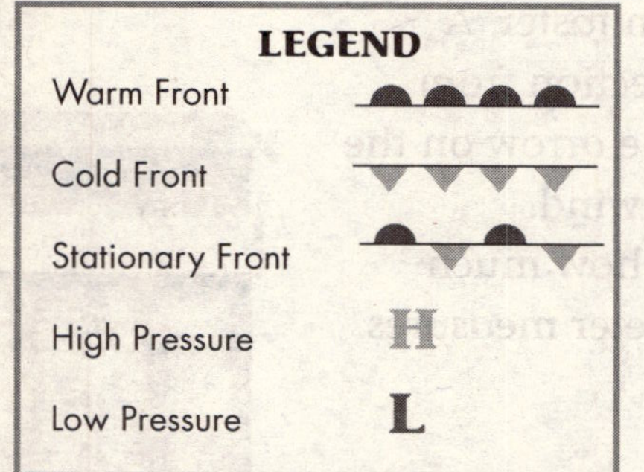

### Precipitation

Water may fall as rain, snow, or hail. If the air temperature is above freezing, the water vapor will condense and fall as rain. If the air temperature is below freezing, water falls as snow, sleet, or hail.

### Storage

The water from precipitation over land sinks into soil and into the ground. Some water runs off the land into streams, rivers, and lakes. Most of it falls, flows, or seeps into the ocean.

## The Earth's Atmosphere

The atmosphere is the blanket of air around Earth. Air has mass. It takes up space. Air is made of invisible gases. Nitrogen makes up nearly $\frac{4}{5}$ of the atmosphere. The rest is mostly oxygen, with some carbon dioxide gas. The part of the atmosphere that is closest to Earth's surface has water vapor. Air over a desert has less water vapor than air over an ocean.

Air pressure is the pushing force of air. Air pushes in all directions with the same amount of force. Air pushing up is balanced by air pushing down.

## Air Pressure

Temperature can change air pressure. The particles of warm air near the surface of Earth move quickly. The air rises and then pushes down with less pressure. This makes an area of low pressure. If the air near the surface of Earth becomes cool, its particles will move slowly. This dense air will sink.

Wind is air moving from an area of high pressure to an area of low pressure. Wind is named for the direction from which it comes. A north wind comes from the north and moves south.

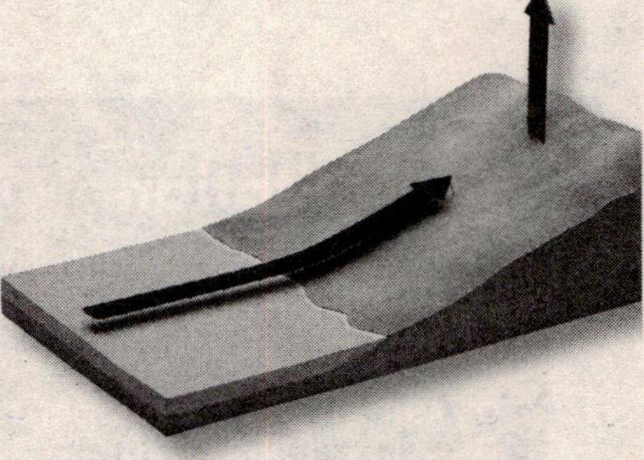
A land breeze moves from land to the sea. At night, the cool air over land sinks and moves toward the water.

A sea breeze moves from the sea to land. During the day, the warm air over land rises. The air over the water moves toward the land.

## Air Pressure and Weather Conditions

You can tell some things about air pressure by looking outside. Weather is often damp and cloudy when air pressure is low. High air pressure often causes dry and clear weather.

An **anemometer** measures wind speed. It has three or four cups on top. The cups spin in the wind. As the wind blows harder, the cups spin faster. A **wind vane** shows the direction from which wind is blowing. The arrow on the wind vane points into the wind.

A rain gauge measures how much rain has fallen. A hygrometer measures humidity.

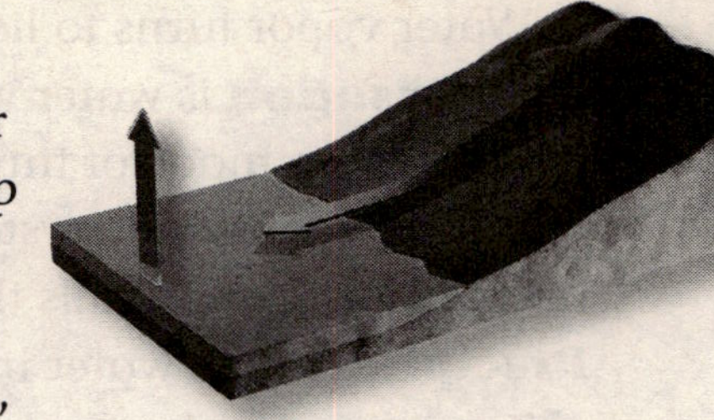
Anemometer

Hygrometer

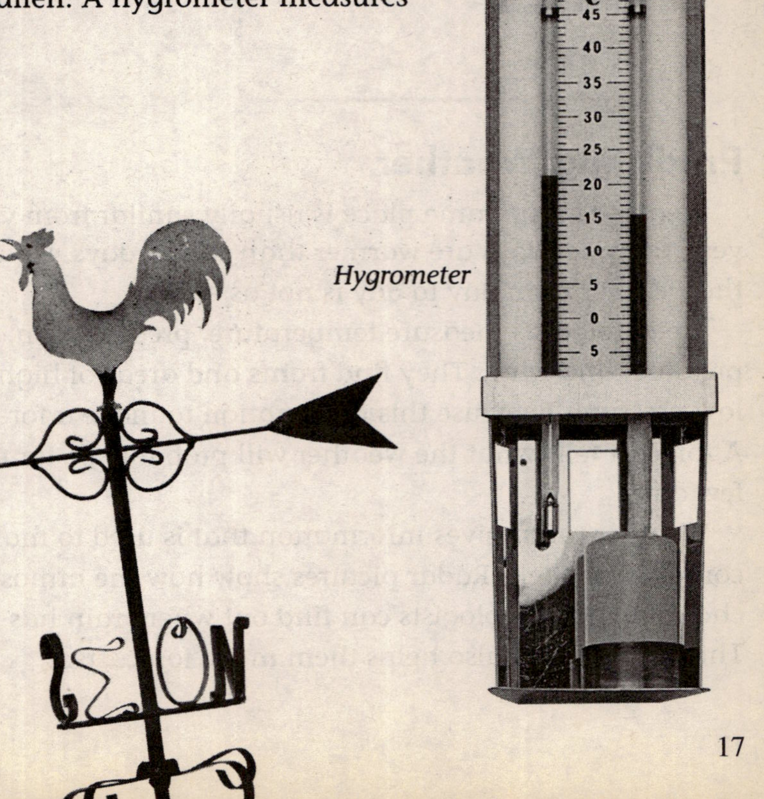
Wind vane





80

# How do we measure and predict weather?

## Measuring Weather

Temperature, air pressure, and water affect weather. Ocean currents move warm water to cold lands. They also move cold water to warm lands. Areas near water may have milder temperatures than areas farther away.

A **meteorologist** is a scientist who studies weather conditions. Meteorologists also study temperature, water, and air movement. They get information from weather observation stations.

A thermometer measures air temperature. A **barometer** measures air pressure. Air pressure is often measured in millibars (mb).



Mercury barometer

Aneroid barometer

Early barometers, such as the one on the right, used mercury. Today scientists use aneroid barometers.



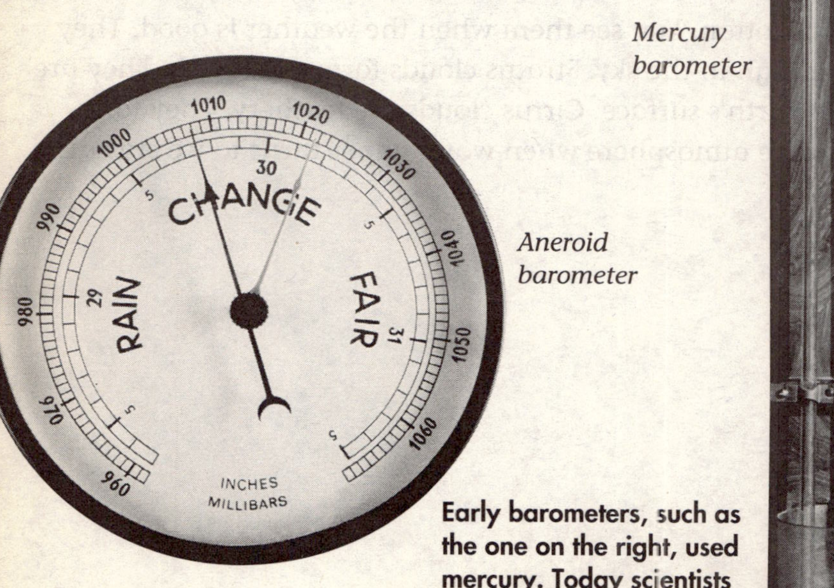

# What are air masses?

## Air Masses

An air mass is a vast body of air with almost the same temperature and humidity. **Humidity** is the amount of water vapor in the air. Most weather comes from how air masses move and interact. Air masses are heated or cooled by the land or water over which they form. This can take several days, or even weeks. A cool or cold air mass forms over polar areas. A warm or hot air mass forms over tropical areas.

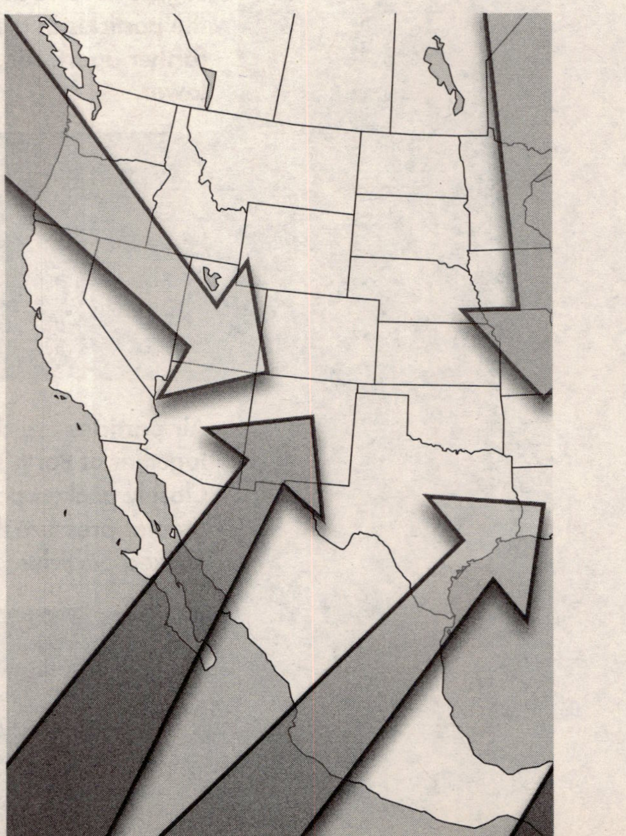

Ten names are used to describe most clouds. The names are combinations of three main types of clouds. The main types of clouds are cumulus, stratus, and cirrus. Adding *alto* to a cloud's name means the cloud is very high. *Nimbo* means a cloud will bring rain.

Cumulus clouds are thick, white, and puffy. They look like pieces of cotton. You see them when the weather is good. They may be high in the sky. Stratus clouds form flat layers. They are close to Earth's surface. Cirrus clouds are feathery. They form high in the atmosphere when water vapor turns to ice crystals.

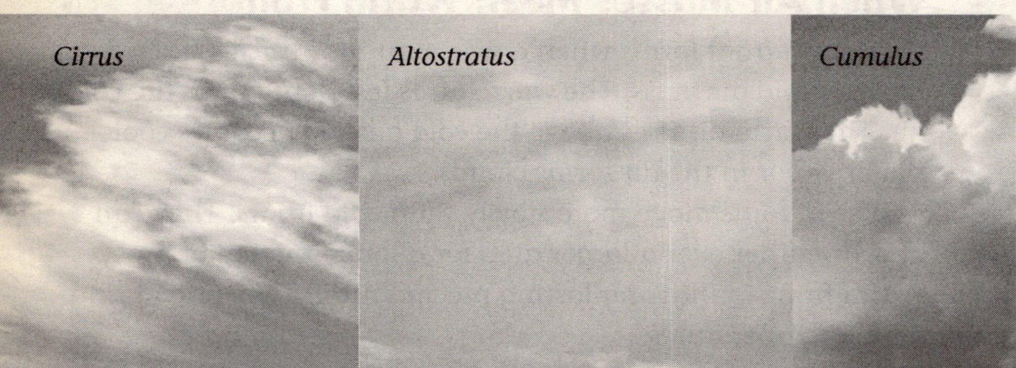



An air mass has water vapor in it. This water vapor is water that has evaporated from the land or body of water below the air mass. An air mass that forms over water has more humidity than one that forms over land. An air mass that forms over a tropical ocean will most likely be warm and humid. An air mass that forms over a cool ocean will be cool and moist.

Temperature and humidity move with air masses. Scientists follow the movement of air masses to predict the weather. They also study where and how air masses will meet. Weather is how air, water, and temperature interact.

## Clouds

Clouds begin to take shape as the Sun warms the water in oceans, rivers, lakes, and the ground. The warm water evaporates and water vapor enters the air. This air is warmed by the Sun. This causes the air to rise and cool. The water vapor forms water drops and ice crystals. These drops and crystals are clouds.

There are many kinds of clouds. They can have different shapes, sizes, and colors. The kind of cloud that forms depends on the atmosphere.

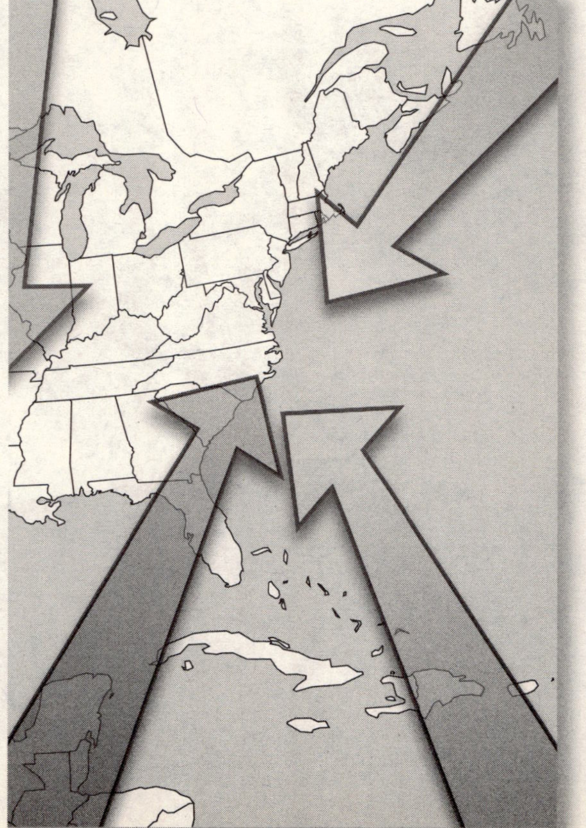

## When Air Masses Meet: Cold Front

An air mass usually moves from west to east. It can meet air masses that have different temperatures and humidity. The air masses do not mix. A **front** is the area where two different air masses meet.

A cold front comes from a cold air mass meeting a slowly moving warm air mass. Cold air is denser than warm air. The dense, cold air moves below the warm air. The warm air becomes cooler as it is pushed up. Water vapor in the cooling air forms clouds.

Cold fronts can cause strong winds and heavy, brief precipitation. Cold fronts move quickly. After they pass, the weather is usually cooler and fair.

## When Air Masses Meet: Warm Front

A warm front forms when a warm air mass meets a slowly moving cold air mass. The warm air is less dense than the cold air. The warm air rises above the cold air and becomes cooler. Water vapor in the air forms clouds.

Warm fronts move more slowly than cold fronts. They can affect weather over a larger area for a longer period of time. Warm fronts bring long-lasting precipitation. They often bring higher temperatures.

# Hurricanes and Tornadoes

by Mariella C. Dinsel

| Genre | Comprehension Skill | Text Features | Science Content |
|---|---|---|---|
| Nonfiction | Main Idea and Details | • Captions<br>• Labels<br>• Maps<br>• Glossary | Severe Storms |

**Scott Foresman Science 4.7**

## What did you learn?

1. How is the eye of a hurricane different from the rest of the storm?

2. What is a storm surge? Why is it dangerous?

3. Why are tornadoes difficult to forecast?

4. **Writing** in Science A tropical storm goes through many stages before it forms a hurricane. Explain on your own paper what these stages are. Include details from the book to support your answer.

5. **Main Idea and Details** Reread the "How Tornadoes Form" section on page 12. What is the main idea of this section? What are some supporting details?

**Illustration:** 12 Tony Randazzo
**Photographs:** Every effort has been made to secure permission and provide appropriate credit for photographic material. The publisher deeply regrets any omission and pledges to correct errors called to its attention in subsequent editions. Unless otherwise acknowledged, all photographs are the property of Scott Foresman, a division of Pearson Education. Photo locators denoted as follows: Top (T), Center (C), Bottom (B), Left (L), Right (R) Background (Bkgd)
Opener: Getty Images Title Page: ©Japan Meteorological Agency 2 ©Reuters/Corbis 4 (L, C) ©Japan Meteorological Agency 5 (CR, R) ©Japan Meteorological Agency 6 ©Japan Meteorological Agency 7 ©Adastra/Getty Images 8 ©DK Images 9 (CR) ©Morton Beebe/Corbis, (BR) ©Cameron Davidson 10 NASA 13 (CL) ©ANT Photo Library/NHPA Limited, (CR) ©H. Hoflinger/FLPA-Images of Nature 14 ©Jim Reed/Photo Researchers, Inc. 15 ©Reuters/Corbis

ISBN: 0-328-13877-0

Copyright © Pearson Education, Inc.

All Rights Reserved. Printed in the United States of America. The blackline masters in this publication are designed for use with appropriate equipment to reproduce copies for classroom use only. Scott Foresman grants permission to classroom teachers to reproduce from these masters.

2 3 4 5 6 7 8 9 10 V004 13 12 11 10 09 08 07 06 05

# Hurricanes and Tornadoes

**by Mariella C. Dinsel**

## Glossary

**hurricane** — a storm with wind speeds of at least 119 kilometers per hour

**storm surge** — a rise in sea level caused by the winds of a hurricane

**tornado** — a spinning column of air that comes from a thunderstorm and touches the ground

**tropical depression** — a storm whose winds have reached a speed of 61 kilometers per hour

**tropical storm** — a storm whose winds blow faster than 62 kilometers per hour

**vortex** — an area where air or liquid spins in circles

# What are hurricanes?

## How Tropical Storms Become Hurricanes

A low pressure area formed over part of the Atlantic Ocean in August 1992. It became stronger and bigger. It grew into a powerful tropical storm named Andrew. It became even more powerful. It became Hurricane Andrew.

The area near the equator is known as the tropics. Tropical storms form there. A **hurricane** is a dangerous storm formed by bands of thunderstorms wrapping around its center. It has wind speeds of at least 119 kilometers per hour.

## Safety

The National Weather Service tells people about tornadoes. A tornado watch means a tornado is likely to form. A tornado warning means a tornado has been observed.

During a tornado, go to a basement or a small space, such as a bathroom or closet. Do not go near outside walls or windows. You are not safe in a car. Tornadoes can pick up cars and then drop them.

## Comparing Tornadoes and Hurricanes

Hurricanes and tornadoes are powerful storms. They have strong winds and cause great damage. But hurricanes are many kilometers wide. They form over the ocean. They can last for many days. Tornadoes are smaller than hurricanes. Most of them form over land. They do not last long. It is important to look for shelter if either of these storms is in your area.

## Forecasting Tornadoes

Only some strong thunderstorms produce tornadoes. It is hard to forecast tornadoes. They form and move quickly.

A tornado can destroy weather equipment. It can destroy everything in its path. Scientists can look inside thunderstorms. They use Doppler radar to do this. Doppler radar finds information, such as the direction and speed of wind.

## Classifying Tornadoes

The damage caused by tornadoes can help scientists learn how strong the storm's winds were. Scientists group tornadoes by damage and wind speed. They use a scale developed by scientist T. Theodore Fujita.

| Fujita Scale | | |
|---|---|---|
| Strength of Tornado | Wind Speed (km/hour) | Damage caused |
| F0 Gale | 64–116 | Tree branches broken, chimneys damaged |
| F1 Moderate | 117–180 | Tree trunks broken, cars pushed off roads |
| F2 Significant | 181–253 | Trees knocked down, weak buildings destroyed |
| F3 Severe | 254–332 | Cars and trains turned over, roofs torn off buildings |
| F4 Devastating | 333–419 | Sturdy wooden buildings destroyed, cars thrown |
| F5 Incredible | over 419 | Houses shattered, cars thrown more than 100 meters |

Hurricane Andrew moved west across the Atlantic. It first hit the Bahama Islands. It moved toward Florida. The winds near the center of the storm may have been as fast as 250 kilometers per hour. You would run an entire mile in less than 25 seconds if you moved that fast!

Hurricane Andrew crossed southern Florida in about four hours. Over land, the storm became weaker. But it became strong again when it reached the warm waters of the Gulf of Mexico. From there, it moved on to Louisiana. Then it continued north. The storm again weakened. But its rain caused a great deal of flooding.

This hurricane was one of the most expensive natural disasters in the history of the United States. It caused many deaths. It damaged and destroyed many businesses and houses.

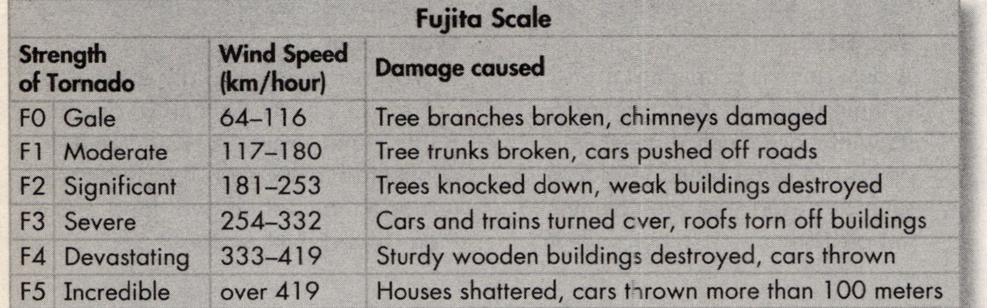

## Stages of Tropical Storms

A tropical storm must have certain things to form. It needs warm ocean water. It also needs an area of low air pressure at the ocean's surface. Winds blow toward this area of low pressure. The warm ocean water provides heat and water vapor. The warm, moist air rises. Water vapor condenses and forms clouds. A tropical disturbance develops.

## How Hurricanes Form

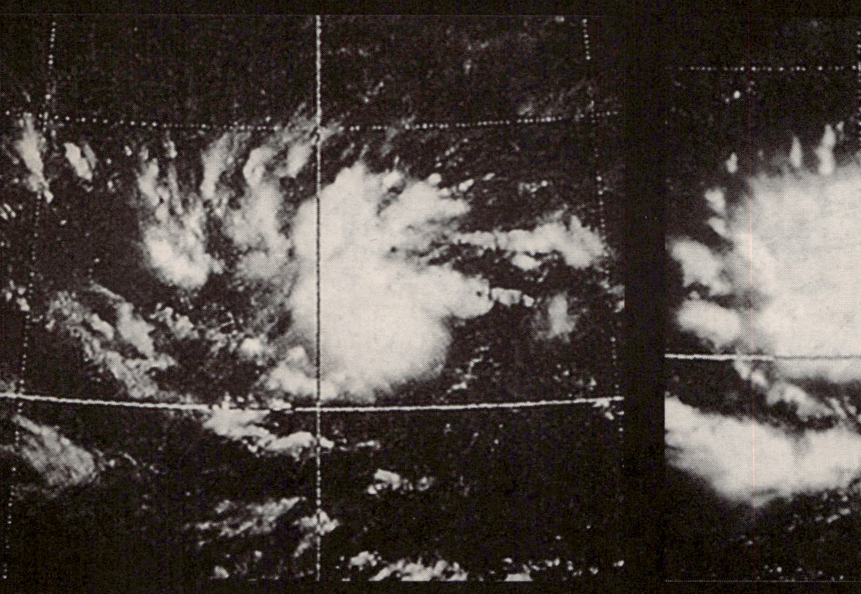

Thunderstorms grow out of a tropical depression.

Air pressure at the ocean's surface drops. Surface winds blow faster and begin to swirl. A tropical storm develops.

## The Vortex

A **vortex** is an area where air or liquid spins in circles. You may see a vortex when water drains from a sink. A tornado is a vortex that forms within a thunderstorm. Air rushes up along the outside of a tornado.

Air moves down through the center of a tornado, where the air pressure is low. Water vapor condenses in the rising air. A funnel cloud may form below the storm. The vortex may become more visible as the funnel cloud picks up dust. But a tornado can be hidden by heavy rain, dust, or nighttime.

**Dust Devil**
A dust devil is a column of spinning air. It is not a tornado. Its winds are much slower. Dust devils are often found in places such as deserts, where columns of hot air rise.

**Waterspout**
A waterspout is a rapidly spinning column of air over a lake or ocean. It lifts water drops. A waterspout is connected to a cloud. It may be a tornado that started over land and then moved over water.

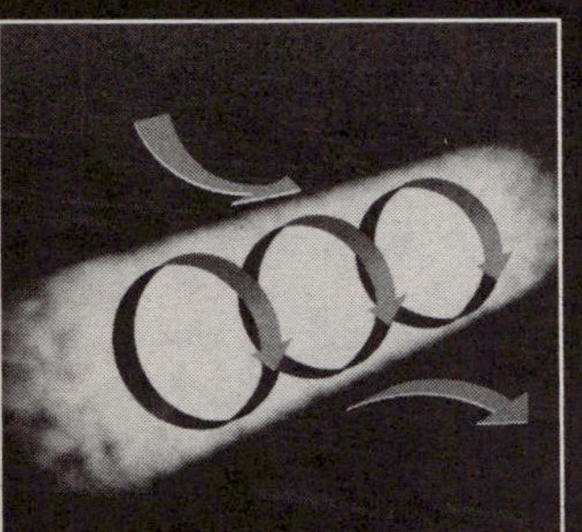

Before thunderstorms form, winds change direction and increase in speed. Winds begin to spin.

As the thunderstorm forms, air within it rises. The spinning air begins to tilt upward.

The area of spinning grows wider.

# What are tornadoes?

## How Tornadoes Form

A funnel cloud is a spinning column of air. It comes out of a thunderstorm. It becomes a **tornado** when it touches the ground. The air pressure is low in the center of a tornado. The wind speeds of most tornadoes are less than 200 kilometers per hour. But the winds can reach 500 kilometers per hour. These are the fastest winds on Earth.

A tornado begins as a spinning column of air. The column may become shaped like a funnel. The funnel becomes longer and thinner. It gains speed. As it moves, it may pick up anything in its path. The funnel cloud reaches down toward the ground. It is a tornado when it actually touches the ground.

The clouds in a tropical disturbance can become thunderstorms. Water vapor condenses, releasing heat energy. The thunderstorms grow as the air inside them becomes warmer. Winds increase and begin to swirl. The storms become a **tropical depression.** A tropical depression can have winds moving as fast as 61 kilometers per hour. These winds can increase and form a **tropical storm.** The winds in a tropical storm blow faster than 62 kilometers per hour. The air pressure in the storm drops.

Thunderstorms begin to move in spiral bands. Air pressure drops lower, and surface winds blow faster. The tropical storm is now a hurricane.

## Hurricane as a System

Thunderstorms move toward the area with the lowest air pressure. They move in a spinning pattern. A lot of air moves out of the top of the storm. Less air moves in at the surface of the ocean. Air pressure keeps dropping. This makes the winds blow even faster. When the wind speeds reach 119 kilometers per hour, the storm is a hurricane.

Parts that work together or affect each other make up a system. The atmosphere and the ocean are two of Earth's systems. Together they produce a hurricane. Hurricanes are systems. They form in the atmosphere. They get energy from the ocean.

Hurricanes can change Earth's systems. They can change the land. They can cause huge waves. They can change the shape of a coastline.

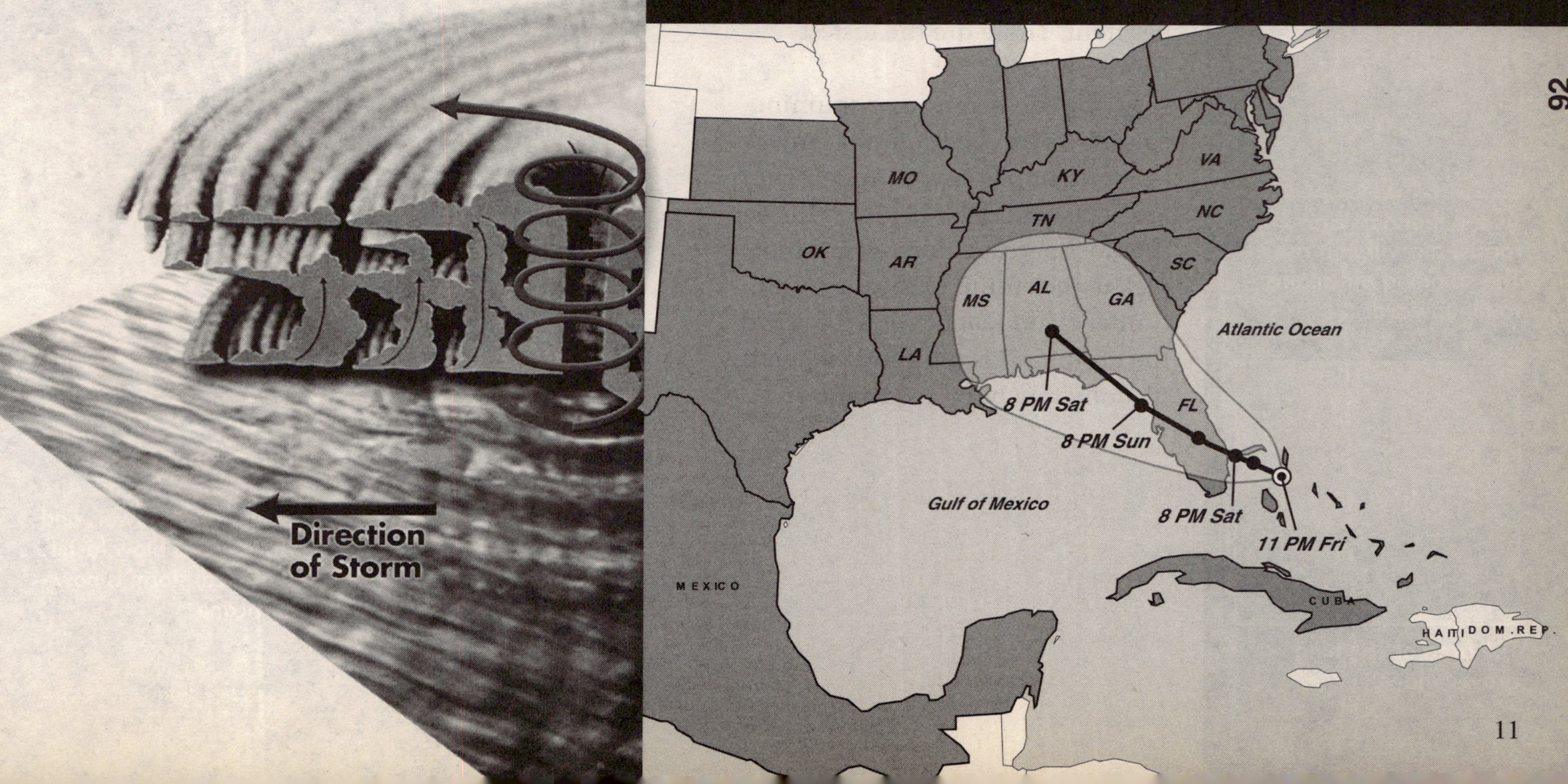


## Hurricane Models

Hurricane models predict what path the storm will take. A forecast shows where a hurricane is and where it might go. The map below is a forecast for Hurricane Frances. Scientists try to predict what path a storm will take, and what areas it will affect. As they predict further into the future, they expand the area that might be affected.

## Teamwork of Scientists

Scientists work together to make predictions about hurricanes. Some may study how heat moves. Others may study how the winds in the atmosphere will affect a hurricane. Scientists share their information to make the best possible forecast.

## How Scientists Predict Hurricanes

It used to be hard to tell when a hurricane was coming. Now scientists make weather forecasts. The weather forecasts tell people about hurricanes that are far away.

Scientists get information from instruments all over the world. There are satellites high above Earth's surface. They can tell about a hurricane's rainfall. Pilots fly special planes into hurricanes to get information. This information helps scientists make computer models. A model shows a system or set of events. Models help people study things that are too big or too dangerous to study directly.

Computer models can predict the strength, direction, and speed of a hurricane. Scientists compare the forecasts made by the models to what really happens. Then they fix the models to make them more accurate.

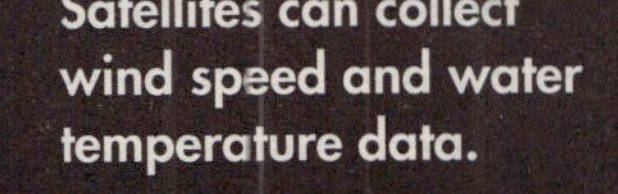

Satellites can collect wind speed and water temperature data.

## The Hurricane's Eye

The eye of a hurricane is the calm area in the middle of the storm. The hurricane spins around its eye. The winds in the eye are gentle. The eye has little or no rain. The thunderstorms around the eye have the strongest winds and heaviest rains. A typical hurricane's eye is about 20 to 50 kilometers across.

People under the eye may think the hurricane has passed. They must be careful. They need to be in a safe place when the other half of the hurricane sweeps in.

## The Effects of Winds and Water

A hurricane can destroy many things on land. Its winds can knock down trees. They can completely flatten buildings. The winds can pick up objects and throw them. Hurricanes are put in categories based on their wind speed.

The water from a hurricane often does the most damage. Rain can mix with soil. This can lead to mudslides. Even though a hurricane loses strength as it moves over land, it can cause deadly floods.

The winds of a hurricane can force large ocean waves onto the shore. A **storm surge** is the rise in sea level caused by a storm's winds. A storm surge can make flooding worse. It can sweep large boats onto land. In 1900, a hurricane over Galveston, Texas caused a storm surge that killed more than 6,000 people.

But a hurricane can be helpful in some ways. The rain reduces the chances of wildfires. The storm can kill non-native plants. This makes room for native plants to grow.

# Minerals and Rocks

by Audrey N. Delmar

| Genre | Comprehension Skill | Text Features | Science Content |
|---|---|---|---|
| Nonfiction | Summarize | • Labels<br>• Captions<br>• Charts<br>• Glossary | Rocks and Minerals |

Scott Foresman Science 4.8

PEARSON
Scott Foresman

DK

ISBN 0-328-13880-0

9 780328 138807

90000

scottforesman.com

## What did you learn?

1. What are some physical properties of minerals that scientists test?

2. What are the three kinds of rock?

3. What are some forces that cause the changes that take place in the rock cycle?

4. **Writing** in Science  Over time, rock changes to soil. On your own paper, describe how this happens. Use details from the book to support your answer.

5. **Summarize** Explain the steps that take place in order for a fossil to form.



**Illustration:** 6, 9, 11, 15 Alan Male

**Photographs:** Every effort has been made to secure permission and provide appropriate credit for photographic material. The publisher deeply regrets any omission and pledges to correct errors called to its attention in subsequent editions. Unless otherwise acknowledged, all photographs are the property of Scott Foresman, a division of Pearson Education. Photo locators denoted as follows: Top (T), Center (C), Bottom (B), Left (L), Right (R) Background (Bkgd)

Opener: (Bkgd) ©Ted Mead/PhotoLibrary, (TC) ©DK Images; Title Page: (CC) ©DK Images; 2 (L, C, CR, BR) ©DK Images, (BR) GeoScience Resources/American Geological Institute; 3 (BR) ©Colin Keates/ Courtesy of the Natural History Museum, London/©DK Images; (T, CL, C) ©DK Images; 4 (1–8,10) ©DK Images, (9) Colin Keates/Courtesy of the Natural History Museum, London/©DK Images; 5 (T, BL) ©DK Images, (CL) Natural History Museum/©DK Images, (C) Colin Keates/Courtesy of the Natural History Museum, London/©DK Images; 7 ©DK Images; 8 (TL, TR) ©DK Images, (CL) Dave King/©DK Images, (BR) ©Danny Lehman/Corbis; 10 (BL) Harry Taylor/Courtesy of the Natural History Museum, London/ ©DK Images, (BR) Colin Keates/Courtesy of the Natural History Museum, London/©DK Images; 12 (TL, TR, BR) ©DK Images, (BL) Colin Keates/Courtesy of the Natural History Museum, London/©DK Images; 13 Alan Williams/©DK Images; 14 (BL) ©DK Images, (B) Richard M. Busch; 15 ©DK Images.

ISBN: 0-328-13880-0

# Minerals and Rocks

## by Audrey N. Delmar

## Glossary

**igneous rock**    rock that forms from cooled molten rock

**luster**    a measure of the way the surface of a mineral reflects light

**metamorphic rock**    rock that has changed as a result of heat and pressure

**mineral**    a natural, nonliving solid crystal that makes up rocks

**sediment**    the eroded material that settles at the bottom of lakes, rivers, and oceans

**sedimentary rock**    rock that forms when layers of sediment particles harden

# What are minerals?

## Mineral Crystals

A **mineral** is a natural, nonliving solid crystal that makes up rocks. The salt you put on your food is a mineral. A metal fork is made of minerals.

Every mineral has crystals. Fluorite crystals are cube-shaped. Corundum crystals are six-sided. A mineral has the same shape crystals and the same chemicals in it no matter where it is found. A piece of quartz in Australia has the same chemical makeup as a piece of quartz in Arkansas.

Granite contains quartz, mica, and feldspar crystals.

Mica can form rocks that are brown or black.

Quartz is hard and glassy.

Feldspar is often white or pink.

## The Rock Cycle

The rock cycle is the recycling of old rock into new. It is an ongoing process. The rock cycle needs forces such as heat, pressure, chemical reactions, weathering, and erosion. All three kinds of rock can change from one form to another. Not all rock completes the entire cycle. Rock deep in the crust may never reach the surface. It may never change. Sedimentary rock can melt and harden into igneous rock.

Slate is a metamorphic rock. It forms from shale, a sedimentary rock. Slate and shale can wear away to form new layers of sediment. These layers can harden into sedimentary rock. Rock under Earth's surface can melt and then form igneous rock. Over time the same materials can change into different types of rock.

The metamorphic rock slate forms from the sedimentary rock shale.

## Metamorphic Rocks

Rock is under pressure below the surface of Earth. It is squeezed by the weight of other rocks. This can cause rocks to change form. Rock that has changed as a result of heat and pressure is called **metamorphic rock.**

Metamorphic rock can form from sedimentary, igneous, or other metamorphic rock. Limestone is sedimentary rock. It can become the metamorphic rock marble. Rock can change form more than once.

Rock can change in many ways as it becomes metamorphic rock. Heat and pressure can cause the rock's mineral crystals to change. They may form again with new crystals of different sizes and shapes. The heat and pressure can also cause minerals to form parallel layers. This means some metamorphic rock may chip into flat sheets and slabs.

Phyllite forms from sedimentary rock. Its minerals are layered.

Gneiss forms from sedimentary or igneous rock.

Scientists have found more than 3,000 minerals. But only a small number of them make up most of the rocks in Earth's crust. These are "rock-forming" minerals. Most rocks are a combination of these minerals. Granite is made of quartz, mica, and feldspar crystals. White marble has only the mineral calcite.

Cinnabar

Orpiment

Pyrite

## Mohs Scale for Hardness

10 Diamond

9 Corundum

8 Topaz

7 Quartz

6 Feldspar

5 Apatite

4 Fluorite

3 Calcite

2 Gypsum

1 Talc

## How to Identify a Mineral

Scientists test different properties in order to identify minerals. Some properties they test are color, luster, hardness, streak, and cleavage.

A mineral's color is easy to see. Feldspar minerals are usually pink or white. But some minerals can be several different colors. Scientists must use other tests such as luster. The **luster** of a mineral is how its surface reflects light. Luster can be dull, metallic, pearly, glassy, greasy, or silky.

## Hardness

The Mohs Scale for Hardness tells scientists how easily a mineral can be scratched. The scale is from 1 to 10. A mineral with a higher number can scratch minerals with lower numbers. Topaz is an 8. Quartz is a 7. Topaz is harder than quartz. It will scratch quartz.

## The Giant's Causeway

A causeway is a road built above water. It is built on pillars. These basalt pillars are called the Giant's Causeway. The tops of these pillars are stepping stones that lead to the sea. There are about 40,000 of these columns. They are located in Northern Ireland. The pillars formed between 50 and 60 million years ago. Lava cooled quickly when it reached the sea. It squeezed together. Cracks from the top to the bottom of the rock formed these pillars. Many of the pillars have six sides.

# What are igneous and metamorphic rocks?

## Igneous Rocks

Some rocks can melt. The layer of rock below Earth's crust is so hot that it is partly melted. This molten, or melted, rock is magma. **Igneous rock** is molten rock that has hardened.

Igneous rock forms above or below Earth's surface. Sometimes magma bursts out of a volcano in hot, gooey clumps. Magma is called lava when it reaches the surface. Lava may flow from a volcano as a hot river. Lava on Earth's surface cools quickly. It may harden into igneous rock in just a few days. Igneous rock that cools very quickly does not form many crystals.

Magma usually rises slowly to Earth's surface. It fills in cracks in the crust. As it slowly cools into rock, large crystals form. This slow cooling can take more than a million years!

Basalt is the most common quickly cooled igneous rock. Most of the ocean floor is basalt.

Gabbro cools slowly. The minerals in it may separate into layers.



## Streak

Streak is measured using a special plate. A mineral is scratched on this plate. The color of the powder that it leaves is its streak. No matter what color a mineral is, its streak is always the same color. The mineral halite can be colorless to white, with pieces of yellow, red, or blue. Halite's streak is always white.

| Mineral | Color | Luster | Streak | Mohs Scale |
|---|---|---|---|---|
| Calcite | Usually colorless or white | Glassy | White | 2 |
| Hornblende | Dark green | Glassy | Pale gray | 5–6 |
| Pyrite | Gold | Metallic | Green-black | 6–6.5 |
| Quartz | Milky | Glassy | White | 7 |

# How are sedimentary rocks formed?

## Layers of Rock

Erosion is the movement of material such as rock, soil, shells, and dead plant and animal matter from one place to another. The material is moved by wind, ice, water, and gravity. It settles at the bottom of lakes, rivers, and oceans. It is called **sediment.**

Sediment is carried into bodies of water. Particles of sediment have different sizes and shapes. Some particles are smooth. Others are sharp. New layers build on old layers, pressing the older layers together. The weight of the layers bonds the particles together. They harden and form **sedimentary rock.**

## How a Fossil Forms

Scientists can form ideas about Earth's history from fossils. They can tell when certain plants and animals lived. To do this, they figure out the age of the layer of rock in which the plant or animal was found. For example, ammonoids were sea creatures that looked like snails. Scientists think ammonoids lived from about 408 to 66 million years ago. An ammonoid fossil means that the layer of rock formed between 408 and 66 million years ago. Different layers of rock tell scientists how living things have changed.

## Geologic Time Scale

Scientists have used their estimates of Earth's history to make a geologic time scale. The earliest period of time is at the bottom of the scale. The scale is in the same order as the layers of sedimentary rock. The layers with the oldest fossils are at the bottom. The newest layers are on top. The four major time periods are the Precambrian era, the Paleozoic era, the Mesozoic era, and the Cenozoic era.

Scientists use what they learn from fossils to make models of extinct animals.



## Types of Sedimentary Rock

One kind of sedimentary rock comes from sediment of material that was once alive. Limestone is made of skeletons and shells of sea animals that lived long ago. Their remains formed layers. These layers are held together by dissolved minerals.

What kind of sediment do you think makes up a sedimentary rock named sandstone? Sandstone comes from pieces of quartz that are about the size of a grain of sand.

Mudstone is a third kind of sedimentary rock. It forms in lakes or oceans from tiny pieces of clay minerals. Mudstone is similar to a sedimentary rock named shale.

Conglomerate forms from round pieces of rock that are stuck together.

## How Rocks Change into Soil

Water can drip into cracks in rock. The water freezes and thaws again and again. As the cracks get bigger, the rock gets weaker. Eventually the pieces of rock break. Plant roots can force themselves into a rock. This also can cause the rock to break into pieces. These natural processes are known as weathering. Weathering can wear away even the tallest mountain over millions of years.

Soil is made of tiny pieces of weathered rock. Soil also has dead and decaying plant and animal matter. Soil even has living things such as bacteria, fungi, worms, and insects. They break up the plant and animal material into nutrients for plants to use.

Weathering wears away these rock formations.

## How Rocks Tell a Story

Sedimentary rocks can tell scientists about life on Earth millions of years ago. Scientists may find a 100-million-year-old dinosaur footprint. They may find a copy of a set of teeth from an animal that became extinct, or died out, 50 million years ago.

The footprints and teeth are fossils. Fossils give scientists clues about life on Earth long ago. Many fossils are found in sedimentary rocks.

Scientists get information from fossils. Fossils might tell how many legs a dinosaur walked on. They might tell what plants and animals looked like. They can even tell how Earth's features and environment have changed.

**1.**

The soft body parts of an animal decay after the animal dies.

**2.**

Sediment settles on top of the remains.

**3.**

Many layers form. Eventually the remains are replaced with minerals that harden into rock.

**4.**

The rock layers weather. The fossil appears at the surface.

# Changes to Earth's Surface

by Marcia K. Miller

| Genre | Comprehension Skill | Text Features | Science Content |
| --- | --- | --- | --- |
| Nonfiction | Compare and Contrast | • Labels<br>• Captions<br>• Diagrams<br>• Glossary | Earth's Surface |

Scott Foresman Science 4.9



PEARSON
Scott Foresman

DK

ISBN 0-328-13883-5

90000

9 780328 138838

scottforesman.com

**Vocabulary**

deposition

earthquake

epicenter

erosion

fault

landform

landslide

volcano

weathering

## What did you learn?

**1.** What can cause a landslide?

**2.** What makes magma rise inside a volcano?

**3.** Why do earthquakes happen at faults?

**4.** **Writing** in Science  Erosion and deposition are two forces that change landforms. Explain in your own words what each force does. Include details from the book to support your answer.

**5.** **Compare and Contrast** How are physical weathering and chemical weathering alike? How are they different?

**Illustration:** 14 Alan Male
**Photographs:** Every effort has been made to secure permission and provide appropriate credit for photographic material. The publisher deeply regrets any omission and pledges to correct errors called to its attention in subsequent editions. Unless otherwise acknowledged, all photographs are the property of Scott Foresman, a division of Pearson Education. Photo locators denoted as follows: Top (T), Center (C), Bottom (B), Left (L), Right (R) Background (Bkgd)
Opener: ©Hubert Stadler/Corbis; Title Page: ©Chris Reynolds and the BBC Team-Modlemakes/DK Images; 4 ©AP/Wide World Photos; 5 ©Jack Dykinga/Getty Images; 7 (T) ©Richard Bickel/Corbis, (B) ©Owaki-Kulla/Corbis; 8 ©Paul A. Souders/Corbis; 10 ©Dave G. Houser/Corbis; 13 (TR, CR) ©Gary Rosenquist; 15 ©George Hall/Corbis

ISBN: 0-328-13883-5

# Changes to Earth's Surface

## by Marcia K. Miller

## Glossary

| | |
|---|---|
| **deposition** | the laying down of pieces of Earth's surface after erosion |
| **earthquake** | the sudden movement of plates that makes Earth's crust shake |
| **epicenter** | the point on Earth's surface above the spot where plates start to move |
| **erosion** | the process of moving weathered rock |
| **fault** | a break or crack in rocks where Earth's crust can move |
| **landform** | a shape or natural feature found on Earth's surface |
| **landslide** | the quick downhill movement of great amounts of rock and soil |
| **volcano** | a landform with an opening out of which lava pours from below Earth's crust |
| **weathering** | the physical or chemical process by which rocks slowly break into smaller pieces |

# How does Earth's surface wear away?

## Earth's Crust

Earth is covered by a rock layer called the crust. The crust is underwater in the ocean.

Earth's crust has many natural features. Each one is called a **landform.** Landforms are many sizes and shapes. Plains are flat landforms on low ground. Plateaus are flat landforms on high ground. Peninsulas are landforms that stick out into water. Valleys and canyons are also landforms.

## Effects of Earthquakes and Volcanoes

Many places on Earth have earthquakes and volcanoes. In 1815 Mount Tambora in Asia erupted. Ash darkened the sky. Less sunlight reached Earth. This caused snow to fall in the northeastern United States in June.

In 1883 Krakatoa erupted in Indonesia. This volcano caused huge waves called tsunamis in Earth's oceans. Earthquakes can also cause tsunamis. Tsunamis can lead to landslides.

Two plates meet in California along the San Andreas Fault. Many earthquakes happen along this fault. Most are small. Some are very powerful.

Weathering, erosion, and deposition change Earth's landforms. So do landslides, earthquakes, and volcanoes. Earth's surface will always be changing.

Earthquakes can cause great damage.

## Earth's Moving Plates

Earth's crust rests on a layer called the upper mantle. These layers form huge moving pieces called plates.

## The Cause of Earthquakes

A **fault** is a break or crack in rocks where Earth's crust can move. Rocks may get stuck along a fault. The plates keep moving. They press on the rocks that are stuck. If the pressure becomes strong enough, the rocks break. The plates shift quickly. An **earthquake** is the sudden movement that makes Earth's crust shake.

The focus is the underground spot where the plates shift and the earthquake begins. The **epicenter** is the point on Earth's surface above the focus. The most damage is usually near the epicenter. Energy from an earthquake moves in waves.



Some landforms develop quickly. Others take a long time. A mountain may take millions of years to form. Rocks rolling downward can change it quickly. Think of how a flood moves soil from one place to another. Think about dust that blows across empty, unplanted fields.

## How Weathering Affects Landforms

Landforms are always changing. Rocks slowly break into smaller pieces. This process is called **weathering.** Water, ice, and temperature changes can cause weathering. Chemicals and living things cause weathering too.

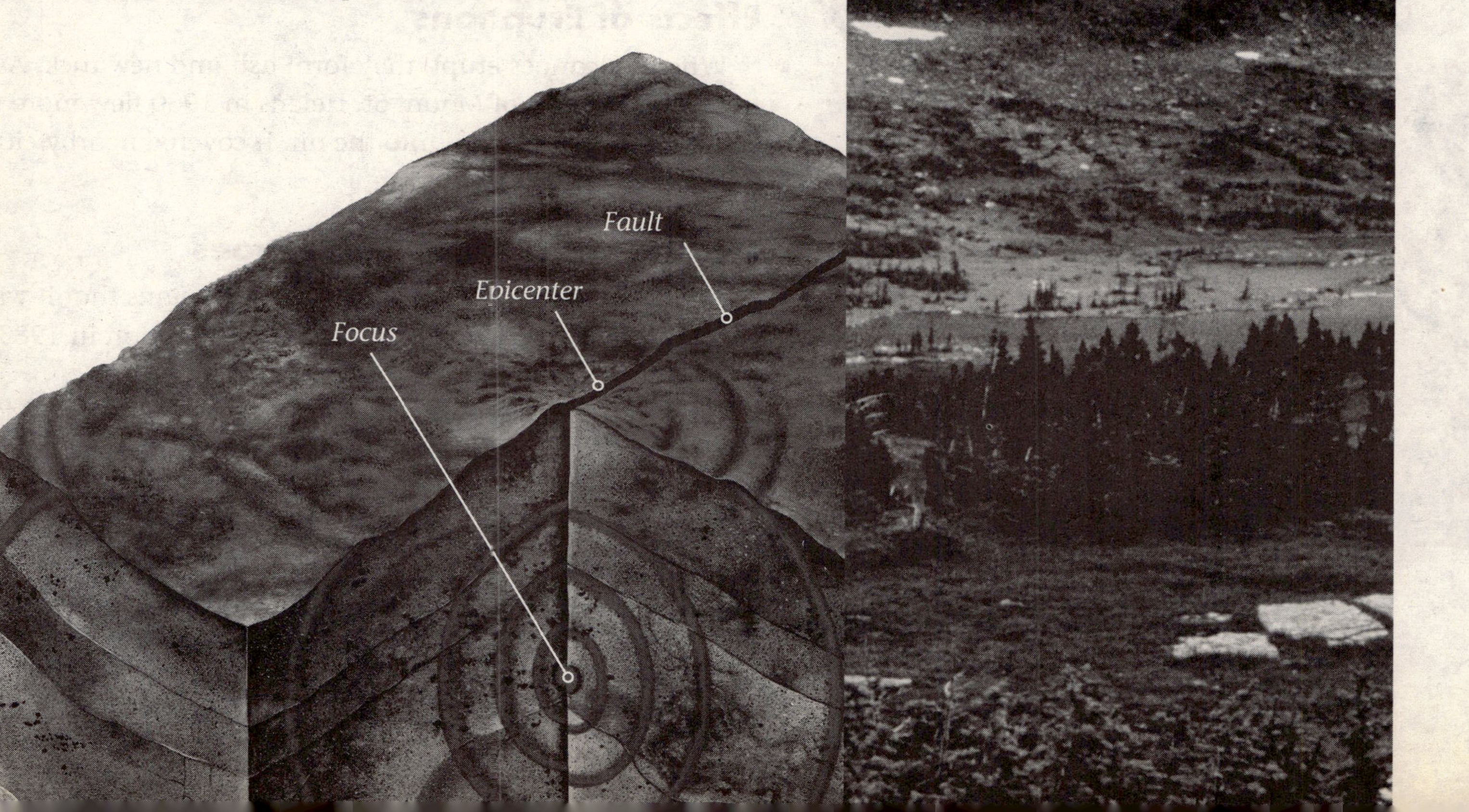

## Physical Weathering

In physical weathering, rock breaks into smaller pieces of the same kind of rock. Water can cause physical weathering. Flowing water carries small bits of soil and sand. These bits scrape against rocks to wear them down.

Ice also causes physical weathering. Rain or melting snow can get into cracks in rocks. If this water freezes, it turns into ice. The ice pushes against the cracks. The cracks become deeper. This process can repeat until the rock finally splits.

Changes in temperature can also weather rocks. A rock's surface grows larger when it gets hot. Its surface shrinks when it gets cold. All this changing may weaken the rock.

Living things can also cause weathering. Have you seen plants living in the cracks of rocks? As plants and roots grow, they can split the rocks.

Weathering changed the rock known as the Old Man of the Mountain in New Hampshire. In 2003 the rock broke off and fell.

The 1980 eruption of Mount St. Helens sent rock and ash into the air.

## Effects of Eruptions

When volcanoes erupt, they form ash and new rock. Ash from the eruption of Mount St. Helens in 1980 flew more than 24 kilometers (15 miles) into the air. It covered nearby cities. It killed trees and animals.

## Active and Dormant Volcanoes

An active volcano erupts often or shows signs that it will erupt. Kilauea in Hawaii began its latest eruption in 1983. It is still actively erupting.

A dormant volcano has not erupted for a long time. Mount Rainier in Washington has not had a big eruption in more than 500 years. If it erupted, it could melt nearby glaciers. This could cause flooding and landslides.

An extinct volcano no longer erupts. Mount Kenya in Africa is one of many extinct volcanoes in the world.

# How can Earth's surface change rapidly?

## Volcanoes

A volcano is a landform. It can cause a rapid change to Earth's surface. Hot rock, called magma, has partly melted into liquid. Gases push the magma up. A **volcano** forms at a weak spot in Earth's crust.

A volcano erupts when magma boils onto the surface. Lava is magma that has come out of a volcano. Lava is still red hot.

Pressure can build so much that the gases in the magma explode. Lava, gases, and ashes burst out of openings called vents. Not all volcanoes erupt so wildly. Magma oozes up and slowly flows out of some volcanoes. A bowl-shaped area, or crater, may form around the volcano's main opening.

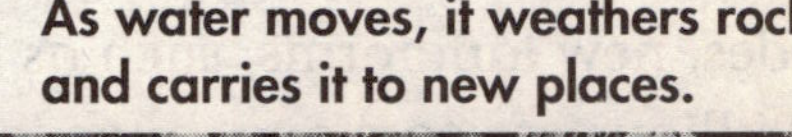

## Chemical Weathering

In chemical weathering, rock breaks into smaller pieces. But the material that the rock is made of also changes.

Different materials can be formed when chemicals come in contact with rock. Carbon dioxide, a chemical in the air, mixes with rainwater and forms a weak acid. When it rains, this acid lands on the rock. It combines with rock material and forms a new chemical. Over time, the new chemical breaks the rock into smaller pieces.

Chemicals can come from animals and plants. These chemicals can cause weathering. So can people and their activities.

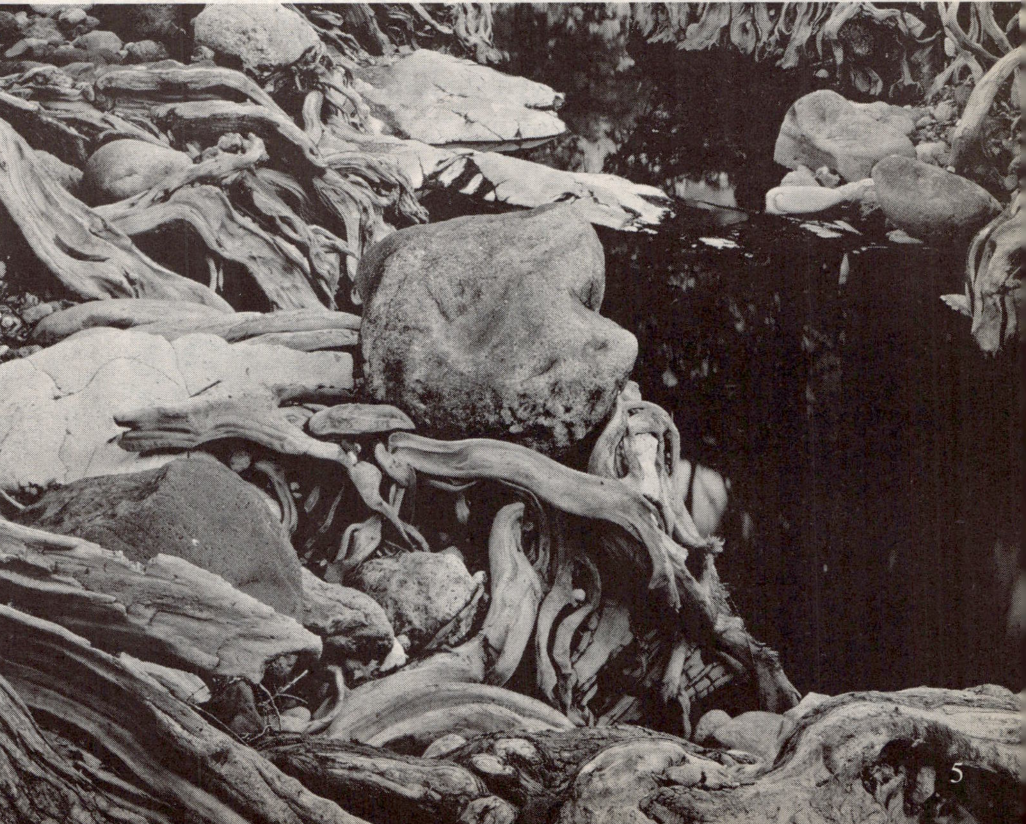

As water moves, it weathers rock and carries it to new places.

# How do weathered materials move?

## Effects of Erosion

**Erosion** is the process of moving weathered rock. Water, ice, gravity, and wind can cause erosion.

Rain can wash away loose rock material into a stream. The stream may carry that material far away.

Over time, water running downhill carves grooves into the land. These grooves become canyons or valleys.

Waves pound against cracks in rocks that are at the shore. Pieces of rock break off and are carried away. As the shore erodes, new landforms, such as beaches, will appear.

Millions of years ago, huge ice sheets, called glaciers, covered parts of Earth. A glacier slowly slides along a thin layer of water below it, wearing away rock. Even small glaciers can rip rocks apart and carry the pieces far away.

Erosion can be a problem along the seashore as well. Waves that pound against the shore carry away material, such as sand. People build barriers to prevent this. Barriers stop waves from eroding sand and rock. Barriers also help protect nearby buildings and roads.

People can reduce deposition. They can dig away deposits from waterways. This helps ships pass through the water more easily.

Terraces slow the movement of water running downhill.

# Controlling Erosion and Deposition

Erosion and deposition often take place in areas with few trees or plants. Trees and plants help keep wind and water from eroding rock and soil.

People have found ways to slow the effects of erosion. They grow plants on the sides of hills. Roots hold soil in place. Plant leaves keep some of the rain from washing soil away. Farmers whose fields are on a hill can plow them into steps, called terraces. Rain forms puddles on the steps instead of washing soil downhill. Crops can then soak up more water.

# Deposition

Wind and water carry bits of rock and soil from one place to another. **Deposition** is the laying down of pieces of Earth's surface. This may happen slowly or very quickly.

When water moves slowly, big pebbles in the water sink first. Then smaller bits, such as sand, sink. Finally the smallest pieces of soil, called silt, fall to the bottom. Rivers deposit material where they meet the ocean. This deposit forms a fan-shaped landform called a delta.

Wind can carry only small bits of rock. In deserts, the wind deposits sand in mounds called sand dunes. Wind will keep shaping the dunes.

## Gravity and Landslides

No place on Earth is completely flat. The force of gravity pulls all objects from high places to lower ones. Gravity causes loose material to roll downhill. Bits of rock and soil may move slowly, only a little at a time. But at times they move very quickly. Heavy rains or earthquakes can loosen material that is on a steep hill or slope. Gravity then pulls this loose material downward. A **landslide** is the quick downhill movement of great amounts of rock and soil. Buildings, trees, and other large objects may be swept down the slope with the sliding soil.

## Gravity and Avalanches

The rapid movement of objects down a slope can occur in cold areas as well. An avalanche is fast-moving snow and ice that race down a mountain. Strong winds, earthquakes, and explosions can cause avalanches. People try to stop avalanches from happening. They may clear snow before it builds up too much. Landslides and avalanches can cause terrible damage, especially on large mountains.

# Using Natural Resources

**by Martin E. Lee**

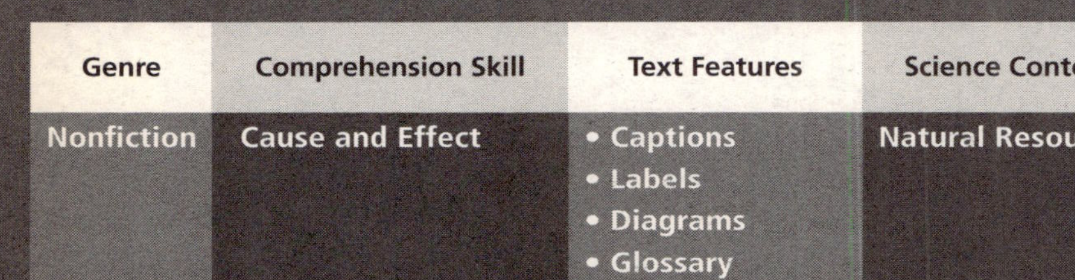

| Genre | Comprehension Skill | Text Features | Science Content |
|---|---|---|---|
| Nonfiction | Cause and Effect | • Captions<br>• Labels<br>• Diagrams<br>• Glossary | Natural Resources |

**Scott Foresman Science 4.10**

ISBN 0-328-13886-X

90000

9 780328 138869

115

## Vocabulary

conservation

fossil fuels

humus

ore

petroleum

recycling

solar cell

solar energy

## What did you learn?

1. What are some materials that make up soil?

2. How do we get and use solar energy?

3. How do Earth's natural resources get used up?

4. **Writing** in Science You read about two kinds of natural resources, renewable and nonrenewable. On your own paper, explain how these resources are alike and different. Use examples from the book to support your answer.

5. **Cause and Effect** What causes rock to become soil?



**Illustrations:** 4, 5, 10, 11 Tony Randazzo
**Photographs:** Every effort has been made to secure permission and provide appropriate credit for photographic material. The publisher deeply regrets any omission and pledges to correct errors called to its attention in subsequent editions. Unless otherwise acknowledged, all photographs are the property of Scott Foresman, a division of Pearson Education. Photo locators denoted as follows: Top (T), Center (C), Bottom (B), Left (L), Right (R) Background (Bkgd)
Opener: ©Alan Schein Photography/Corbis; Title Page: (B) ©Sylvain Saustier/Corbis; 2 ©Layne Kennedy/Corbis; 5 ©Deborah Kopp/Visuals Unlimited; 6 (CR) ©DK Images, (CC) Colin Keats/Courtesy of the Natural History Museum, London/©DK Images, (B) ©Sylvain Saustier/Corbis; 8 (TR) ©Layne Kennedy/Corbis, (B) ©Kevin Burke/Getty Images; 12 ©Charles E. Rotkin/Corbis; 13 (BL) Getty Images, (BC) ©Carin Krasner/Corbis, (CR) ©Liz Hymans/Corbis, 15 ©Owaki-Kulla/Corbis

ISBN: 0-328-13886-X

# Using Natural Resources

**by Martin E. Lee**

## Glossary

| | |
|---|---|
| **conservation** | the act of using only the resources you need without wasting them |
| **fossil fuels** | nonrenewable resources that come from the remains of organisms that lived long ago |
| **humus** | bits of rich soil formed from the decaying remains of living things |
| **ore** | a rock that is rich with minerals |
| **petroleum** | another name for the fossil fuel commonly known as oil |
| **recycling** | saving, collecting, or using materials again |
| **solar cell** | a device that changes energy from the Sun into electricity |
| **solar energy** | energy that comes from the Sun |

# What are natural resources?

## How Resources Are Used

We use natural resources to make what we need. We also use natural resources for energy.

Natural resources are the materials we get from nature. Some natural resources are living things, such as plants and animals. Some resources such as soil, water, minerals, and sunlight, were never alive. Air is an important natural resource. All natural resources help support life on Earth.

## Recycling

**Recycling** is saving, collecting, or using materials again. Recycling helps us reuse raw materials. There are ways to recycle glass, cardboard, aluminum, tin, paper, steel, and some plastics. Look for the recycling symbol on containers before you throw them away. It looks like three arrows chasing each other around a triangle.

Nature provides many materials that support life. These natural resources help us to live and grow. Some can be renewed. Others will be used up someday. It helps all life on Earth when people use natural resources wisely.

The recycling symbol shows materials that can be reused.

## Methods of Energy Conservation

**Conservation** means using only what you need. When you conserve, you use resources carefully and without wasting them. You can cut back energy use in many ways. You can walk or ride a bike to go short distances. For longer trips, you can share rides with others. Turn off lights you don't need.

Some cars and appliances use less energy to do the same amount of work as others. Less energy is needed to heat buildings that have good insulation. If we conserve energy, our resources will last longer.

Living things need natural resources. Plants must have air, sunlight, soil, and water to grow. Plants and animals give people the resources they need for food. Everything we eat, use, or buy either is a natural resource or is made from one or more natural resources.

## Renewable Natural Resources

Earth has renewable and nonrenewable natural resources. Renewable resources can't run out. They can be replaced. **Solar energy** is power that comes from the Sun. It is renewable. Air, water, trees, and soil are also renewable natural resources.

Nearly everything in this car's trunk can be recycled.

Water is a renewable natural resource.

## Why Soil Is a Renewable Resource

Soil covers most of Earth's land areas. Some animals and plants make their homes in the soil. Animals and plants provide food for other living things, including people. Soil is a nonliving natural resource.

## How Soil Is Renewed

Rock breaks apart during weathering. Plant roots and ice erode rock by breaking it into pieces. Wind and water carry bits of rock and deposit them in new areas. After a long time, broken rock becomes soil.

Plant roots cause rock to crack.

More plants growing weathers the rock even more.

## How Resources Can Last Longer

People use nonrenewable resources to meet most of their energy needs. But as people need more energy, fossil fuels will be used up faster than ever. Fuel costs will go up.

Water, air, soil, and trees are resources that help all living things. We must use them carefully. We must not waste or destroy them. It is hard to restore forests, soil, and fishing areas. It costs a lot of money too. So does cleaning up polluted air, water, and soil.

To help our fossil fuels last, we can use less energy. We should also use wind power, water power, solar energy, and other renewable energy sources.

Old tires can be used to make a wall.



Do you recycle paper? The paper in a notepad may once have been your newspaper.

## Impact of Fossil Fuels

Removing fossil fuels from under the ocean floor can harm Earth. An oil spill can result from drilling under the ocean. Oil spills kill sea life. Spills can also kill or harm living things along the coast. Companies are working to make drilling safer and cleaner.

Using fossil fuels also has unsafe effects. Air is polluted when fossil fuels burn. Too much carbon dioxide in the air may lead to global warming. Gases from burned fossil fuels can break up in rainwater to form a weak acid. The acid falls to Earth as acid rain. It can damage buildings. It can harm living things.

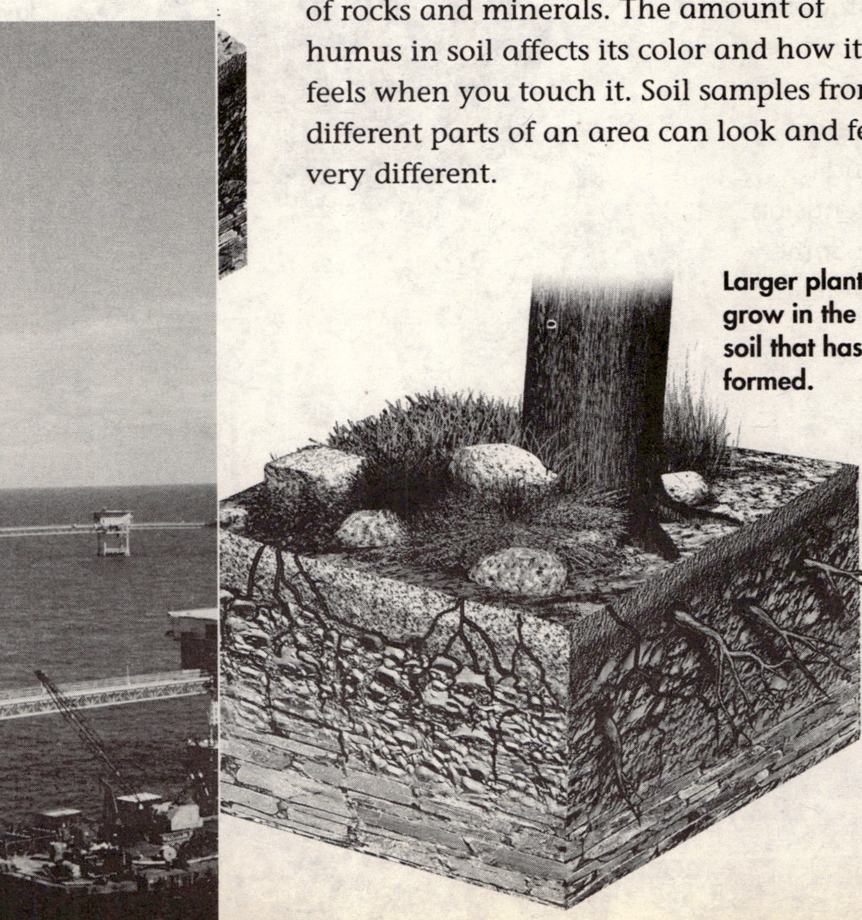

This oil rig digs deep into the ocean floor to get petroleum.





## Ingredients in Soil

Soil is made of bits of weathered rock. Soil contains humus. **Humus** is decaying plant and animal material. Humus adds nutrients to soil.

Some animals, such as prairie dogs, dig entire towns under the ground. Tiny organisms such as bacteria, fungi, worms, spiders, and insects, also live in soil. They break down plant and animal remains that plants can use as food.

Different soils come from different kinds of rocks and minerals. The amount of humus in soil affects its color and how it feels when you touch it. Soil samples from different parts of an area can look and feel very different.

Larger plants grow in the soil that has formed.

Topsoil is the top layer of soil.

Subsoil is part soil and part rock.

Bedrock is mostly solid rock.

## Properties of Soil

Each kind of soil has certain properties. Topsoil has a lot of humus and bits of weathered rock. These bits can be different sizes.

## Clay, Silt, and Sand

Clay is soil made mostly from the smallest bits of broken rock. The materials in clay make it different colors. Red clay has bits of iron in it.

Silt is soil with slightly larger particles in it. Silt feels smooth. Sand is soil with even larger particles. Sandy soil has bits of different materials. Quartz is the most common material in sand.

The color of sand depends on what materials are in it. Some sand is tan. Sand from volcanic rock can be black.

**Petroleum** is commonly known as oil. Petroleum is made from ancient sea life. Bacteria, algae, and other organisms used the energy in sunlight to live. Their bodies stored energy they didn't use. After they died, their remains fell to the ocean floor.

More and more dead organisms fell to the ocean floor. They formed thick layers called sediments. Millions of years passed. The heavy top layers pushed down on the lower layers. Pressure, heat, and decay changed the remains. Chemicals in the bodies of those tiny organisms turned into fossil fuels.

Thick layers of dead plants were buried. Over time, the layers turned into rock.

Today we remove coal from the layer of rock.

# Nonrenewable Energy Sources

Some resources are nonrenewable because they are used up faster than they are put back naturally. Others cannot be replaced at all. People use many nonrenewable resources for energy. Ore is a nonrenewable resource. **Ore** is a rock that is rich with minerals.

## Fossil Fuels

Coal, natural gas, and oil are nonrenewable energy sources. They are fuels that we burn for heat. **Fossil fuels** come from organisms that lived long ago. The Sun is the source of energy stored in coal, oil, and natural gas.

# Soil for Growing Plants

Plants grow best in soil with many nutrients. Sandy soil does not hold nutrients. Clay can hold nutrients. But it is so hard that most plant roots cannot spread very easily. The best soil for plants has some clay, silt, sand, and humus.

## Soil as a Renewable Natural Resource

Some plants can put nutrients back in soil. Plants that get plowed under at the end of a growing season also renew soil. Renewing just a few centimeters of nutrient-rich topsoil can take 1,000 years. That same amount of topsoil can wear away in only ten years.

## Other Uses of Soil

Soil has many uses besides farming. Clay is used to make tile, bricks, and pottery. Sand is used to make concrete, glass, and other things.

Swamps once covered the land.

# How are resources used for energy?

## Renewable Energy Sources

People use energy in many ways. We use energy to run machines, make heat, and grow food. We can use the Sun's energy without even trying. A room becomes warmer when sunlight shines in.

Solar energy warms Earth. The air near Earth's surface heats up when it meets the warm ground. The cycle of heating and cooling air makes wind energy. The Sun also powers the water cycle by making water evaporate.

Solar panels take in energy from the Sun. Solar cells in the panels turn the energy into electricity.

## How We Use Solar Energy

A **solar cell** changes energy from the Sun into electrical energy. Solar cells are put together to make large solar panels. Fields of solar panels collect energy. Solar energy is changed into electric energy or heat energy.

In a solar heat system, solar energy heats water. The heated water runs through solar panels into a storage tank. A pump forces the water into pipes. The hot water can be used to heat buildings.

## Energy from Flowing Water

Moving water has energy. Today people use this energy to run machines that make electricity. Dams are built to control how the water moves. Water forms a lake behind a dam. It flows through gates in the dam when its energy is needed.

Science
Science

# Properties of Matter

## by Gregory K. George

125

| Genre | Comprehension Skill | Text Features | Science Content |
| --- | --- | --- | --- |
| Nonfiction | Compare and Contrast | • Labels<br>• Captions<br>• Charts<br>• Glossary | Matter |

Scott Foresman Science 4.11

## What did you learn?

1. What are the most common states of matter?

2. What is a pan balance used to measure? How does it work?

3. Explain why condensation is a physical change.

4. **Writing** in Science   Sugar cubes dissolve in water. On your own paper, explain how the solubility of a sugar cube can be increased. Include details from the book to support your answer.

5. **Compare and Contrast** Suppose you have two mixtures. One mixture is beads and water. The other is salt and water. How are they alike? How are they different?



**Illustrations:** 5, 20, 21 Big Sesh Studios
**Photographs:** Every effort has been made to secure permission and provide appropriate credit for photographic material. The publisher deeply regrets any omission and pledges to correct errors called to its attention in subsequent editions. Unless otherwise acknowledged, all photographs are the property of Scott Foresman, a division of Pearson Education. Photo locators denoted as follows: Top (T), Center (C), Bottom (B), Left (L), Right (R), Background (Bkgd).
Opener: PhotoLibrary; Title Page: (CC, TR) ©DK Images; 2 ©Kevin Schafer/Getty Images; 4 ©Bernhard Edmaier/Photo Researchers, Inc.; 12 ©DK Images; 22 (CL, CR) ©Royalty-Free/Corbis, (BL) ©DK Images.

ISBN: 0-328-13889-4

# Properties of Matter

## by Gregory K. George

## Glossary

**chemical change**  a change that occurs when the particles of one substance change to make particles of a new substance with different properties

**density**  the amount of mass in a certain volume of matter

**mixture**  a blend of two or more substances whose properties do not change when they are combined

**physical change**  any change in the size, shape, or state of matter

**solubility**  a measure of how much of a substance will dissolve in another substance

**solute**  the substance that is dissolved in a solution

**solution**  a combination that results when one or more substances are dissolved in another substance

**solvent**  the substance that dissolves another substance

# What is matter?

## Properties of Matter

Matter is anything that has mass and takes up space. All living and nonliving things are made of matter. Scientists use the properties of matter to identify it. Your senses can help you find many of these properties. You can see the color, size, and shape of some matter. You can touch matter to tell if it is smooth or rough. You can taste and smell some matter too.

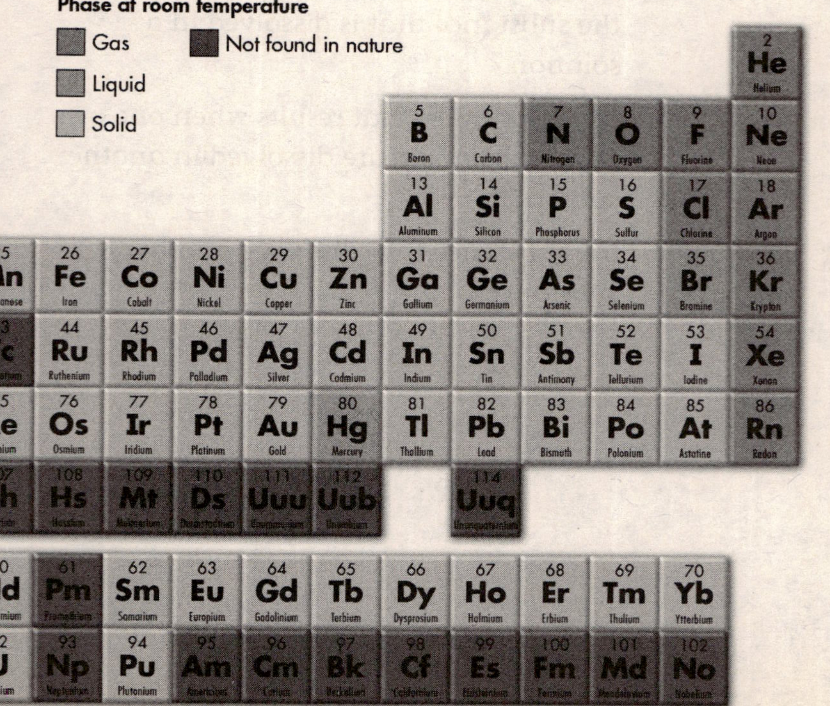

## Elements

All particles in a pure substance are alike. The simplest pure substances are elements. Information about the elements is in a chart called the Periodic Table. The row and column the element is in tells scientists about its properties. Each element has a letter or letters as its symbol.

Elements are matter. In fact, everything is made of matter. All matter can be measured. You can find out the mass, volume, or density of any kind of matter. All matter can go through chemical and physical changes.

**Phase at room temperature**

- Gas
- Liquid
- Solid
- Not found in nature

| 7 | 8 | 9 | 10 | 11 | 12 | 13 | 14 | 15 | 16 | 17 | 18 |
|---|---|---|---|---|---|---|---|---|---|---|---|
| | | | | | | | | | | | 2 He Helium |
| | | | | | | 5 B Boron | 6 C Carbon | 7 N Nitrogen | 8 O Oxygen | 9 F Fluorine | 10 Ne Neon |
| | | | | | | 13 Al Aluminum | 14 Si Silicon | 15 P Phosphorus | 16 S Sulfur | 17 Cl Chlorine | 18 Ar Argon |
| 25 Mn Manganese | 26 Fe Iron | 27 Co Cobalt | 28 Ni Nickel | 29 Cu Copper | 30 Zn Zinc | 31 Ga Gallium | 32 Ge Germanium | 33 As Arsenic | 34 Se Selenium | 35 Br Bromine | 36 Kr Krypton |
| 43 Tc Technetium | 44 Ru Ruthenium | 45 Rh Rhodium | 46 Pd Palladium | 47 Ag Silver | 48 Cd Cadmium | 49 In Indium | 50 Sn Tin | 51 Sb Antimony | 52 Te Tellurium | 53 I Iodine | 54 Xe Xenon |
| 75 Re Rhenium | 76 Os Osmium | 77 Ir Iridium | 78 Pt Platinum | 79 Au Gold | 80 Hg Mercury | 81 Tl Thallium | 82 Pb Lead | 83 Bi Bismuth | 84 Po Polonium | 85 At Astatine | 86 Rn Radon |
| 107 Bh Bohrium | 108 Hs Hassium | 109 Mt Meitnerium | 110 Ds Darmstadtium | 111 Uuu Unununium | 112 Uub Ununbium | | 114 Uuq Ununquadium | | | | |

| 60 Nd Neodymium | 61 Pm Promethium | 62 Sm Samarium | 63 Eu Europium | 64 Gd Gadolinium | 65 Tb Terbium | 66 Dy Dysprosium | 67 Ho Holmium | 68 Er Erbium | 69 Tm Thulium | 70 Yb Ytterbium |
|---|---|---|---|---|---|---|---|---|---|---|
| 92 U Uranium | 93 Np Neptunium | 94 Pu Plutonium | 95 Am Americium | 96 Cm Curium | 97 Bk Berkelium | 98 Cf Californium | 99 Es Einsteinium | 100 Fm Fermium | 101 Md Mendelevium | 102 No Nobelium |

## Chemical Changes

An iron nail will rust if it is in a damp place. If you compared the iron nail to the rust, you would find that the nail and the rust have different properties. Rust is a new, different substance. It results from a chemical change. In a **chemical change,** particles of one substance are changed to make particles of a new substance with different properties. A chemical change is taking place when wood burns or silver tarnishes.

The color of a substance may be different after a chemical change. The substance may have a different smell. Its temperature may change. Heat often comes from a chemical change.

### The Periodic Table

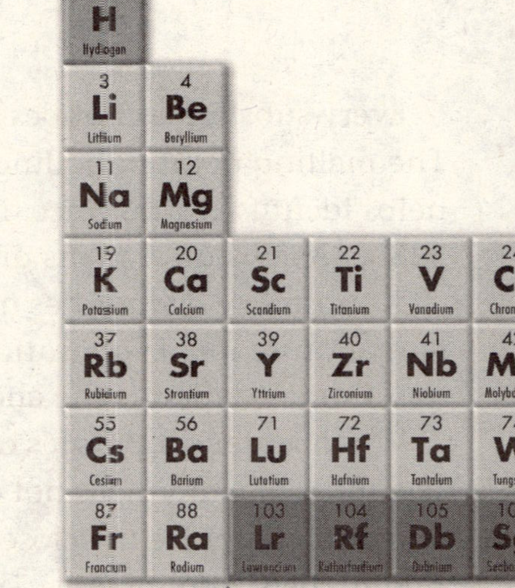
Rust forms as oxygen combines with the iron in this gear.

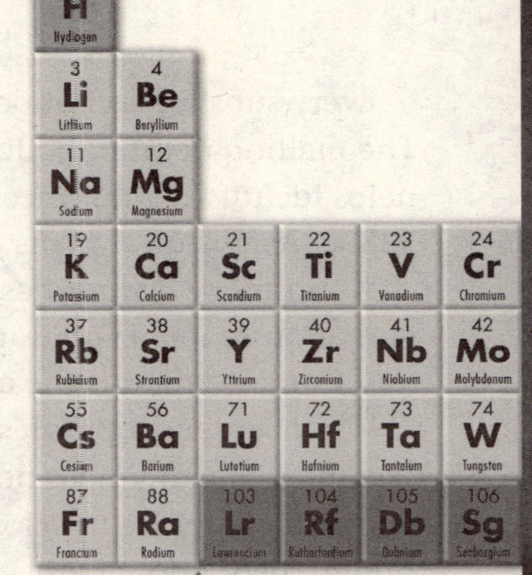
Burning wood reacts with oxygen to form ashes, carbon dioxide gas, and water vapor.





## Testing Matter

You can also test matter to find out about its properties. How does it react if you heat or cool it? Is it affected by a magnet? Does electricity pass through it? If you hit it with a hammer, does it break or just bend? If you put it in water, does it sink or float? What happens if you mix it with other matter?

Look at the ice and water. What are some properties that you can see?

## States of Matter

Matter is made of tiny particles. These tiny particles can move. They are also arranged in different ways. The way these particles move and the way they are arranged tell the form, or state, of the matter. The most common states of matter are solid, liquid, and gas.

Most substances are found in just one state in nature. Water is the most common substance that can be found naturally in all three states of matter.



Every substance changes phases at a different temperature. The melting point or boiling point is a physical property. Each helps identify a substance. Ice melts at 0°C. Lead melts at 328°C. A substance melts and freezes at the same temperature.

A substance evaporates and condenses at the same temperature too. Evaporation is the change from a liquid to a gas. Condensation is the change from a gas to a liquid.

When water evaporates or condenses, it is changing phase. The mass of water does not change when it changes phase. The particles of ice are close together. They do not move much. Adding heat adds energy. The particles move more. Ice becomes a liquid. Boiling water has even more energy. Particles move even more. The liquid water changes to water vapor.

## Phase Changes

Water can be a liquid, a solid, or a gas. If you melt solid water, or ice, it becomes liquid water. If you heat water to a temperature of 100°C, it becomes a gas, or water vapor. Liquid, solid, and gas are called phases.

What causes matter to be in one phase and not another? Energy causes particles to move faster and farther apart. Adding or taking away energy causes a substance to change phases. You add energy to water when you heat it. You take energy away from water when you freeze it. Phase changes are physical changes.

## Effects of Temperature on Matter

230°C
Paper starts burning.

100°C
Water boils.
Water vapor condenses.

0°C
Water freezes into ice.
Ice melts into water.

## Solids

An ice cube is solid water that forms at temperatures of 0°C or below. A solid is any kind of matter that has a definite shape and takes up a definite amount of space. The particles of a solid are packed closely together.

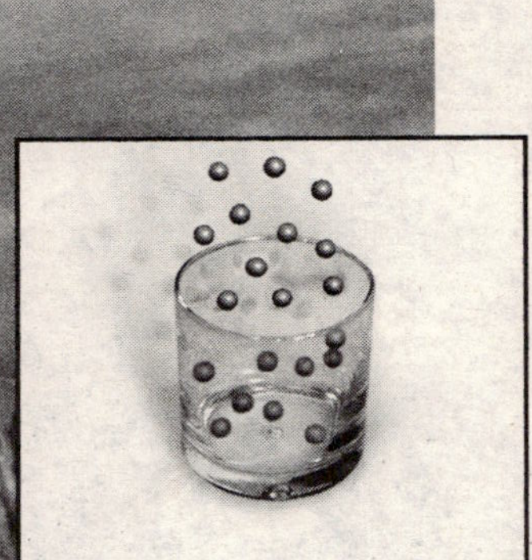


## Liquids

Water is a liquid. A liquid is any kind of matter that has no definite shape but takes up a definite amount of space. The particles of a liquid are not packed as closely together as particles are in a solid. The particles can slide past each other.



## Gases

Water vapor is an invisible gas. Water vapor and other gases make up the air around us. A gas is any kind of matter that has no definite shape and does not take up a definite space. The particles of a gas are not close together. They move in all directions.

# How is matter measured?

## Mass

You weigh more on Earth than you would on the Moon. Why is that? Weight depends on the force of gravity. The Moon has less gravity than Earth does. So your weight on the Moon would be less than it is on Earth.

Mass does not change. Mass is the amount of matter an object has. Since mass stays the same wherever an object is, measuring mass is useful for scientists. Mass changes only if matter is added or taken away.

The mass of the toy is equal to the total mass of its parts. The pan balance is level.

Mixing salt and water is a physical change. The particles of the salt and the water do not change when they mix. Salt and water make a mixture. The parts of a mixture do not change, and they can be separated. So making a mixture is a physical change.

Another example of a physical change is breaking a pencil. The pieces of a broken pencil have the same kinds of particles as a pencil that is in not broken.

Tearing a sheet of paper is also a physical change. No matter how many pieces the sheet of paper is in, it still has the same particles that it had before it was torn.



If you unfold the shape, you will have the same piece of paper you started with.

The shape is finished.

# How does matter change?

## Physical Changes

Origami is folding paper to make shapes. When you do origami, you are not changing the particles that make up the paper. You are only changing the size and shape of the paper.

Any change in the size, shape, or state of matter is a **physical change.** In a physical change, the particles that make up matter do not change. It is the arrangement of those particles that changes.

Origami begins with a plain square of paper.

The paper is folded many times.

## Using a Pan Balance

A pan balance helps you find the mass of an object. You can use a pan balance to compare a mass that you know with one that you do not know. The masses are equal when the two sides are level.

The mass of the toy in the picture is 23 grams. What if you took the toy apart and measured each part? The mass of all the parts would add up to 23 grams. The total mass of the parts is equal to the mass of the toy that is put together.

The pan balance shows this. The toy is on one side of the pan balance. It is in many pieces on the other side. Both sides have a mass of 23 grams. The masses are equal. This would be true even if all of the pieces were put together in a different way.

## Metric Units of Mass

Scientists do not use ounces and pounds to measure matter. They use metric units. The base unit of mass in the metric system is the gram (g). Other metric units that are often used are the milligram (mg) and the kilogram (kg).

The metric system is based on tens. A prefix before a base unit changes what it is worth. For example, 1 gram is the same as 1,000 milligrams. A mass of 1,000 grams is the same as a mass of 1 kilogram. A grape has a mass of about 1 gram. A cantaloupe has a mass of about 1 kilogram.

The mass of a large paper clip is about 1 g.

The mass of a nickel is about 5 g.

The mass of the milk in this carton is about 1,000 g, or 1 kg.

Sand does not dissolve in water.

## Common Solutions

A solution does not have to be a liquid. The air we breathe is a solution made of gases. Steel used for buildings and cars is a solution of carbon and iron.

## Solubility

**Solubility** measures how much of a substance will dissolve in another substance. Sand does not dissolve in water. This means the solubility of sand in water is zero.

By raising the temperature of a solvent, you can dissolve a solute faster. It is easier to dissolve sugar in warm water than in cold water.

Crushing a solute also makes it dissolve faster. A sugar cube will dissolve slowly in a cup of water. The sugar cube will dissolve faster if it is crushed first.

## Solutions

Salt and water stirred together make a mixture. But you cannot see the salt in the water. The salt has dissolved. It has broken into very small parts. The salt and water have made a special mixture called a solution. A **solution** is made when one or more substances are dissolved in another substance.

The most common kind of solution is a solid dissolved in a liquid. The substance that is dissolved is the **solute.** In a solution of salt and water, salt is the solute. The substance that takes in the other substance is the **solvent.** In the salt and water solution, the water is the solvent. Ocean water is a solution.

Salt dissolves in water.

## Volume

Volume is the amount of space that matter takes up. When you take a deep breath, your lungs expand. As they fill with air, their volume increases.

You can use a metric ruler to measure the length, width, and height of a solid, such as a box. To find the volume, multiply these numbers together. Suppose the length of a box is 6 centimeters (cm), the width is 2 cm, and the height is 5 cm. Then the volume of the box is 6 cm × 2 cm × 5 cm, or 60 cubic centimeters.

Like mass, volume is also measured in metric units. Scientists use metric units such as the cubic centimeter ($cm^3$) and the cubic meter ($m^3$) when they measure solids. Look at the chart to see some other metric units.

### Comparing Metric Units of Length

| Metric Unit | Equivalent |
| --- | --- |
| 1 millimeter | 0.001 meter |
| 1 centimeter | 10 millimeters |
| 1 decimeter | 10 centimeters |
| 1 meter | 100 centimeters or 1,000 millimeters |
| 1 decameter | 10 meters |
| 1 hectometer | 100 meters |
| 1 kilometer | 1,000 meters |

## Volume of Liquids

Unlike solids, liquids do not have exact shapes. So when scientists measure the volume of a liquid, they use a measuring container, such as a graduated cylinder. Some metric units used for volume are the milliliter (mL) and the liter (L). A graduated cylinder is marked with milliliters. One liter is the same volume as 1,000 milliliters.

The water level rose 5 mL when the ball was dropped in. The volume of the ball is 5 mL.

Look at the mixture of marbles, beads, sand, safety pins, and salt. How can these parts be separated? Safety pins are attracted to a magnet. So you can use a magnet to pull out the safety pins. You pick out the marbles. Then you can put the mixture in water, to help separate what is left. Some beads float to the top. You can use a spoon to take those out. Then you can pour the rest of the mixture through a filter. The filter will separate the sand and any remaining beads from the water. You can evaporate the water by heating it. Then the salt will be left.

The properties of each of the substances do not change when the mixture is separated. Each substance is the same as it was before it was added to the mixture.

# How do substances mix?

## Mixtures

A **mixture** is a blend of two or more substances. These substances can easily be separated. They are not chemically combined.

Think of a bag of frozen vegetables from the store. The vegetables have been combined into a mixture. But they can be separated. When the vegetables are separated, they have the same properties that they had before they were mixed.

## Volume of Other Objects

A graduated cylinder can measure the volume of a liquid or a solid. A solid must sink in water in order for a graduated cylinder to measure it. To measure the volume of a ball, fill a graduated cylinder with water. Notice the height of the water. Then put the ball in the water. Notice the new height of the water. It is higher because the ball has pushed away some of the water. The number of milliliters the water has risen is equal to the volume of the ball. A volume of 1 mL is the same volume as 1 cm$^3$.

| Examples of Metric Lengths | |
| --- | --- |
| **What Was Measured** | **Measurement** |
| Thickness of a CD | 1 mm |
| Length of a paper clip | 32 mm |
| Thickness of a CD case | 1 cm or 10 mm |
| Height of a doorknob from the floor | 1 meter |
| Length of a school bus | 12 meters |
| Length of 440 blue whales placed end to end | 11 km or 11,000 m |
| Distance from the North Pole to the equator | 10,000 km |

## Density

You may need to know how much mass is in a certain volume of matter. Does steel have more mass than wood? To find out, you need to know the sizes of the pieces of steel and wood. You need an equal volume of the objects you are measuring. **Density** is the amount of mass in a certain volume of matter. If the pieces of wood and steel are the same size, then the steel has more mass and more density than the wood.

## Finding Density

You divide the mass of an object by its volume to find its density. Like mass and volume, density is measured in metric units. The units to measure density are grams per cubic centimeter. Density is written as a fraction: $\frac{\text{mass in grams}}{\text{volume in cubic centimeters}}$ or $\frac{g}{cm^3}$.

## Comparing Densities

The density of an object tells if the object will sink or float in a liquid. Some liquids float on other liquids. As you can see in the picture, water floats on top of corn syrup. The density of water is less than the density of corn syrup. Cooking oil floats on top of water. So the density of cooking oil is less than the density of water.

The grape is floating on top of the corn syrup and at the bottom of the water. This is because the density of the grape is less than the density of the corn syrup, but more than the density of the water. The cork has the least density of anything in the container.

The density of an ice cube is a little less than the density of water. This makes the ice cube float. But the difference in density between water and an ice cube is very small. So most of an ice cube is below the surface.

Science  Science

# Heat

## by Kim Fields

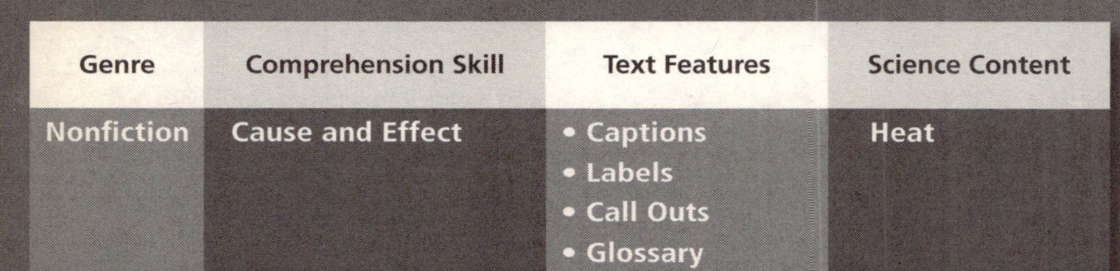

| Genre | Comprehension Skill | Text Features | Science Content |
|---|---|---|---|
| Nonfiction | Cause and Effect | • Captions<br>• Labels<br>• Call Outs<br>• Glossary | Heat |

Scott Foresman Science 4.12

**Vocabulary**

conduction

conductor

convection current

insulator

radiation

thermal energy

**What did you learn?**

1. What causes a metal spoon to get hot when one end of it is placed in hot water?

2. Why are many hot foods served in foam containers?

3. How does energy from the Sun get to Earth?

4. **Writing** in Science The meanings of heat and temperature are often confused. On your own paper, explain the difference between heat and temperature. Use details from the book to support your answer.

5. **Cause and Effect** What causes the movement of air in a convection current?

**Photographs:** Every effort has been made to secure permission and provide appropriate credit for photographic material. The publisher deeply regrets any omission and pledges to correct errors called to its attention in subsequent editions. Unless otherwise acknowledged, all photographs are the property of Scott Foresman, a division of Pearson Education. Photo locators denoted as follows: Top (T), Center (C), Bottom (B), Left (L), Right (R) Background (Bkgd)
Opener: ©Charles O'Rear/Corbis; Title Page: ©A. Pasieka/Photo Researchers, Inc.; 2 ©William Taufic/Corbis; 3 ©A. Pasieka/Photo Researchers, Inc.; 4 ©Paul Seheult/Eye Ubiquitous/Corbis; 5 Brand X Pictures; 11 (BR) ©DK Images, (TR) Getty Images; 13 ©DK Images; 14 ©Chris Andrews Publications/Corbis

ISBN: 0-328-13892-4

Copyright © Pearson Education, Inc.

# Heat

**by Kim Fields**

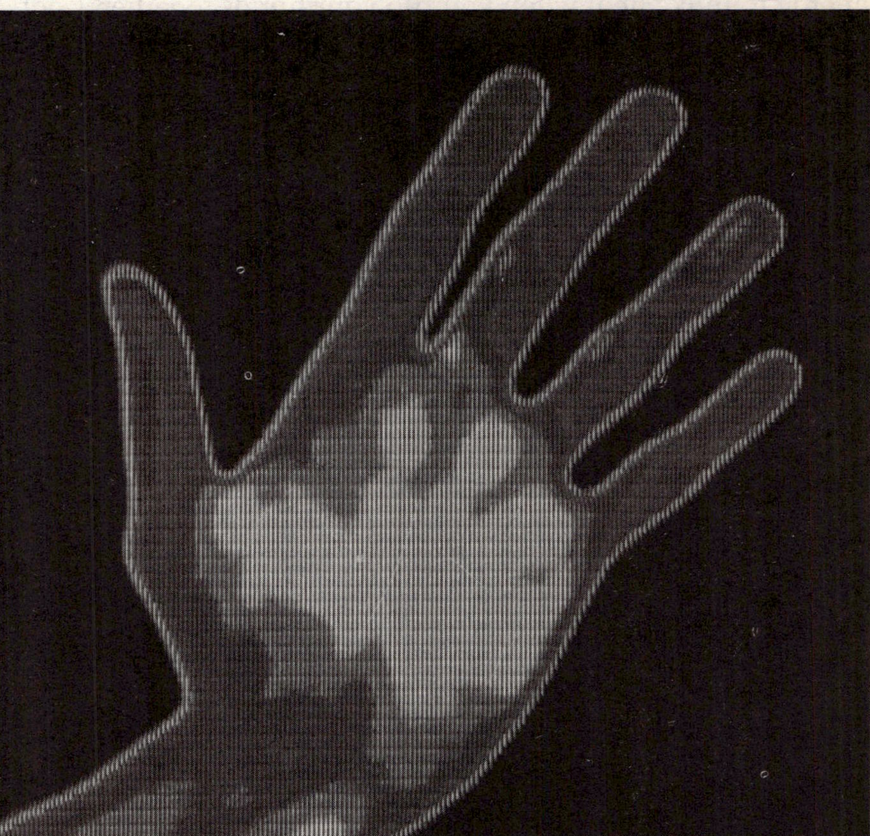

**Glossary**

| | |
|---|---|
| **conduction** | the transfer of heat energy by one thing touching another |
| **conductor** | a material that allows heat to move easily through it |
| **convection current** | a pattern of flowing heat energy |
| **insulator** | a material that limits the amount of heat that passes through it |
| **radiation** | energy sent out in little bundles |
| **thermal energy** | energy due to moving particles that make up matter |

# Why does matter have energy?

## Energy in Matter

Energy is the ability to do work or cause a change. You use energy to make heat when you rub your hands together. Cool hands become warmer ones. All changes need energy. Energy is used when there is a change to how something looks, what it is made of, or where it is.

## Conduction, Convection, and Radiation

Energy from the Sun heats Earth's surface through radiation. The surface transfers heat to the air and warms it through conduction. Convection currents also form as Earth's surface heats the air. These currents cause Earth's wind and rain patterns.

Energy is the ability to do work. Heat is the transfer of thermal energy. It can be moved in several ways. Conduction, convection, and radiation are all ways that heat is moved. Think about how heat moves the next time you drink hot cocoa, sit in a warm sunbeam, or take a hot bath.

## Radiation

**Radiation** is energy sent out in little bundles. You feel radiation when you get warm in the Sun or sit by a fire.

Radiation can travel through empty space or through matter. It is absorbed by dark, dull surfaces. Shiny surfaces reflect radiation. Clear surfaces allow radiation inside. A greenhouse is made of plastic or glass. Radiation from sunlight makes a greenhouse warm even when it is cold outside.

Radiation is unlike conduction and convection. Conduction happens when materials are touching each other. Convection needs the heated particles of a fluid to carry energy. Radiation does not need particles of solids, liquids, or gases. Radiation can move energy great distances, even from the Sun to Earth.

Tiny moving particles make up all matter. Particles are tightly packed in a solid. They only move slightly. In a liquid, particles are close together. They flow freely. Particles are far apart in a gas. They move all around. Particles move because they have energy.

**Thermal energy** is energy due to moving particles that make up matter. We feel the flow of thermal energy as heat. An object's particles move faster as it gets hotter. An object's particles move more slowly as it cools.

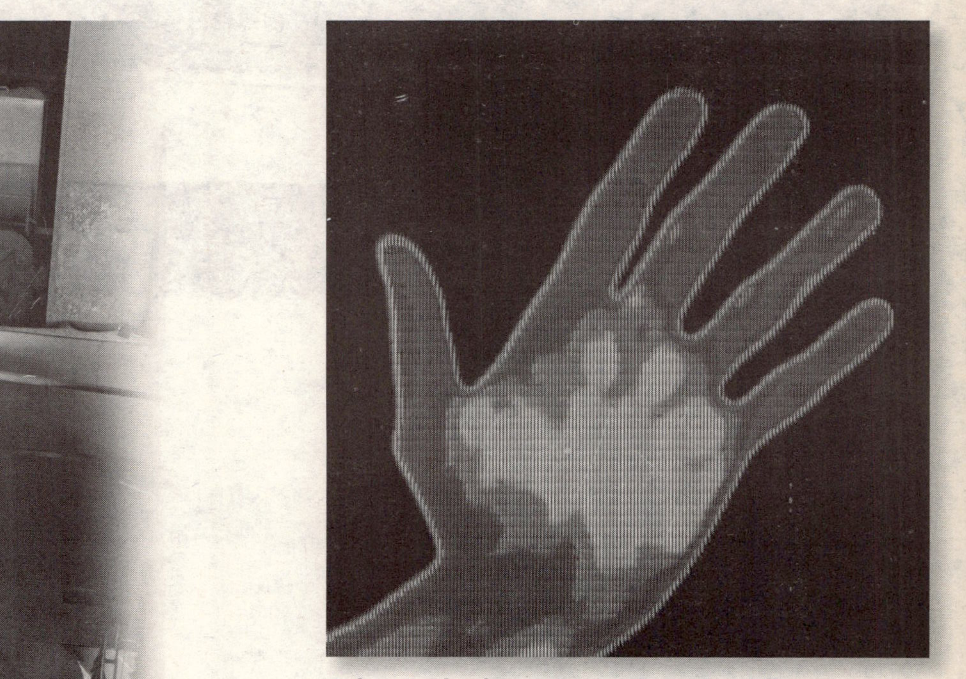

Colors in this heat picture show the different amounts of heat energy.

## Measuring Moving Particles

Temperature is often measured with a thermometer. A thermometer is usually a glass tube with a bulb that holds colored alcohol. The degrees are shown by number lines on the outside of the glass tube. The lines on one side of the tube tell the degrees Fahrenheit. The lines on the other side tell the degrees Celsius.

What is the heat source in this photo? It's the candles. As long as the candles are burning, movement of the rising warm air will make the objects above the candles move. The energy from the flames heats the air above them. The air particles move faster and farther apart. This makes the air less dense. Cooler air rushes under the less dense air. It pushes the warm air upward.

Much larger convection currents change our weather. Uneven heating of the air around Earth causes large currents. They make Earth's major wind patterns.

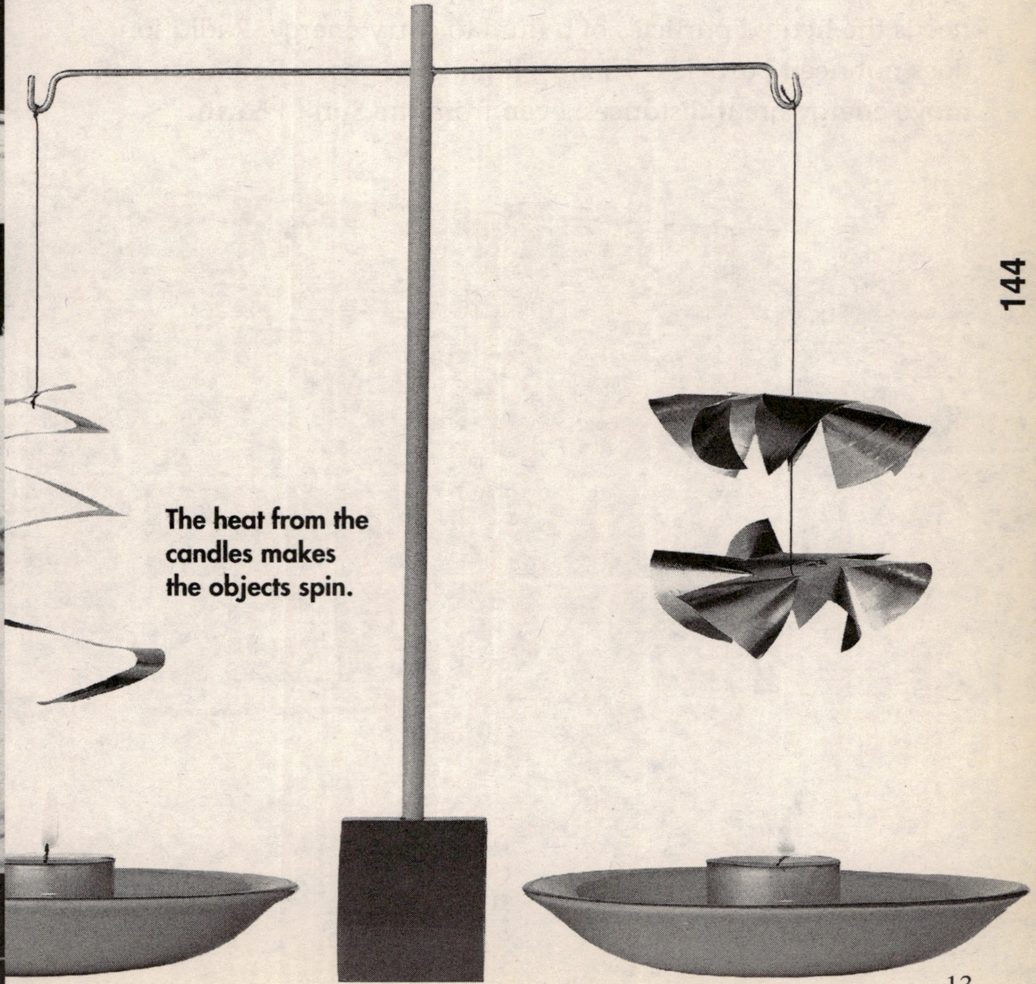

**The heat from the candles makes the objects spin.**

## Convection

A fluid is matter that does not have a definite shape. Water and air are fluids. Heated fluids can move from place to place in a process called convection.

A **convection current** is a pattern of flowing heat energy. A convection current forms when a heated fluid expands. Heat moves through air in a convection current. When air is heated, it becomes less dense than the cooler air around it. The cooler air sinks below the warmer air. This forces the warm air upward. The cycle continues as more cool air is warmed and is forced upward by colder air.

A radiator heats the air by convection.

Matter expands, or gets larger, when its particles move faster. It contracts, or gets smaller, when particles slow down. If a thermometer touches matter with fast-moving particles, the particles in the colored alcohol speed up. They also move farther apart. The liquid expands and moves up inside the tube. The reading on the line shows a higher temperature. The liquid in the tube contracts if the particles slow down. The reading on the number line shows a lower temperature.

The thermometer has to be on or in what it's measuring. If the thermometer is not touching the substance, it might not measure the motion of the particles correctly.

## Heat and Temperature

The particles of a material move fast when the material has a high temperature. But temperature is not a measure of how much heat a material has.

People often mix up the meanings of heat and temperature. Temperature is the measure of the average amount of particle motion in matter. It measures the average energy. Thermal energy measures the total energy of moving particles. It measures how fast particles move and how many are moving. Heat is the movement of thermal energy from one material to another.

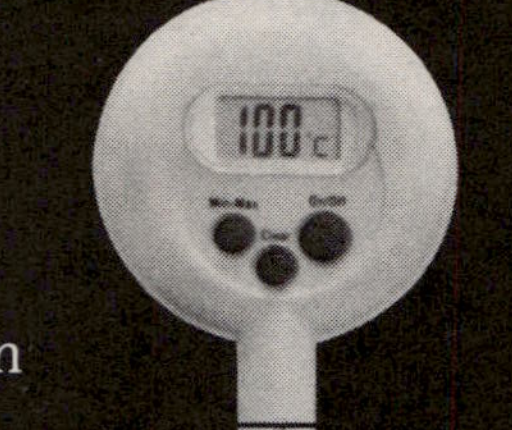

Some things do not get warm even when they touch something hot. An **insulator** is a material that doesn't let much heat pass through it. Wood is a very good insulator. That is why many pots have wooden handles.

Marble is an insulator. It has been used in buildings since ancient times. Plastic foam combines two good insulators: plastic and air. Plastic foam containers keep your food warm and your hands cool.

*Plastic foam cup*

*Marble tray*

## Conductors and Insulators

A **conductor** is a material that allows heat to move through it easily. Many metals, such as iron, aluminum, and copper, are good conductors. An iron pan gets hot quickly when it is placed on a heat source, such as a burner. A metal spoon is also a good conductor.

*Iron pan*

Suppose you filled a large pot and a small pot halfway with boiling water. The large pot holds more water. It has many more moving water particles. This means it has more energy of motion. Because of this, the large pot has more thermal energy. The temperature of the water in both pots is the same because the water in each pot is boiling. The average amount of particle motion is also the same. The size of the pot does not change the temperature.

# How does heat move?

## Conduction

Thermal energy flows from a warmer material to a cooler one. The movement is what we feel as heat. A heat source gives off energy that can be taken in by particles of matter. Heat energy moves by conduction between two solids that are touching. **Conduction** happens when heat energy is transferred by one thing touching another.

Place one end of a cool metal spoon in boiling water. What happens? The spoon gets hot! Particles in the spoon touch the hot water. They start to move quickly. The particles crash into other particles in the spoon's handle. Soon heat energy moves throughout the spoon. The transfer of energy continues until the water and the spoon are the same temperature.

If you do the same thing with a wooden spoon, its handle will stay cool. That is because the wooden spoon does not conduct heat energy very well.

The metal spoon conducts heat well. This causes the piece of wax on the spoon to melt. The wooden spoon does not conduct heat well. The piece of wax on this spoon does not melt.

Science

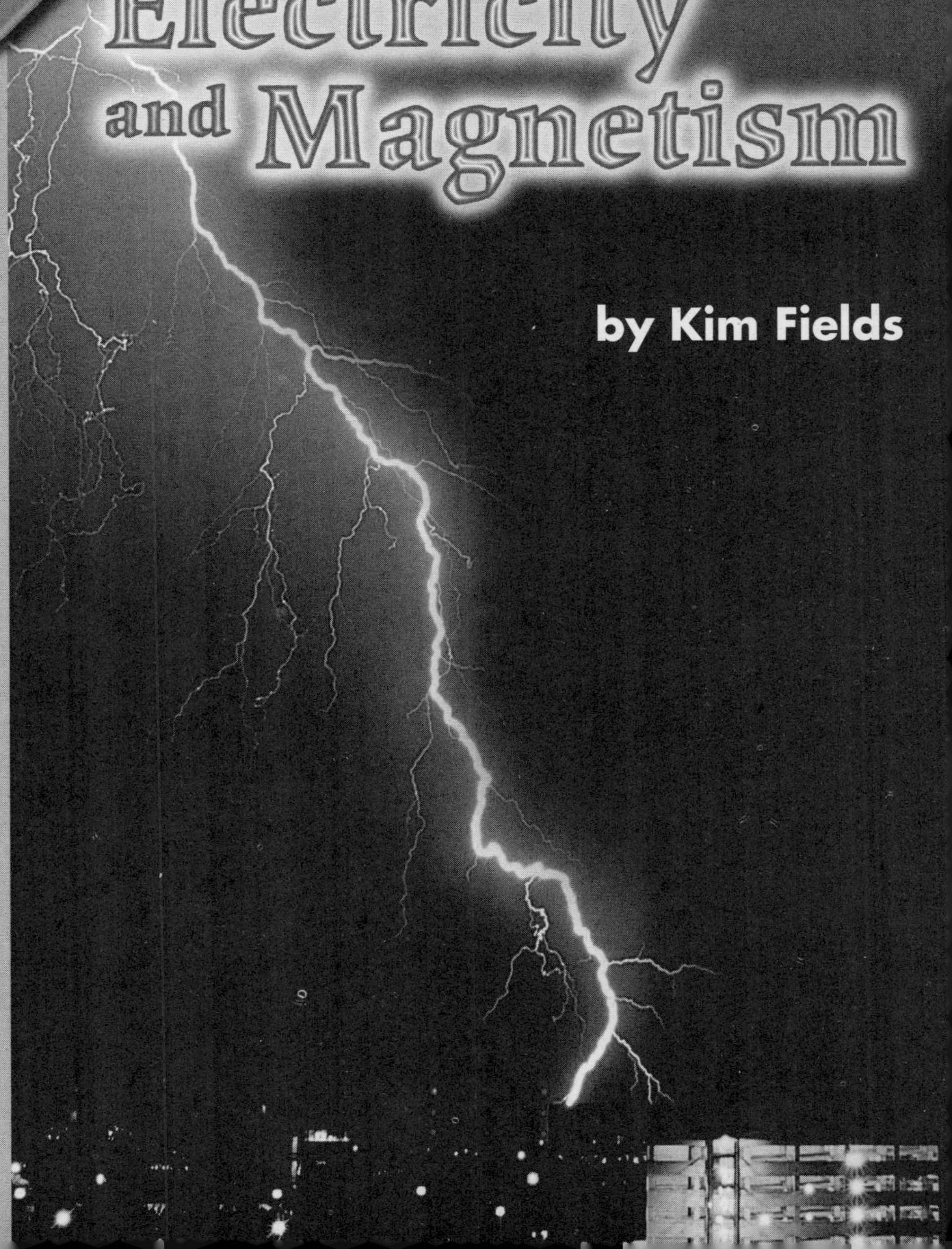

| Genre | Comprehension Skill | Text Features | Science Content |
|---|---|---|---|
| Nonfiction | Cause and Effect | • Captions<br>• Labels<br>• Diagrams<br>• Glossary | Electricity and Magnetism |

Scott Foresman Science 4.13

PEARSON Scott Foresman

DK

ISBN 0-328-13895-9

9 780328 138951 90000

scottforesman.com



Science

Physical Science

# Electricity and Magnetism

by Kim Fields

## Vocabulary

electric current

electromagnet

magnetic field

magnetism

parallel circuit

resistance

series circuit

static electricity

## What did you learn?

1. How do like charges behave? unlike charges?

2. How are magnets used to make electricity?

3. How can you make an electromagnet stronger?

4. **Writing** in Science   In a series circuit, if one bulb burns out, it opens the circuit and the other bulbs won't receive the energy they need. On your own paper, write to explain why this does not happen in a parallel circuit. Include details from the book to support your answer.

5. **Cause and Effect** What causes lightning?



**Illustrations:** 8, 9 Peter Bollinger
**Photographs:** Every effort has been made to secure permission and provide appropriate credit for photographic material. The publisher deeply regrets any omission and pledges to correct errors called to its attention in subsequent editions. Unless otherwise acknowledged, all photographs are the property of Scott Foresman, a division of Pearson Education. Photo locators denoted as follows: Top (T), Center (C), Bottom (B), Left (L), Right (R) Background (Bkgd)
Opener: (Bkgd) Digital Vision; 2 ©Byron Aughenbaugh/Getty Images; 4 Stephen Oliver/©DK Images; 7 (BC) ©Richard Megna/Fundamental Photographs, (TC) ©DK Images; 10 ©Cordelia Molloy/Photo Researchers, Inc.; 11 ©Loren Winters/Visuals Unlimited; 15 ©Kennan Ward/Corbis; 18 ©DK Images; 19 ©DK Images; 22 ©Sheila Terry/Photo Researchers, Inc.; 23 (B) ©Royalty-Free/Corbis, (TR) Getty Images

ISBN: 0-328-13895-9

# Electricity and Magnetism

## by Kim Fields

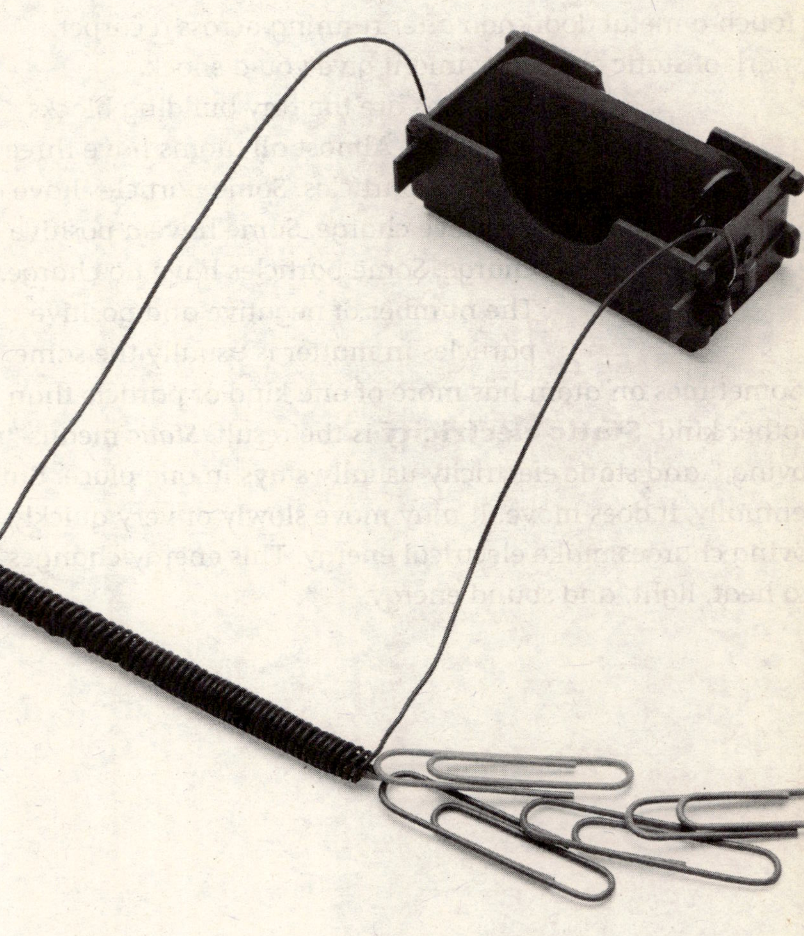

## Glossary

**electric current** — an electric charge in motion

**electromagnet** — a core of iron with wire coiled around it; when electricity goes through the wire, it causes a magnetic field

**magnetic field** — an invisible field around a magnet where the force of magnetism can be felt

**magnetism** — a force that pushes or pulls magnetic materials near a magnet

**parallel circuit** — a circuit in which an electric charge can follow two or more paths

**resistance** — the ability of a substance to keep an electric charge from flowing through it easily

**series circuit** — a circuit in which electric charge flows in one path

**static electricity** — the result of positive and negative particles not in balance

# How does matter become charged?

## Electric Charges

Touch a metal doorknob after running across a carpet. A spark of static electricity might give you a shock.

Atoms are the tiny building blocks of matter. Almost all atoms have three kinds of particles. Some particles have a negative charge. Some have a positive charge. Some particles have no charge. The number of negative and positive particles in matter is usually the same.

Sometimes an atom has more of one kind of particle than another kind. **Static electricity** is the result. *Static* means "not moving," and static electricity usually stays in one place. But eventually, it does move. It may move slowly or very quickly. Moving charges make electrical energy. This energy changes into heat, light, and sound energy.

## Discoveries in Using Electrical Energy

Many people have made many discoveries about electricity. In the 1740s Benjamin Franklin and Ebenezer Kinnersley described electric charges as positive or negative. Zenobe Gramme developed the electric generator in 1870. Thomas Edison demonstrated the first light bulb in 1879. And those are just a few examples!

## How Generators Are Powered

Some generators make electrical energy by using the energy of the wind. Others use falling water. Some generators are powered by steam. This steam may be from the hot temperatures deep below Earth's surface or from nuclear energy heating water. In each kind of generator, a coil of wire spins around a magnet. Electricity and magnetism work together in generators to provide energy for many things.

## A Flashlight Without Batteries

Michael Faraday was a British scientist. In 1831 he invented a machine that used magnets to change motion into an electric current. He made electrical energy by turning a crank on the machine. He called this a dynamo. This is the same technology that is used today in an emergency flashlight. It does not use batteries. It makes electricity when you squeeze the handle.

## Currents Currently

A generator makes electric energy by turning coils of wire around powerful magnets. It uses magnets and wires to produce electrical energy. Most businesses, homes, and schools use electricity from generators.





## Static Electricity

Storm clouds become charged when particles move between atoms. The positive particles usually gather near the top of the clouds. The negative particles move toward the bottom of the clouds. The static electricity is released as lightning. Lightning heats the air around it. The heated air glows. Lightning makes the sound that we call thunder.

## How Charged Objects Behave

Objects with opposite charges are attracted to each other. An object with a positive charge and an object with a negative charge will pull toward each other. This attraction makes an electric force. An electric force is the push or pull between objects with opposite charges.

An object with a charge can attract something without a charge. Rub a blown-up balloon on your head. It picks up negative particles from your hair. This gives the balloon a negative charge. Then hold the balloon near lightweight objects that are neutral, such as small pieces of paper. The pieces of paper stick to the balloon! Eventually, the balloon loses its negative charge. The pieces of paper fall off.

The magnetic field of a magnet moves when the magnet moves. You can make electricity by changing a magnetic field. If you move the coiled wire or the magnet faster, you make the current stronger. If you move the coiled wire or the magnet is moved more slowly, you make the current weaker. The strength of the current is also affected by the number of coils wrapped around the magnet. More coils mean the magnet makes a stronger current.

# How is magnetism transformed to electricity?

## Electrical Energy

Most people use electrical energy without thinking about it. They find it hard to think of life without electricity. The electrical energy that powers televisions, lamps, and refrigerators has come a long way.

We use magnetism to make electricity. We can make electricity by sliding coiled wire back and forth over a magnet. We can also make electricity by spinning the wire around a magnet.

## An Electric Field

An electric field is the space around electrically charged objects. It is invisible. The electric field is strongest close to the charged object. It gets weaker as it gets farther away.

A negative electric field attracts positive charges. It pushes away, or repels, negative ones. A positive electric field attracts negative charges and pushes away positive ones.

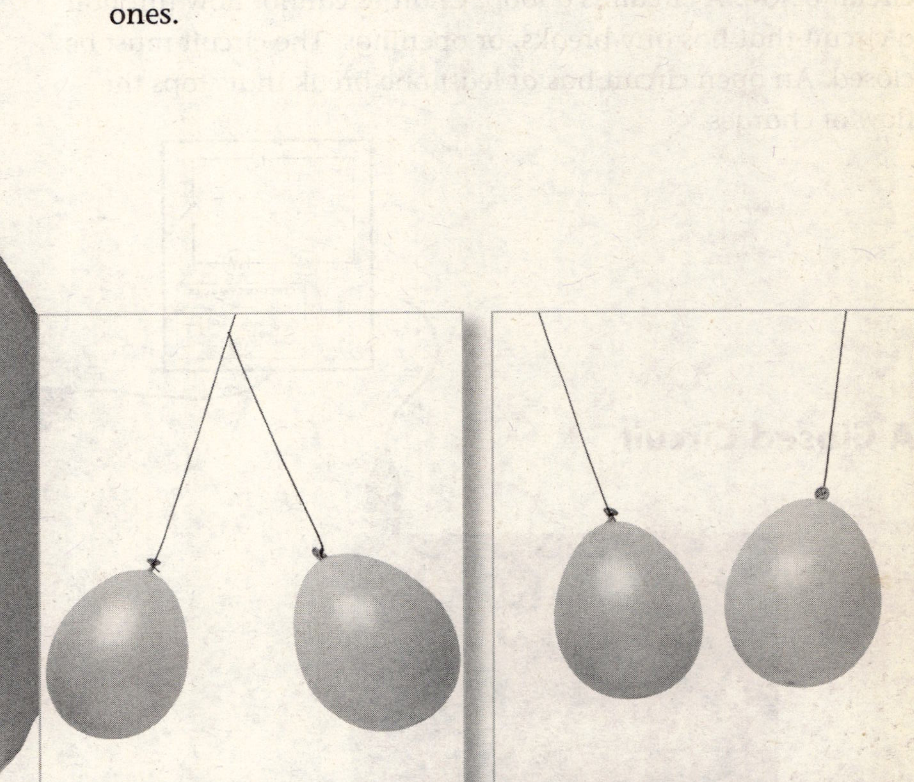

These balloons have the same charge. They repel each other.

These balloons have opposite charges. They attract each other.

# How do electric charges flow?

## How Electric Charges Move

Most electricity moves. An electric charge in motion is called an **electric current.** An electric current travels quickly Electricity can be very dangerous. You cannot see it. Look at the circuit below. A circuit is a loop. Charges cannot flow through a circuit that has any breaks, or openings. The circuit must be closed. An open circuit has at least one break that stops the flow of charges.

## A Closed Circuit

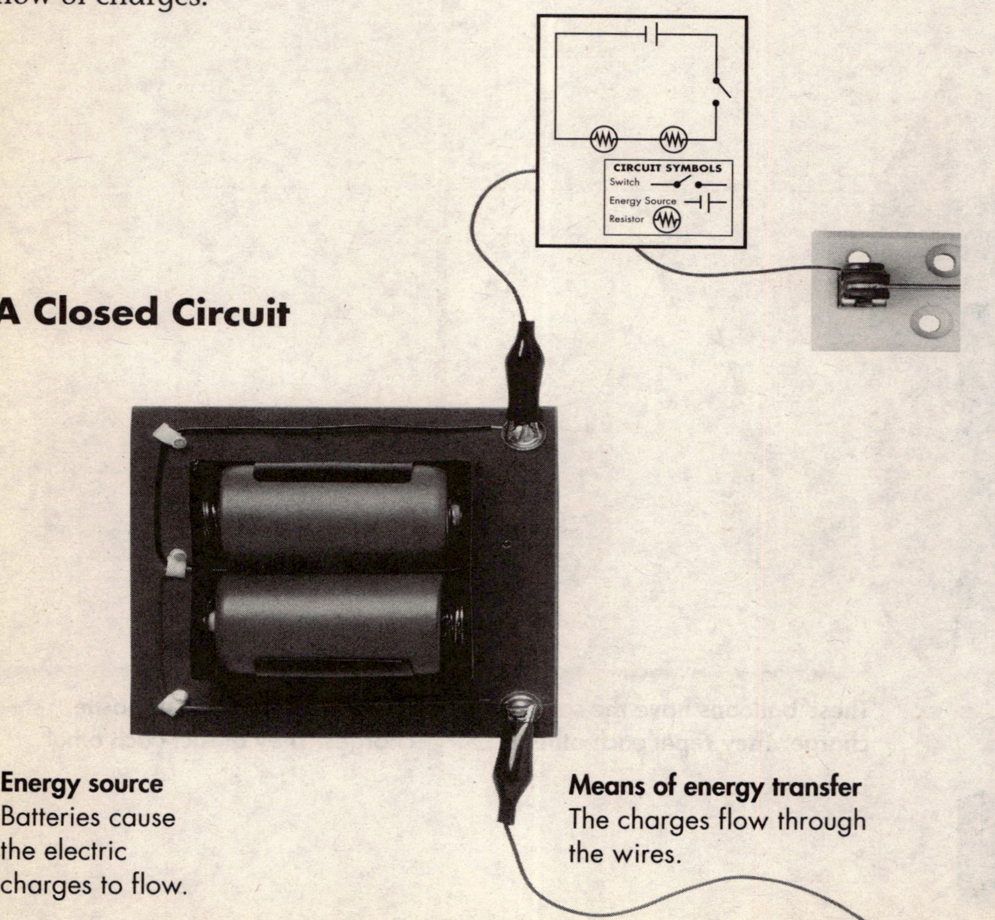



**Energy source**
Batteries cause the electric charges to flow.

**Means of energy transfer**
The charges flow through the wires.

## Simple Electric Motor

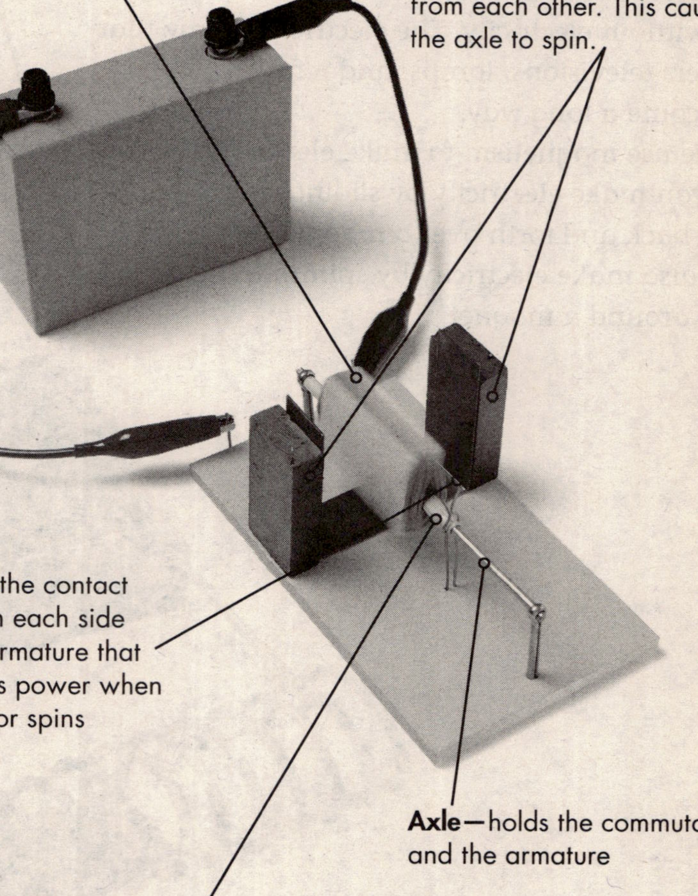





156

## Uses for Electromagnets

Electromagnets are used to lift heavy objects. Electromagnets are also in many machines that scientists and doctors use.

Electronic devices that you use each day have electromagnets. DVD players, fans, computers, and televisions work because of electromagnets. Electromagnets help change electric energy into magnetic energy and then into other kinds of energy.

## How a Doorbell Works

Press the button on a doorbell. This closes the electrical circuit. The current flows to a part called the transformer. The transformer controls how much current is sent to the electromagnet. Electricity flowing into the coil of wire causes the electromagnet to become magnetized. This magnetism pulls up the contact arm. The arm is attached to the metal clapper. The clapper hits the bell. The bell rings. Magnetic energy has been changed into the sound you hear.

## Going with the Flow

An electric charge does not flow the same way through all materials. The atoms of some materials are charged more easily than others. These materials are called conductors. Most metals are good conductors. The copper wire in the circuit below is a good conductor. Silver is also a good conductor.

Electric charge moves through the atoms of some materials slowly. These materials are called insulators. Dry wood, rubber, plastic, and glass are good insulators. The wire in the picture is insulated. This stops the electric charges from traveling to other wires. The wire in each light bulb is made of a material with high resistance. **Resistance** means the material does not allow electric charges to flow easily.

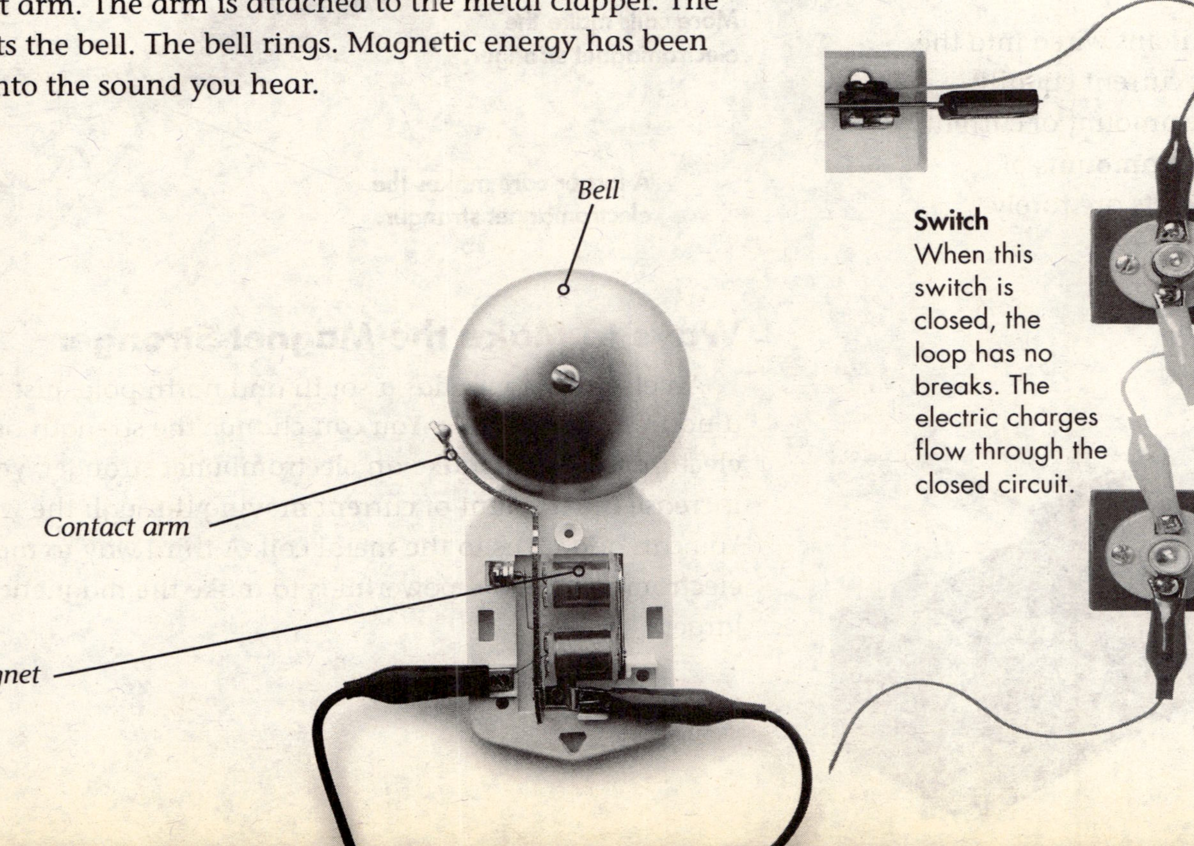

## Types of Circuits

In a **series circuit,** an electric charge can flow in only one path. Look at the string of lights. A power source is turned on. The charged particles in the wire flow in one direction around a loop. Each light bulb around the path receives the same amount of electrical energy. If all the bulbs are the same, each will have the same brightness.

If one bulb burns out, it opens the circuit. The electricity cannot cross the break in the circuit. The other bulbs won't receive the energy they need. So no bulbs are able to light.

In a series circuit, all items wired into the circuit share the electric current equally. Each item gets the same amount of current. Appliances need different amounts of current. Today series circuits are rarely used.

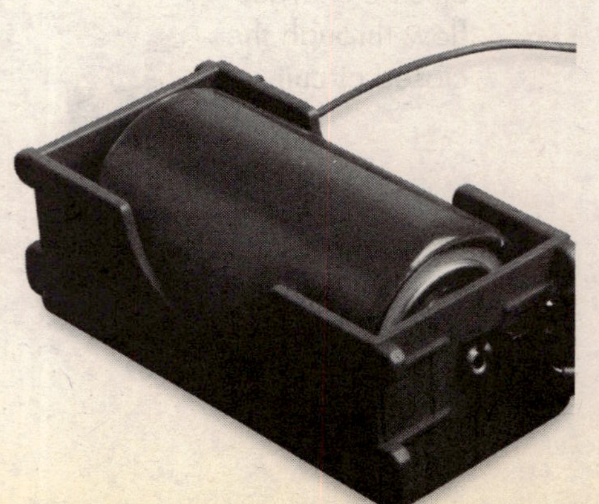

*Series circuit*

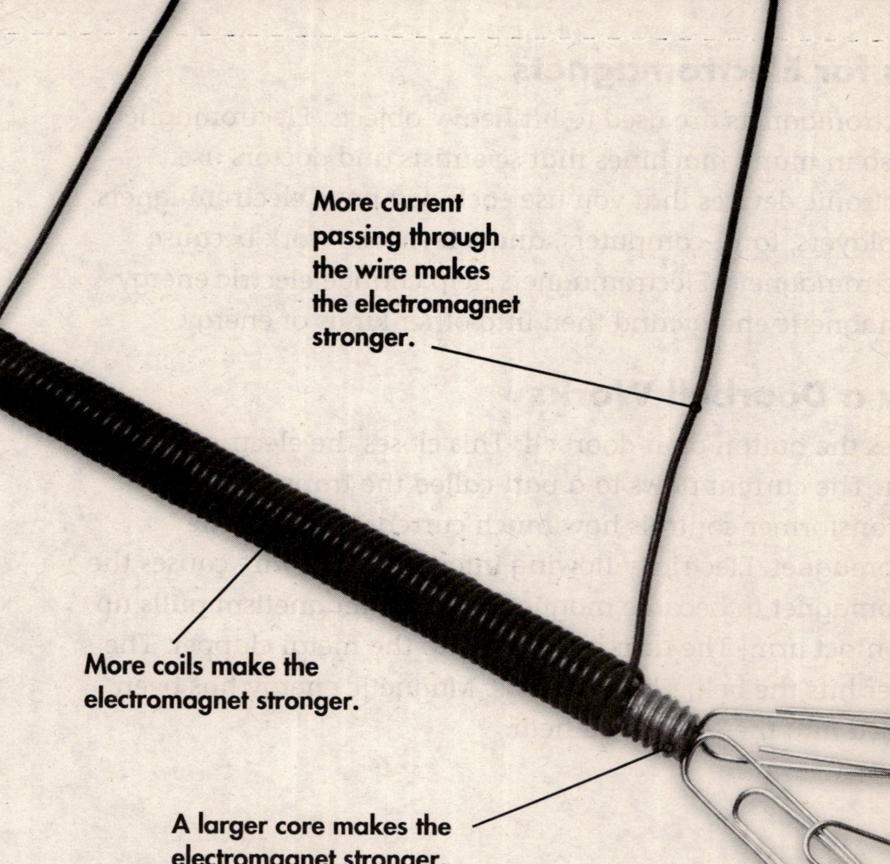


## Ways to Make the Magnet Stronger

An electromagnet has a south and north pole, just as a natural magnet has. You can change the strength of an electromagnet. To make an electromagnet stronger, you can increase the amount of current moving through the wire. You can add turns to the metal coil. A third way to make the electromagnet more powerful is to make the magnetic core larger.

# How is electricity transformed to magnetism?

## Electromagnets

In 1820 scientist Hans Christian Oersted was showing how electric current flowed through a wire. He saw that the needle on a nearby compass moved each time he turned on the electric current. Oersted realized the flowing current made a magnetic field. This led to the invention of the electromagnet.

An **electromagnet** is a coil of wire wrapped around an iron core. An electromagnet changes electrical energy into magnetic energy. A current moving through the wire causes a magnetic field around the electromagnet. The wire loses its magnetic power when the current stops.

## Parallel Circuits

A **parallel circuit** has two or more paths for electric charges to take. All the lights in a circuit don't go out when one light burns out. In a parallel circuit the main loop starts and stops at the power source. Along the loop there are smaller loops. Each smaller loop is a separate path for the electric charges. If electricity stops flowing through one of the smaller loops, it can still flow through the large loop.

Circuits used in buildings are parallel circuits. A parallel circuit can handle electric devices that need different amounts of current.

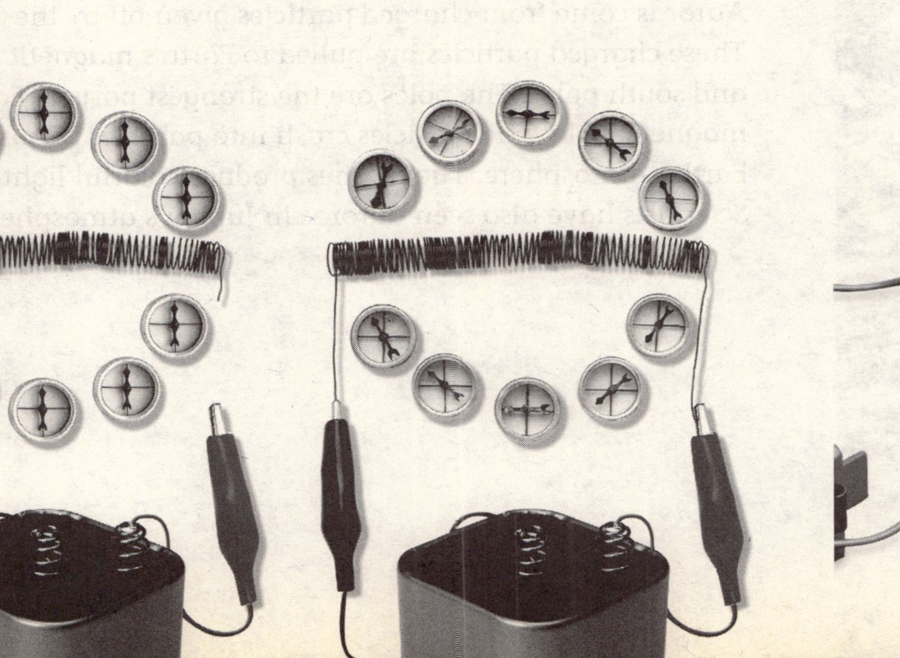

*Parallel circuits*

# What are magnetic fields?

## Magnetism

A magnet is an object that attracts other objects made of steel, iron, and certain other metals. **Magnetism** is the force that pushes or pulls magnetic items near a magnet.

## Magnetic Fields

Magnets have an invisible field surrounding them. This is called a **magnetic field.** The shape of the magnetic field depends on the shape of the magnet. Look at the pattern of iron filings near the horseshoe magnet. The pattern is different from the pattern around the bar magnet on the next page. The magnetic fields have different shapes because the magnets have different shapes. Any magnetic field is strongest at the magnet's ends, or poles. The pushing or pulling force is also strongest at the poles.

## The Northern Lights

The Aurora Borealis, or the Northern Lights, is a natural light show that is visible at different times during the year. Auroras come from charged particles given off by the Sun. These charged particles are pulled to Earth's magnetic north and south poles. The poles are the strongest parts of Earth's magnetic field. The particles crash into particles of gas in Earth's atmosphere. The crashes produce colorful light. Scientists have also seen auroras in Jupiter's atmosphere.

## How Compasses Work

A compass is a small, handy tool. No matter where you are on Earth, one end of a compass needle will always point north. It is drawn to the pull of Earth's magnetic north pole. When you know which direction is north, you can easily find east, west, and south.

A compass needle has to be light. It must turn easily to work properly. The compass cannot be near a magnet. If it is, the needle will be pulled by the magnet. The needle will respond to the magnet's pull instead of Earth's pull.

## Magnetic Poles

All magnets have a south-seeking pole and a north-seeking pole. Opposite poles have opposite charges. Opposite charges pull toward each other. Like charges push away from each other. The south-seeking pole on one magnet and the north-seeking pole on another magnet pull toward each other. But two south-seeking poles push apart.

Breaking a magnet into two parts makes two magnets. Each has a north-seeking pole and a south-seeking pole. The two poles of a magnet are like the two sides of a coin. You cannot have one without the other.

## 12

## The Largest Magnet in the World

Ancient sailors used compasses. But they didn't know why the compasses worked. Then around 1600 a British scientist named William Gilbert claimed that the world's largest magnet is Earth! The huge magnetic field that surrounds Earth makes one end of a compass needle point north.

Scientists don't know why Earth acts as a magnet. But they have an idea. Scientists think that Earth's outer core is made of iron. They think that this iron is so hot that it has melted. As Earth rotates, the liquid iron flows. The moving iron makes a magnetic field. The inner core is probably solid iron. It doesn't melt because it is under extremely high pressure.

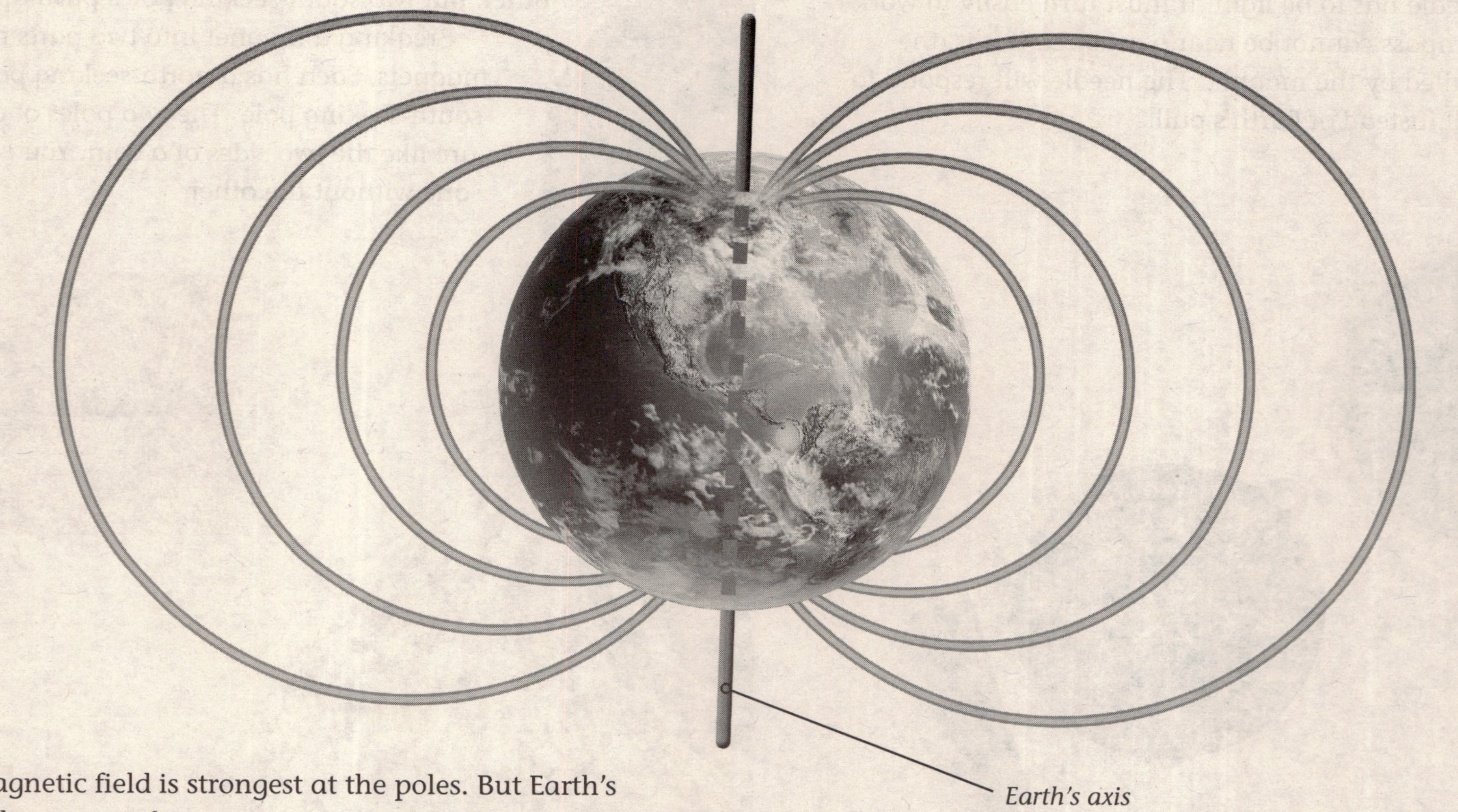


Earth's magnetic field is strongest at the poles. But Earth's magnetic poles are not the same as its geographic poles. The geographic poles are on Earth's axis. This is the invisible line that Earth rotates around. Earth's magnetic north pole is in Canada. It is about 1,000 kilometers (600 miles) from the geographic North Pole. The magnetic south pole is in the Southern Ocean near Antarctica.

## 13

Science

Science

163

# Sound and Light

## by Colin Kong

| Genre | Comprehension Skill | Text Features | Science Content |
|---|---|---|---|
| Nonfiction | Draw Conclusions | • Captions<br>• Labels<br>• Diagrams<br>• Glossary | Sound and Light |

Scott Foresman Science 4.14

PEARSON
Scott Foresman

DK

ISBN 0-328-13898-3

9 780328 138982

90000

scottforesman.com

## Vocabulary

absorption

compression

frequency

opaque

pitch

reflection

refraction

translucent

transparent

wavelength

## What did you learn?

1. Why is there no sound in outer space?

2. How are some invisible electromagnetic waves helpful to us? How can they be harmful?

3. What makes light bend?

4. **Writing** in Science Sound waves and light waves have similarities and differences. On your own paper, write to explain these similarities and differences. Use details from the book to support your answer.

5. **Draw Conclusions** A diver uses a flashlight while swimming to try to find something underwater. A person walking down the street uses a flashlight to try to find her way through the fog. Will the light travel faster underwater or on land? Explain your answer.

164

**Illustrations:** Title Page: Peter Bollinger 3, 4, 6, 7, 15 Peter Bollinger
**Photographs:** Every effort has been made to secure permission and provide appropriate credit for photographic material. The publisher deeply regrets any omission and pledges to correct errors called to its attention in subsequent editions. Unless otherwise acknowledged, all photographs are the property of Scott Foresman, a division of Pearson Education. Photo locators denoted as follows: Top (T), Center (C), Bottom (B), Left (L), Right (R), Background (Bkgd)
Opener: (CR) ©Cameron/Corbis, (Bkgd) Getty Images, (CC) ©Cooperphoto/Corbis; 2 Getty Images; 8 (C) ©DK Images, (B) Getty Images; 9 (CR) ©DK Images, (BL) Getty Images; 10 ©DK Images; 11 ©Bo Veisland, Mi & I/Photo Researchers, Inc.; 12 (BL) ©Chris Bjornberg/Photo Researchers, Inc., (CR) ©DK Images; 13 Mike Dunning/©DK Images; 14 ©Adina Tovy/Robert Harding Picture Library Ltd.; 15 ©Maxine Hall/Corbis; 16 Steve Gorton and Kari Shone/©DK Images; 17 Andy Crawfosd/Courtesy of the Football Museum, Preston/©DK Images; 18 ©NOAO/Photo Researchers, Inc.; 20 ©Southern Illinois University Biomedical Communications/Custom Medical Stock Photo; 21 ©David Parker/Photo Researchers, Inc.; 22 Getty Images.; 23 (R, L) ©E. R. Degginger/Color-Pic, Inc.

ISBN: 0-328-13898-3

# Sound and Light

## by Colin Kong

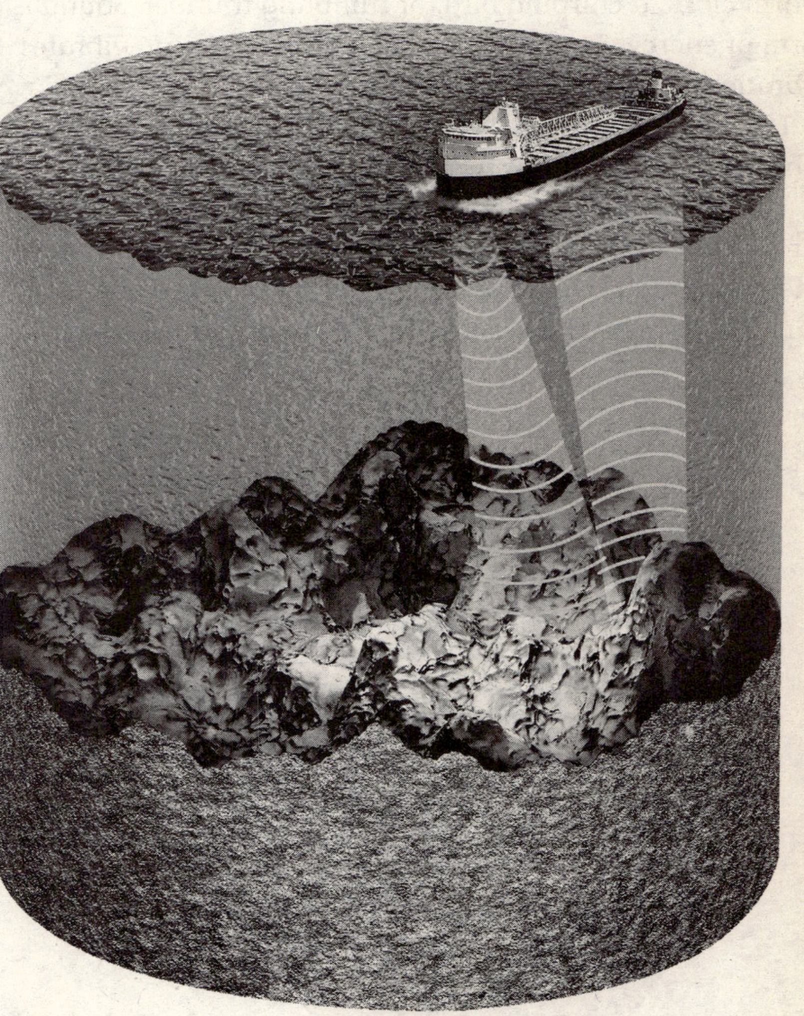

## Glossary

**absorption**   the taking in of light waves

**compression**   the part of a sound wave where the particles are close together

**frequency**   the number of waves that pass a certain point in a certain amount of time

**opaque**   allowing no light rays to pass through

**pitch**   a characteristic of sound that makes it seem high or low

**reflection**   the bouncing of light rays off a surface

**refraction**   the bending of light rays

**translucent**   allowing some light rays to pass through a material and scattering others

**transparent**   allowing nearly all light rays to pass through

**wavelength**   the distance between a point on one wave and a similar point on the next wave

# What is sound energy?

## What Sound Is

What sounds will you hear today? You may hear a buzzing alarm clock, a chirping bird, or rumbling thunder. Sound is a form of energy. Sounds are made when something vibrates. A vibration is a quick back-and-forth movement.

Think of a guitar string. When you pluck it, the string vibrates. The vibrating string sends energy into the air around it. This makes the air vibrate. Vibrations move through the air as sound waves. A sound wave is a disturbance. It moves energy through matter. Sound waves carry sound energy to our ears. Then we hear the sound made by the guitar string.

## Lenses

Lenses are curved pieces of clear glass or plastic. They refract light that passes through them. Lenses help people see things that are small or far away.

## Convex Lenses

A convex lens is thicker in the middle than at the edges. Light rays bend toward the middle of the lens when they pass through. These bent rays meet at one point on the other side of the lens. Convex lenses make things look larger.

## Concave Lenses

A concave lens is thinner in the middle than at the edges. Light rays bend outward and spread apart when they pass through. Objects appear smaller than they are.

Concave and convex lenses can be used together to make details look clearer. Many telescopes use both kinds of lenses.



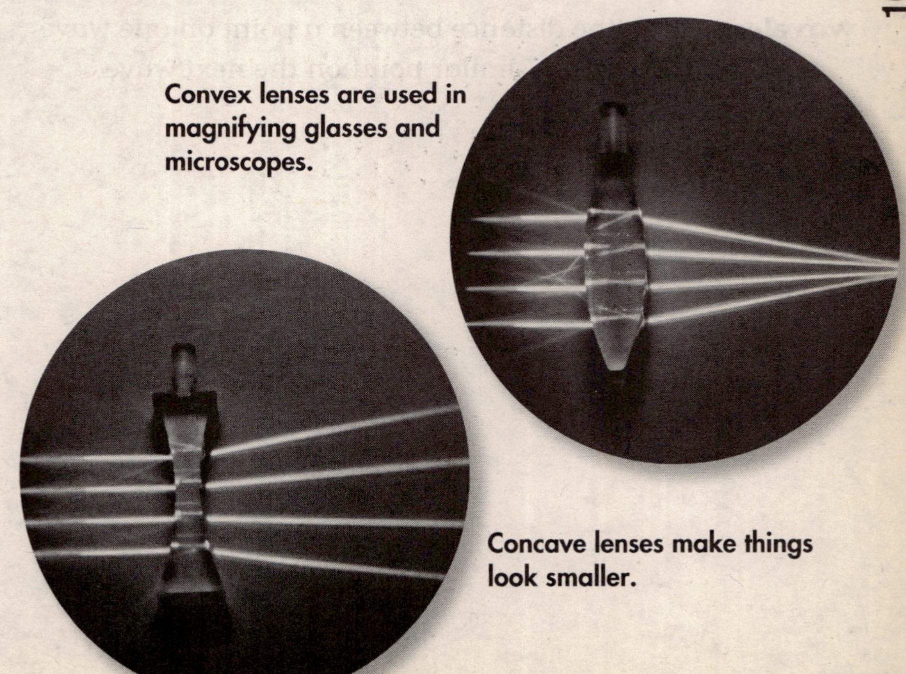

Convex lenses are used in magnifying glasses and microscopes.

Concave lenses make things look smaller.

## The Human Eye

The eye is a fluid-filled ball. It has a bony area around it. The front of the eye has a transparent cover over it for protection. This cover also refracts entering light. The iris is a donut-shaped muscle behind the cover. It is the colored part of the eye. The pupil is the dark opening in the center of the iris.

The iris controls the amount of light that enters the eye. When bright light hits the eye, the iris closes and the pupil gets smaller. The iris opens and the pupil gets larger in dim light. Light then passes through the lens. The lens refracts the light rays even more. An upside-down image forms on the retina at the back of the eye. Cells in the retina change the light into signals. These signals travel through the optic nerve to the brain. You see the image right-side up.

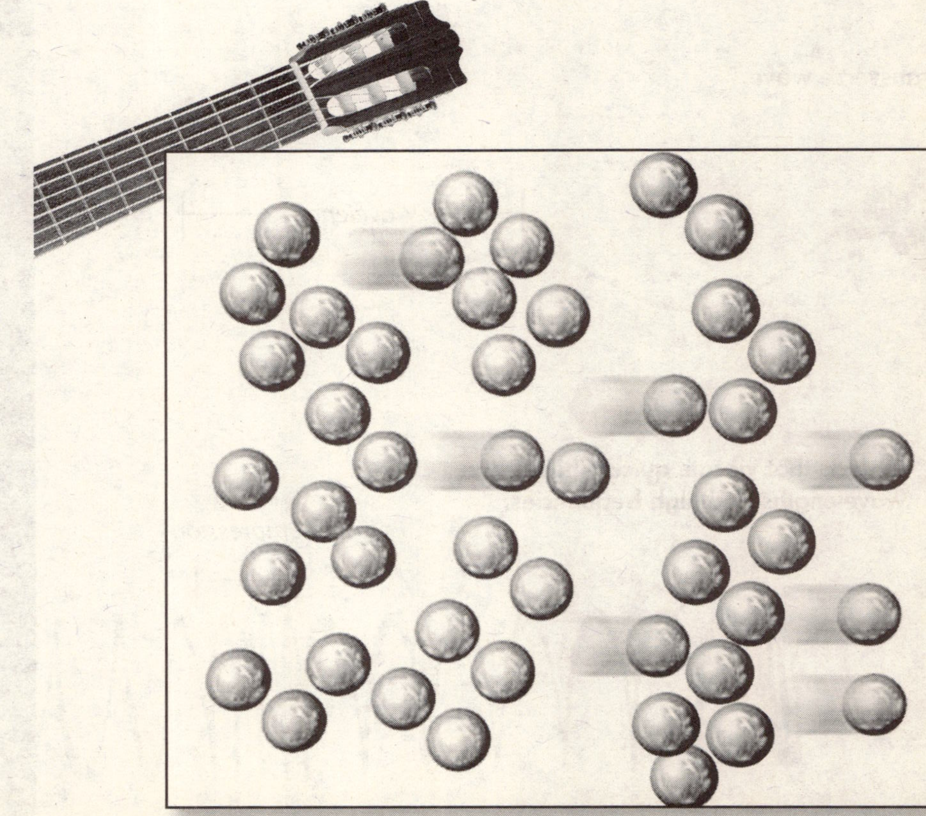


## Types of Sound Waves

Air particles move when sound waves move. Air particles form a pattern when they move. Particles are far apart in one section of the wave. In another section, particles are close together. The section where the particles are close together is called a **compression.** Each type of section follows the other in a wave. Waves are classified by how they move through matter. There are two main kinds of waves.

## Transverse Waves

Suppose you and your friend are holding opposite ends of a jump rope. You quickly flick your wrist. This sends energy through the rope. It causes a wave. The wave moves through the rope to your friend's hand. But the rope vibrates only up and down. This is a transverse wave. In a transverse wave, the particles in the material move at a right angle to the direction of the wave. This means that as the wave moved across to your friend, the rope moved up and down.

**Transverse wave**

Wavelength

**Objects that vibrate quickly have short wavelengths and high frequencies.**

Compression



Light sometimes moves at an angle from one medium to another. Some light is reflected, some is absorbed, and some passes through. But light can also change directions and bend! **Refraction** occurs when light bends. A light ray changes speed as it moves at an angle from one transparent medium to another. Light refracts, or bends, because of the change in speed. Each color of the visible spectrum bends differently. A color with a long wavelength bends less than a color with a short wavelength. This is how white light is separated.

## How Light Changes Direction

You know that light can move through objects. It can also be reflected or absorbed. Did you know that light can be bent?

This pencil looks broken because the light rays refract, or bend, as they move from air to water.



Unlike sound, light does not have to travel through a medium. It actually travels the fastest through a vacuum. Light moves slower in a gas than it does in a vacuum. If light moved from a vacuum into a gas, it would slow down.

Light travels even more slowly through a liquid. This is because particles are packed more closely in a liquid than they are in a gas. Light moves slowest through solids. The particles in a solid are very close together.

## Longitudinal Waves

Particles in longitudinal waves move in the same direction that the wave travels. Hold one end of a spring toy and have a friend hold the other end. Pull on your end and then push it in. This sends energy through the spring. Some of the coils crowd close together. Once the vibrations pass, the coils move farther apart. Sound waves are longitudinal waves.

## Frequency and Wavelength

**Frequency** is the number of waves that pass a certain point in a certain amount of time. Sound waves have different frequencies. **Wavelength** is the distance between a point on one wave and a point on the next wave.

Wavelength can be measured between two high points or two low points.

Longitudinal wave

## How Sound Travels

A sound wave needs a medium to move through. A medium is a kind of matter, such as a solid, a liquid, or a gas. A sound wave can travel through all three mediums.

The particles of a solid are close together. A vibration moves quickly from one particle to the next. A sound wave moves quickly through a solid.

The particles of a liquid are slightly farther apart. A vibration takes longer to move from one particle to another. So sound waves travel more slowly through a liquid.

A **translucent** material lets some light rays pass through and scatters other rays. Light passes through the material. But anything on the other side of the material looks blurry. Some translucent materials are wax paper, lampshades, frosted glass, and beeswax.

An **opaque** material does not let any light pass through. You cannot see through an opaque material. It either reflects or absorbs the light rays that reach it. Aluminum foil is an opaque material. It reflects light. Light bounces off its surface. This makes it look shiny and bright. Wood is also an opaque material. It's not shiny. It absorbs light.

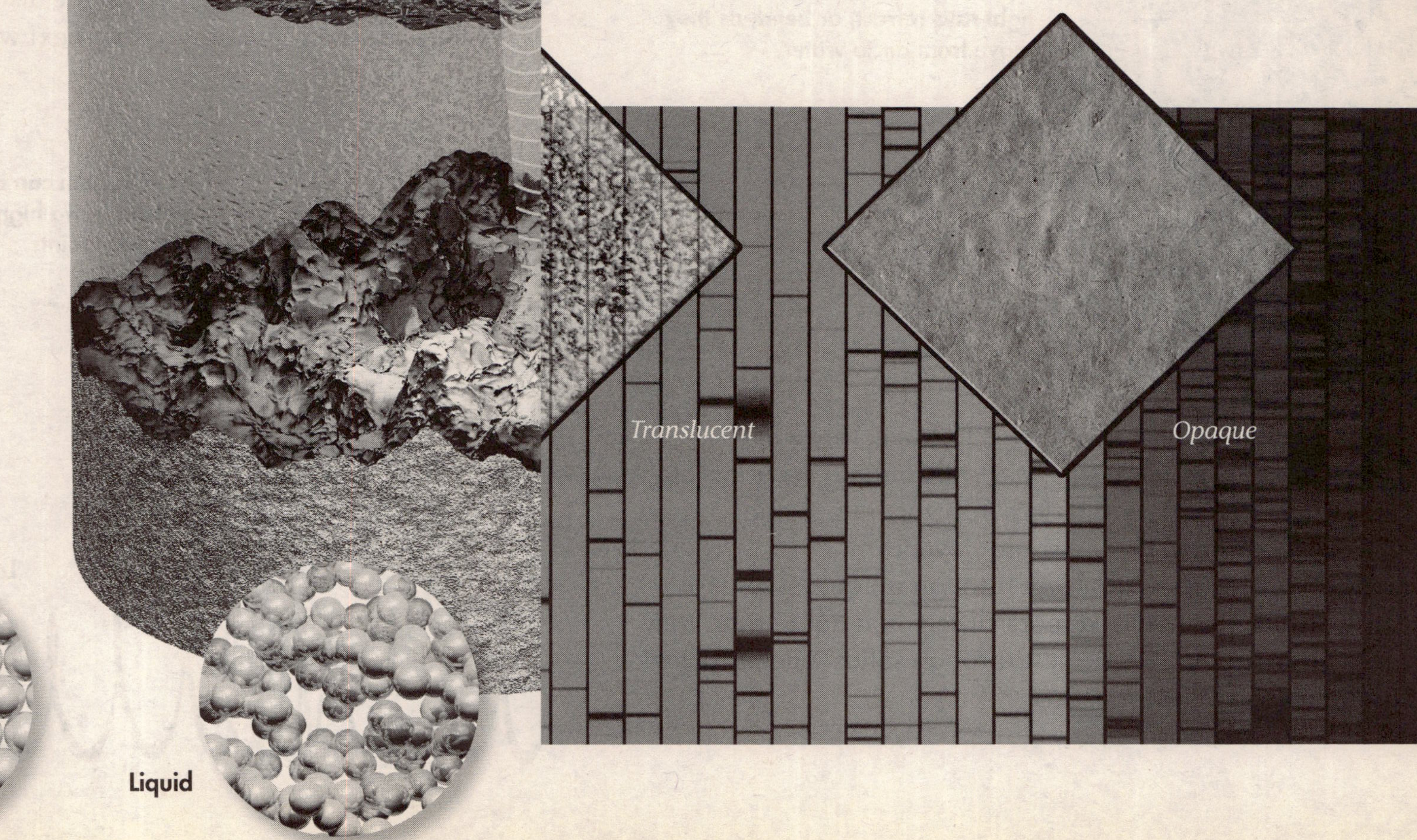

## Letting Light Through

Different materials react differently when light hits them. A **transparent** material lets light rays pass through it. Objects on the other side of a transparent material are clear and easy to see. Air, clean water, and most windows are transparent. Colored transparent objects reflect only that color. All other colors are absorbed. Have you ever seen sunglasses that are tinted blue? They reflect blue frequencies. If you wore them, everything would look blue! They absorb all other colors.

Particles of a gas are the farthest apart. One vibrating gas particle takes time to reach another particle. Sound waves travel slowest in a gas.

Space is a vacuum, or an empty place with no particles of matter. There is no medium for sound to travel through. There is total silence in outer space.

## Echoes

If a sound wave hits a hard, smooth surface, it bounces back. The reflected sound is called an echo. Scientists send sound waves to hit the ocean floor. These waves then bounce back to the ocean's surface. Scientists measure the time the echo takes to come back. This tells them how deep the ocean is.

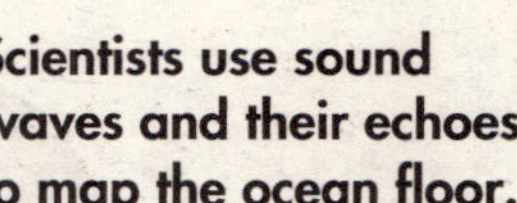

Scientists use sound waves and their echoes to map the ocean floor.

# How is sound made?

## Loudness

One way to describe a sound is by how loud it is. A shout is much louder than a whisper. Loudness is a measure of how strong a sound is to our ears. Loudness depends on the amount of energy in a sound wave.

A sound gets louder as you get closer to it. It is softer when you are farther away. Sound waves do not lose their energy when they travel through air. The sound is softer when you are farther away because the energy spreads out over a larger area.

Blowing across the hole in a flute makes the column of air inside it vibrate.

Rubbing a bow across the strings of a violin makes them vibrate.

*Absorption*

## Color and Light

We see objects of many different colors because objects absorb some frequencies of light and reflect others. The red shirt below reflects light rays of the red frequency. The shirt absorbs rays of other visible color frequencies.

An object that is white, such as a white shirt, does not absorb color frequencies in the visible spectrum. It reflects all of them. When all light frequencies are blended together, they look white. Objects that are black, however, absorb all color frequencies. No light rays are reflected. On a sunny day, black objects feel warm. The light energy they absorb turns into heat energy.

# How do light and matter interact?

## Light and Matter

Light rays can pass through an object. They can reflect off the object. They can also be absorbed by the object.

Light waves reflect off most objects. Sometimes they reflect only a little bit. **Reflection** means that light rays bounce, or reflect, off a surface back to our eyes. A mirror reflects almost all the light rays that hit it. The rays reflect back to your eyes at the same angle, letting you see a clear image of yourself.

Some light waves are absorbed. **Absorption** means that an object takes in light waves. Light waves become a form of heat energy when they are absorbed.

*Reflection*

## Pitch

Sounds also have different pitches. **Pitch** is how high or low a sound seems. It depends on the sound's frequency. Objects that vibrate quickly have a high frequency. They also have a high pitch. Objects that vibrate slowly have a low frequency. They also have a low pitch. The material an object is made of affects how it vibrates. The size and shape of an object also have an effect on the sound.

A tuning fork has a single pitch when it is struck.

A gong vibrates when it is hit. It produces a blend of pitches.

## How Instruments Make Sound

Guitars, violins, and harps make sounds when their strings are plucked, rubbed, or hit. The vibrations move through the instrument.

Tightening the strings on a guitar makes a higher-pitched sound. Loosening the strings will lower the pitch. Sound waves travel slowly through thick, heavy strings. These strings produce lower pitches. Waves travel faster through the thinner strings. These strings have higher pitches.

A tuning key is used to tighten or loosen each string.

## Percussion Instruments

Percussion instruments make sounds when you shake or hit them. The material stretched across the top of a drum vibrates to make a sound. Other percussion instruments are xylophones and maracas.

## The Piano

When a piano key is pressed, a padded hammer hits a group of strings. The strings vibrate. They produce a tone.

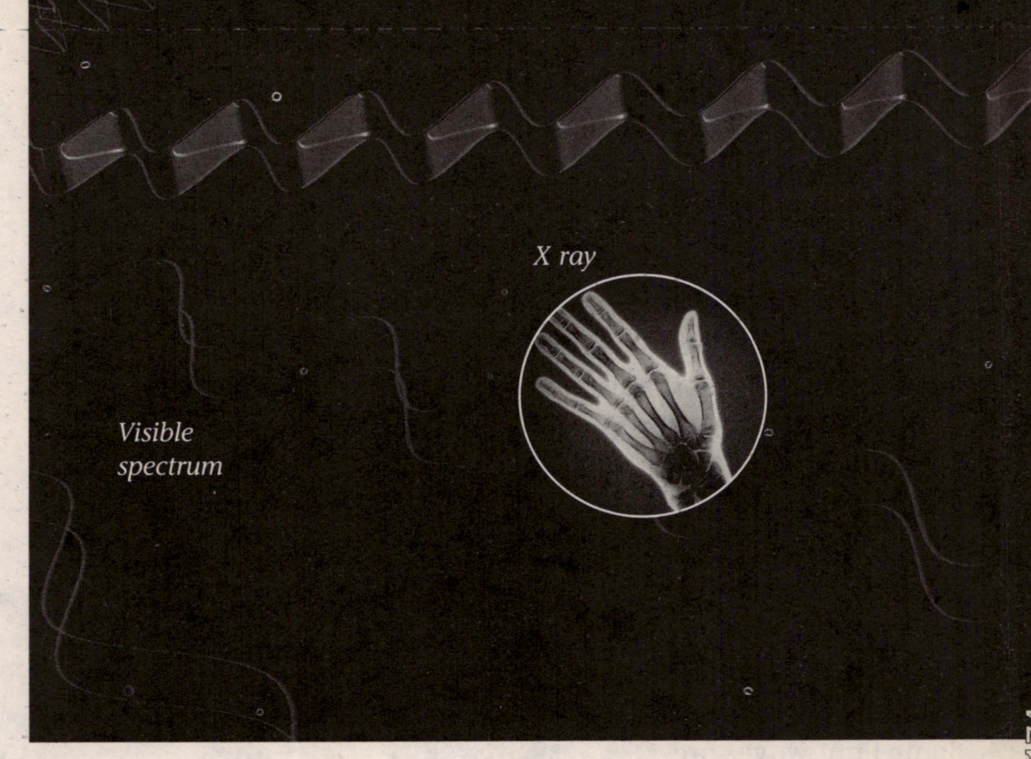


## Electromagnetic Waves We Cannot See

Radio waves, microwaves, and infrared waves have wavelengths that are too long for us to see. Ultraviolet waves, X rays, and gamma rays have wavelengths that are too short for us to see. The shortest waves have the highest energy.

All waves on the electromagnetic spectrum travel at the same speed through space. They carry energy. Objects can absorb this energy and change it into different forms of energy, such as heat.

High-energy waves can be helpful. In small amounts, ultraviolet waves can kill bacteria. Doctors use X rays to see broken bones. But high-energy waves can also have harmful effects. Too much exposure to ultraviolet waves from the Sun can damage your eyes or cause sunburn or cancer.

## Wind Instruments

Musicians blow air into wind instruments. Particles of air inside the instrument vibrate to make sounds. Shorter wind instruments make sounds with a higher pitch.

## How We Hear

Sound waves hit the eardrum, making it vibrate. This causes three tiny bones to vibrate. Because of their shapes, the bones are called the hammer, the stirrup, and the anvil. Next, the vibration moves to an organ called the cochlea. Liquid in the cochlea vibrates, making tiny hairs in the cochlea move. These vibrations travel as signals to the brain. The brain understands the signals as sounds.

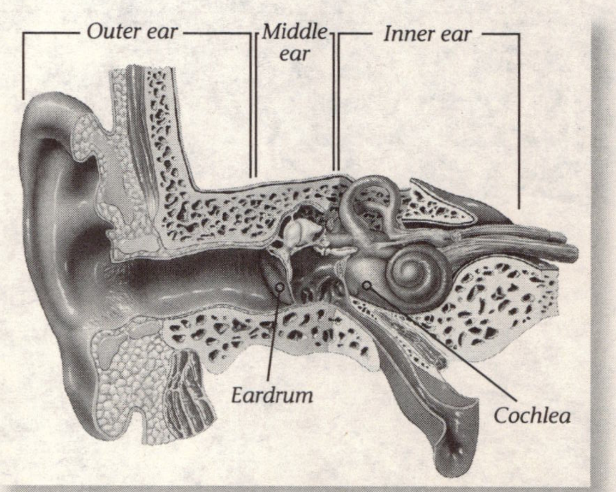




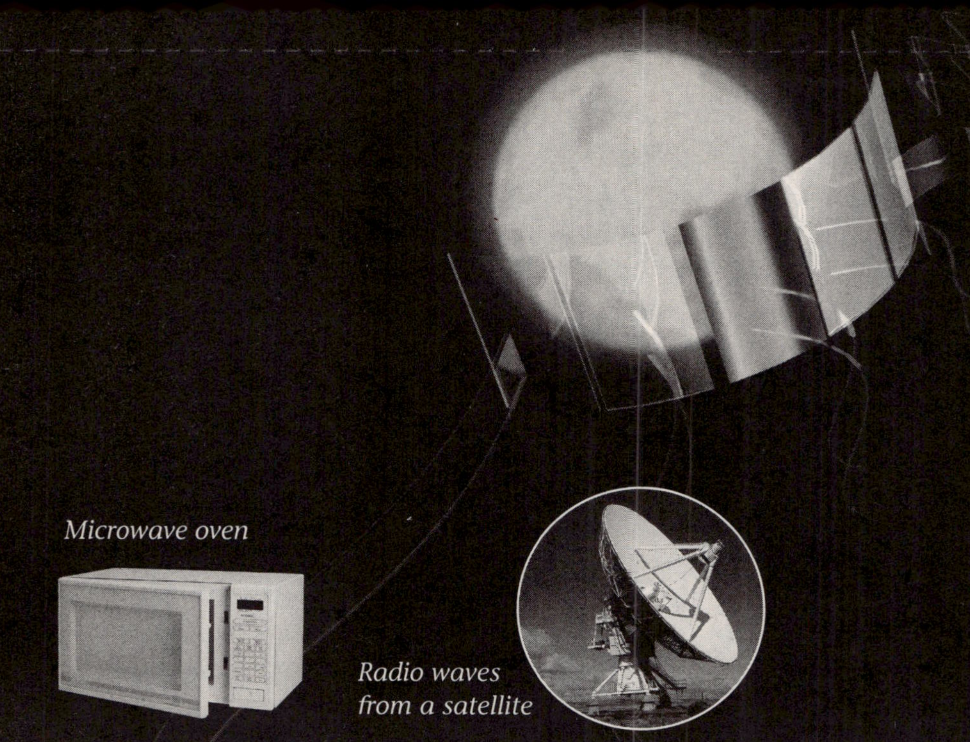


## Light Waves We See

All forms of light energy are called electromagnetic radiation. The most familiar form of electromagnetic waves is visible light, which is the light we see.

Light energy travels as waves. But your eyes can see only certain wavelengths and frequencies. These are the colors in the visible spectrum. White light, such as the light from a lamp or the Sun, is a blend of the colors in a rainbow. White light can separate into its colors when it travels through raindrops. The colors that make up white light are red, orange, yellow, green, blue, and violet.

The order of the colors in a rainbow is always the same. Each color has a certain wavelength and frequency. As you move from left to right on the visible spectrum, wavelength decreases. But frequency increases.

# What is light energy?

## Sources of Light

Light is a form of energy, just as sound is. Light can come from different sources, such as the Sun, a firefly, and a bonfire. The Sun provides Earth with a constant supply of heat and energy. Plants would not be able to grow without sunlight. People and animals cannot survive without plants.

Some animals give off light. This is called bioluminescence. Chemical reactions inside their bodies produce this light.

The discovery of fire allowed humans to make their own light. People could start fires to stay warm, cook food, and work after it was dark.

The firefly is bioluminescent.

## Shadows

Light travels in straight lines called rays. Light rays spread out from the light source. Look at a shadow to see how light travels.

Hold your hand in front of a wall. Shine a flashlight on it. You will see a shadow in the shape of your hand on the wall. Your hand is blocking the light rays. They cannot reach the wall. The size of a shadow can change. If your hand is close to the flashlight but far from the wall, the shadow will be larger than your hand.

The angle from which light strikes an object also changes the size of the shadow. Your shadow is small at noon, when the Sun appears high in the sky. Your shadow is longer early or late in the day, when the Sun appears lower in the sky.

Physical Science

# Objects in Motion

by Kimberly Taylor

| Genre | Comprehension Skill | Text Features | Science Content |
|---|---|---|---|
| Nonfiction | Sequence | • Captions<br>• Labels<br>• Call Outs<br>• Glossary | Motion |

Scott Foresman Science 4.15

PEARSON
Scott Foresman

DK

scottforesman.com

ISBN 0-328-13901-7

90000

9 780328 139019

## What did you learn?

1. How is motion measured?

2. What are some effects that force can have on moving objects?

3. List two types of energy. Give an example of how energy can change from one type to another.

4. **Writing** in Science The amount of friction between objects depends on each object's surface and weight. On your own paper, write a description of the effect that friction has on objects of different surfaces and weights. Include details from the book to support your answer.

5. **Sequence** Two dogs pull a toy with the same size force but in opposite directions. What will happen next if one dog pulls with more force?



**Photographs:** Every effort has been made to secure permission and provide appropriate credit for photographic material. The publisher deeply regrets any omission and pledges to correct errors called to its attention in subsequent editions. Unless otherwise acknowledged, all photographs are the property of Scott Foresman, a division of Pearson Education. Photo locators denoted as follows: Top (T), Center (C), Bottom (B), Left (L), Right (R), Background (Bkgd).
Opener: ©Alan Schein Photography/Corbis; Title Page: ©Michael S. Lewis/Corbis; 1 Getty Images; 3 ©Jim Craigmyle/Corbis; 4 ©Scott T. Smith/Corbis; 5 ©Tom & Dee Ann McCarthy/Corbis; 6 ©Robin Smith/Getty Images; 9 Jane Burton/©DK Images; 10 ©Bill Bachmann/PhotoEdit; 11 ©Stanley R. Shoneman/Omni-Photo Communications, Inc.; 12 (BL) ©World Perspectives/Getty Images, (TR) ©DK Images; 13 ©DK Images; 14 (BL) ©John Lund/Getty Images, (BR) ©Michael S. Lewis/Corbis; 15 ©Royalty-Free/Corbis

ISBN: 0-328-13901-7

## Glossary

| | |
|---|---|
| **force** | any push or pull |
| **frame of reference** | the point of view from which you detect motion |
| **friction** | the force that acts when two surfaces rub together |
| **gravity** | the force that makes objects pull toward each other |
| **kinetic energy** | the energy of motion |
| **potential energy** | stored kinetic energy |
| **relative motion** | the change in one object's position compared to another object's position |
| **speed** | the rate at which an object changes position |
| **velocity** | the speed and the direction in which an object is moving |
| **work** | the ability to move something or make a change |

# Objects in Motion

## by Kimberly Taylor

# What is motion?

## Types of Motion

An object can move in a straight line. A train on a track often travels in a straight line. A baseball player usually runs from base to base in a straight line.

An object can also move in a curved path. A car moves in a curved path when it turns a corner. Curved motion takes place around a center point. A bicycle wheel moves in a curved path around its axle.

An object can also move back and forth. Plucking a guitar string makes it move back and forth. This motion is called a vibration.

## Changing Kinds of Energy

Wind the spring of a toy bird. Each turn winds the spring inside the toy tighter. This adds more stored, or potential, energy. When you release the toy, the bird hops forward as the spring unwinds. The energy stored in the spring changes into kinetic energy.

You can change a rock's potential energy into kinetic energy by pushing it so that it starts to roll down a hill. The total amount of energy always stays the same. Energy cannot be made or destroyed.

## Energy and Motion

Energy is the ability to do work. **Work** is the ability to move something. Work causes a change. Any change in motion requires energy.

**Kinetic energy** is the energy of motion. All moving things have kinetic energy. The faster an object moves, the more kinetic energy it has. The amount of kinetic energy depends on an object's mass and speed.

## Stored Energy

The swing in the picture stops briefly when it reaches the top of its path. The stopped swing has **potential energy,** or energy that is stored. Potential energy changes into kinetic energy once the swing begins to move again.

An object that has been stretched or squeezed has potential energy. A wind up toy has potential energy in its tightened spring.

A wrecking ball has a lot of kinetic energy before it crashes into a building.



When you walk down the street, you pass objects that do not move. You know you are moving when you pass a fixed object. If you stand still, you know that a car is moving because its position changes. You can compare how objects seem to change their positions. The change in an object's position compared to another object's position is **relative motion.**

From your position on the sidewalk, you see the bus change position as it moves toward you.

The toy cars move in different paths around the track.

## How You Know You Are Moving

How do you know if someone on a water slide is moving? How do you know if the water moves? You can see how the positions of the water and the person change. You see their positions changing compared to the slide.

Your **frame of reference** is made up of the objects you use to notice movement. It is your point of view. How an object seems to move depends on your frame of reference.

## Measuring Force

You can measure force with a spring scale. A spring scale has a hook on the bottom. When you hang an object from the hook, the spring inside stretches. The object's weight determines how much the spring stretches. Weight is a measure of the force of gravity that acts on an object's mass. A heavy object has a strong force. A strong force will make the spring stretch more.

A marker on the scale moves along a number line as the spring stretches. The numbers on the scale show a unit of force called the newton. The newton was named after Sir Isaac Newton, who explained how motion and force are related. It takes about one newton of force to lift a small apple.

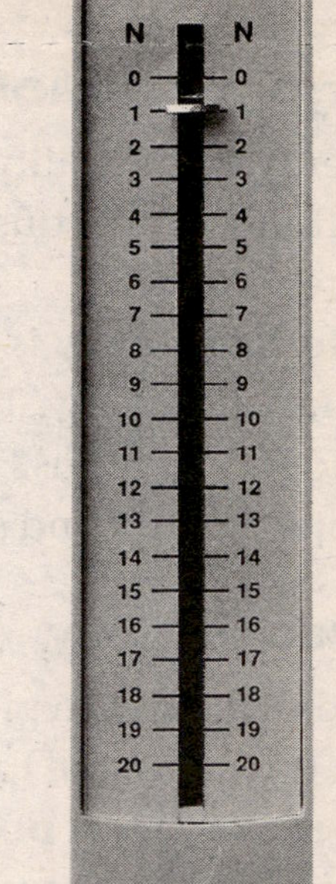


Spring scale

# How are force, mass, and energy related?

## The Force of Gravity

A ball falls to the ground when you drop it. The force that acts on the ball to make it fall is called gravity. **Gravity** is a force that makes objects pull toward each other. The amount of force between two objects depends on the distance between them and their masses.

If objects are close together, the force of gravity is strong. Gravity is weaker when the objects are farther apart. As the mass of the objects is reduced, the force of gravity between them is also reduced. If the mass of one object doubles, the force of gravity between it and another object doubles.

Earth's mass pulls on a ball, causing it to fall. The ball also pulls on Earth. But the ball does not have enough mass to move Earth.

Suppose you are riding on a float in a parade. The float moves past people watching the parade, and you wave at them. From your frame of reference, the people seem to be moving. But the people haven't moved! As the parade moves, people on the sidewalk see you pass by. From their frame of reference, you are moving.

Suppose you are sitting at your desk in school. You would say you are not moving. If you use the Sun as your frame of reference, however, you would say that you, your desk, and your school are all moving. This is because you travel with Earth as it moves around the Sun.

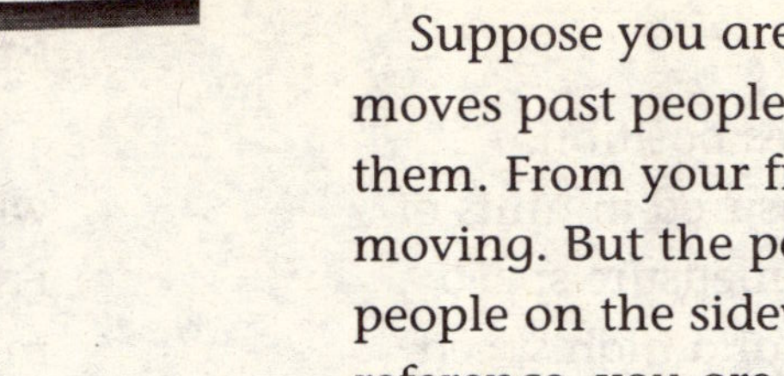

From your frame of reference on the bus, everything on the bus seems to be staying in the same place, and everything outside the bus seems to be moving.

The Moon has less mass than Earth. The force of gravity is not as strong on the Moon.

## Measuring Motion

**Speed** is the rate at which an object changes position. It tells how fast an object moves. Speed is measured in units of distance divided by units of time. One way to measure speed is in kilometers per hour. If one car is moving at a high speed and one is moving at a low speed, which one changes position faster? The car moving at a high speed does. You can find the average speed of an object. To do this, you divide the distance the object moves by the time it takes.

## Friction

**Friction** is a force that acts when two surfaces rub together. Friction can keep objects from moving. It can slow or stop moving objects. Friction depends on an object's surface and weight.

Rubbing together objects with rough surfaces causes a lot of friction. Rubbing together objects with smooth surfaces causes less friction.

A box of feathers is easy to push. The same box filled with books presses against the floor with more force. The box is harder to move.

You can reduce friction between objects. Wax or oil can make surfaces smoother. You need less force to move objects with less friction between them.

This Super Slide has a very smooth surface.

## Force and Motion

Two or more forces acting on an object in opposite directions can be balanced. The object does not move. A still object starts to move only when the forces acting on it change. Inertia is the resistance an object has to any change in motion.

A moving object also changes its motion only when a force acts on it. A moving object will keep moving at the same speed and in the same direction as long as balanced forces are acting on it. An object can change speed or direction if the force acting on it changes.

More force is needed to change the motion of an object with more mass. You can easily pull an empty wagon. When you put objects in the wagon, you add mass. You must pull with more force to move the wagon.

**Velocity** is both the speed and the direction an object is moving. Direction can be given by words such as *east, west, south,* and *north.* Other words that tell direction are *down, up, left,* and *right.*

An acceleration is any change in an object's speed or direction. Speeding up is an acceleration. Slowing down is also an acceleration. The speed of a roller coaster on a curved path does not have to change in order for it to accelerate. It accelerates because it changes direction as it travels on the curved path.

**These horses are using force to move the plow.**

185

# How does force affect moving objects?

## Force

A **force** is a push or pull. Force can make a fixed object move. It can also make a moving object stop, change direction, slow down, or move faster.

Sometimes a force must touch an object to have an effect on it. This is a contact force. You must hit a marble with an object, such as your finger, in order to make it move on a level surface.

Some forces can act on an object without touching it. A magnet can pull a piece of iron toward it without touching the iron.

Pushing or pulling can change an object's position and motion. A strong magnet can pull a piece of iron toward it from farther away than a weak magnet can. The change that takes place depends on how strong the force is.

## Combining Forces

Forces have size and direction. These dogs are combining forces. But they are working against each other. They are pulling the toy in opposite directions, but they are pulling with the same size force. The forces are balanced. The toy does not move. If one dog pulls with more force, the forces will not be balanced. The toy will move toward the dog that is using more force.

Sometimes more than one force acts on objects. If you and your friend push on opposite sides of a door with the same size force, the forces are balanced. The door will not move. If you push one side of the door while your friend pulls the other side, the forces are acting in the same direction. The door will move toward your friend. The total force on an object is found by adding all of the forces.

A moving marble hits one that is standing still. The contact force of the moving marble makes the other marble move.





186

# Simple Machines

by Martin E. Lee



| Genre | Comprehension Skill | Text Features | Science Content |
| --- | --- | --- | --- |
| Nonfiction | Summarize | • Captions<br>• Call Outs<br>• Diagrams<br>• Glossary | Simple Machines |

Scott Foresman Science 4.16

PEARSON
Scott Foresman

DK

scottforesman.com

ISBN 0-328-13904-1

9 780328 139040

90000

187

## Vocabulary

effort

fulcrum

inclined plane

lever

load

pulley

screw

wedge

wheel and axle

## What did you learn?

1. How is it possible to use force but not do work?

2. How can a pulley help you lift a load?

3. How is a screw a type of inclined plane?

4. **Writing** in Science A can opener is made of many simple machines. On your own paper, write a description of what simple machines are in a can opener. Use details from the book to support your answer.

5. **Summarize** Write a summary of how the three different groups of levers work.



**Photographs:** Every effort has been made to secure permission and provide appropriate credit for photographic material. The publisher deeply regrets any omission and pledges to correct errors called to its attention in subsequent editions. Unless otherwise acknowledged, all photographs are the property of Scott Foresman, a division of Pearson Education. Photo locators denoted as follows: Top (T), Center (C), Bottom (B), Left (L), Right (R), Background (Bkgd).
Opener: ©Royalty-Free/Corbis; Title Page: ©Lester Lefkowitz/Corbis; 2 Digital Vision; 4 (CL, BL) ©DK Images; 5 (TR, CR, BR) ©DK Images; 6 (CL) Brand X Pictures, (BC) Getty Images; 7 (CR) ©Tony Freeman/PhotoEdit, (BL) Andy Crawford/©DK Images; 8 (BR) ©DK Images, (BL) Andy Crawford/©DK Images; 9 ©Paul Almasy/Corbis; 11 (CC) Peter Arnold, Inc., (BC) Getty Images; 12 ©DK Images; 13 (L) ©Joe McBride/Getty Images, (CLT) Getty Images, (BL) Brand X Pictures, (BC, BCT) ©DK Images; 14 Corbis; 15 ©DK Images

ISBN: 0-328-13904-1

# Simple Machines

**by Martin E. Lee**

**Glossary**

| | |
|---|---|
| **effort** | a push or pull that makes a load move in some way |
| **fulcrum** | the support on which a lever and its load rest |
| **inclined plane** | a simple machine also called a ramp |
| **lever** | a simple machine made of a bar on a fulcrum |
| **load** | an object to lift or move |
| **pulley** | a simple machine made of a wheel with a rope, wire, or chain around it |
| **screw** | a simple machine made of an inclined plane wrapped around a rod |
| **wedge** | a simple machine made of two inclined planes put together in the shape of a V |
| **wheel and axle** | a simple machine that turns in order to move objects |

# What is a machine?

## Machines and Work

There are many kinds of machines. A machine can be just one piece, or it can have many parts. Machines make work easier. In science, work does not mean doing homework or chores. Work means using force to change or move something. The force can be a push or a pull.

How can you use a lot of force but not do any work? Suppose you push very hard on a brick wall. No matter how hard you push, you won't move the wall. Nothing moved and nothing changed. So you didn't do any work. Something must move or change for work to be done.

Here is another complex machine. It has a different power source than the can opener does. The can opener needs your muscle power. This machine gets its power from the Sun. The box on the left holds solar cells. These solar cells change energy from the Sun into electric energy that powers the machine.

Look at the rest of the machine. You can see wheels and axles. You can see gears. How do you think the gears change the direction of motion?

The machine is lifting a heavy load. The lifting part is a simple machine. Which one is it?

There are many kinds of machines. Some are simple, and some are very complicated. But they all help us do work with less force. They make our lives easier in many ways.





190

## Complex Machines

You can put simple machines together to do bigger or harder jobs. Complex machines are made of two or more simple machines that work together.

You may have a can opener in your kitchen. Is it like the one shown here? Look at it closely. Do you see the simple machines that make it work?

The circles you see may be wheels and axles. Some of the wheels have spikes or points. They are gears. The spikes are called teeth. Gears are often used in pairs. They change the speed or direction of motion.

Machines make work easier. Some simple machines help so you use less force to do a hard job such as moving heavy things. It takes more force to move a heavy object than a light one.

Other simple machines change the direction of force. You may push or pull in one direction. The simple machine helps you by changing the force to a different direction.

Some simple machines have just one or two parts. But they can help you do work. The lever, the wheel and axle, and the pulley are simple machines. The inclined plane, the wedge, and the screw are also simple machines.

## Levers

A **lever** is a long bar on a support. The support is called the **fulcrum.** The object you want to lift or move is the **load.** A push or a pull on the bar that makes the load move is the **effort.**

A lever adds to your force. It can also change the direction of the force.

The effort and the load on Lever A below are both four units from the fulcrum. The effort used is equal to the downward force of the load. The load on Lever B is closer to the fulcrum. You use the same effort to balance a larger load.

You can use math to show how a lever helps effort. Multiply effort by the distance from the fulcrum. The product is equal to the load times its distance from the fulcrum.

| Effort | × | Distance | = | Load | × | Distance |
|---|---|---|---|---|---|---|
| 4 | × | 4 | = | 8 | × | 2 |
|  |  | 16 | = | 16 |  |  |

### Lever A

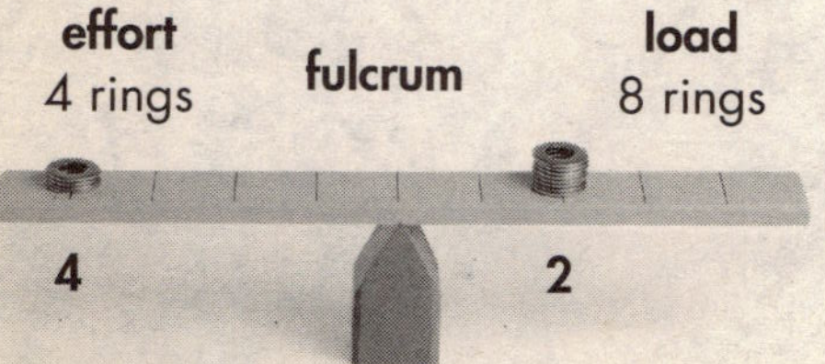


The fulcrum of Lever A is the same distance from the load as from the effort.

### Lever B



The fulcrum of Lever B is closer to the load than it is to the effort. The same effort balances a larger load.

## Screws

A **screw** is a small rod with slanting ridges wrapped around it. These ridges are called threads. The screw is a type of inclined plane. If you could unwrap a screw's threads, you would clearly see the inclined plane, pictured below.

Screws have many uses. They can lift things. They can hold things in place. A screw holds pieces of wood together better than a nail does. Why? A nail can slip out. But the threads make it hard to pull out a screw.

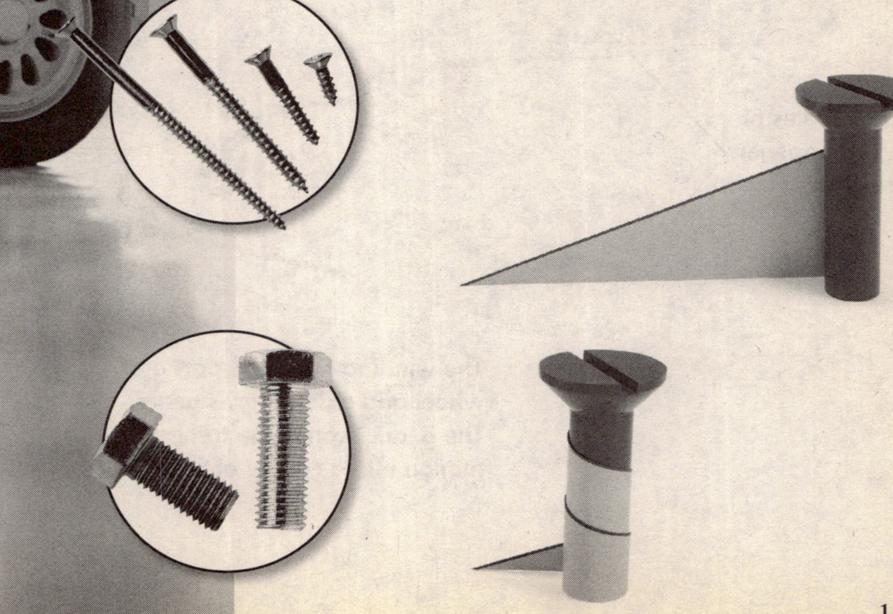

## Wedges

A **wedge** is a special kind of inclined plane. It is two inclined planes in the shape of a V. Usually a wedge must move to do its work. A force is applied to the wider end of the wedge. This makes the wedge move forward. The force drives the thin edge of the wedge into an object.

Wedges are used to move or split things apart. Sometimes wedges are used to hold things in place.

Look at the picture below. The force of the hammer pounds against the wider end of the wedge. This force drives the pointed end of the wedge into the wood. The wedge changes the downward force of the hammer into a sideways force. The sideways force splits the log apart.

**This wedge stops large objects from moving.**

193

12

## Types of Levers

You can sort levers into three groups. The fulcrum, load, and effort are in different places in each group.

### Groups of Levers

Some levers have two bars that work together.

### Group 1

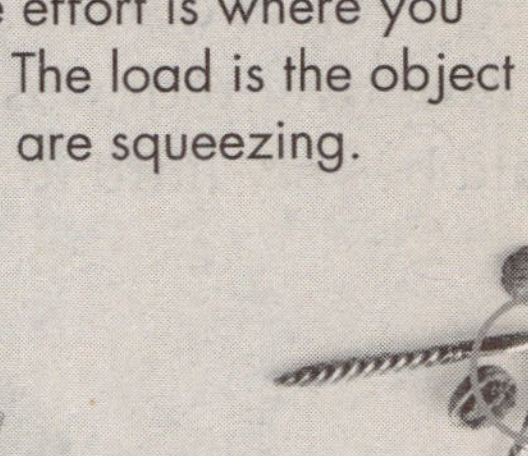

The fulcrum of the pliers is between the effort and the load. The effort is where you squeeze. The load is the object the pliers are squeezing.

### Group 2

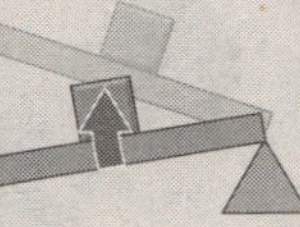

The fulcrum of the nutcracker is at the closed end. The effort is at the open end, where you squeeze. The load is the nut to be cracked.

### Group 3

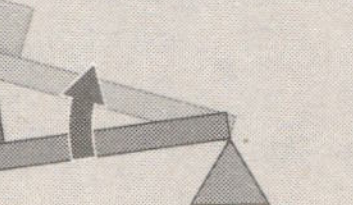

The fulcrum of the tongs is at the closed end. The load is at the open end, where you grab objects. The effort is between the fulcrum and the load, where you squeeze.

5

## Wheel and Axle

The **wheel and axle** is a special kind of lever. It moves or turns objects. The axle is a rod. It goes through the center of the wheel.

The steering wheel on a car is a wheel and axle. The axle is connected to the car's front wheels. This axle turns when the driver turns the steering wheel. The force the driver uses to turn the steering wheel is increased. This makes it easier for the driver to turn the car's wheels.

A screwdriver is also a wheel and axle. The handle is the wheel. The metal blade is the axle. The end of the blade fits into the top of a screw. The wheel increases the force you use. A screwdriver that was just a thin metal rod with no handle would be very hard to use!

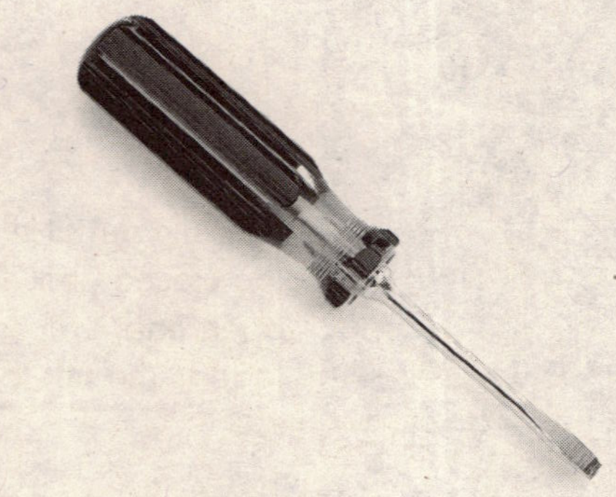

## Factors that Affect Force

Objects can move up or down on an inclined plane. It takes more force to move an object up a short, steep ramp.

Friction is a force that exists between two surfaces that rub against each other. Friction can slow things down. It makes it harder to drag, push, or slide objects.

A box at the top of a ramp stays there. Why? The force of friction balances the downward force of gravity. But suppose you put wheels on the box. Wheels take away most of the friction. The force of friction is now weaker than the pull of gravity. The box rolls down the ramp.

You need more force to move a heavy box up a ramp than you need to move a light box. Using more force allows you to move an object faster.

Less force is needed to go up inclined planes that aren't very steep.

More force is needed to go up a steep inclined plane.

# How can machines work together?

## Inclined Plane

Suppose you are trying to get a very heavy box of books onto your desk. The box is too heavy to lift. You might try pushing it up a ramp instead of lifting it. You could use a long, sturdy board for your ramp. Pushing the heavy object up the ramp would be easier than lifting it.

A ramp is a simple machine called an **inclined plane.** You use the same total force to lift an object straight up as you do when you slide it up an inclined plane. But with an inclined plane, you don't have to apply the force all at once. You apply less force over a longer distance.

Pushing the smaller box up the inclined plane takes less force than pushing the larger box up the same inclined plane.

A doorknob is a wheel and axle. You use force to turn it. The outer part is the wheel. This force is increased as it turns the small axle. The axle is a shaft inside the doorknob. The knob makes it easier to turn the thin shaft.

Look at the picture of the hose reel. The crank is the wheel. It is joined to the axle, which goes through the center of the reel. You use effort to turn the crank. With each turn, you wind up more of the hose. Soon you wind all of the long hose onto the reel. And it was easy to do!

## Pulley

A **pulley** is a wheel with a rope, wire, or chain around it. The pulley in the picture below is actually two pulleys. The top one is fixed in place. The bottom one moves up and down with the load.

A pulley changes the direction of force. In the picture, the force scale is measuring the force needed to raise the weight. The weight is pulling down on the pulley. The pulley changes the direction of the force. When you pull the hook at the end of the force scale down, the weight goes up.

You can reduce the amount of force you need to move a load by using two or more pulleys together. Look at the picture. There is only one length of rope between the top pulley and the force scale. But there are two lengths of rope between the pulleys. Both ropes carry weight. This means that less force is needed to lift the load.

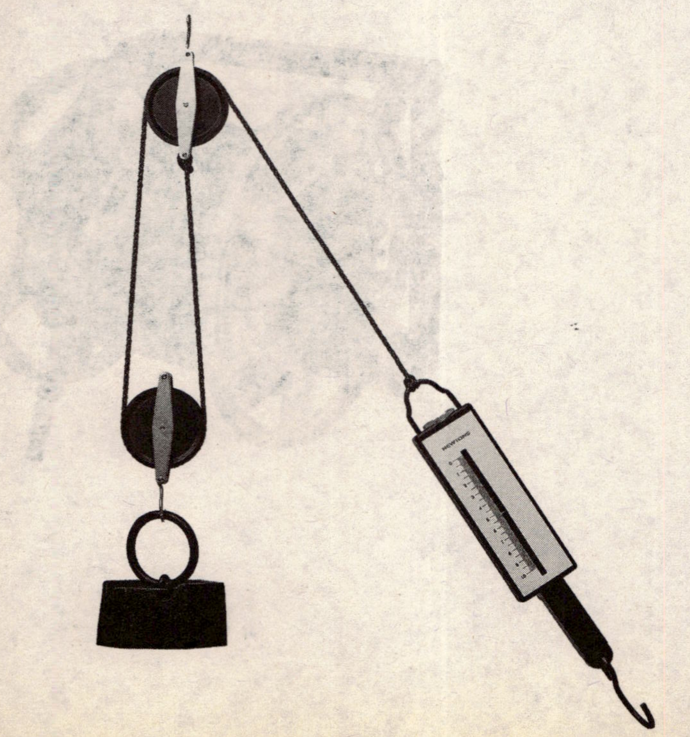

## Block and Tackle

Two or more pulleys make a system of pulleys. If one of these pulleys is fixed in place, the compound pulley is called a block and tackle. Adding more pulleys to the system reduces the effort you need to lift a load. Using more pulleys allows you to use the same force to lift more weight. The system on the left uses one pulley to lift a smaller weight. The system on the right uses more pulleys to lift a larger weight.

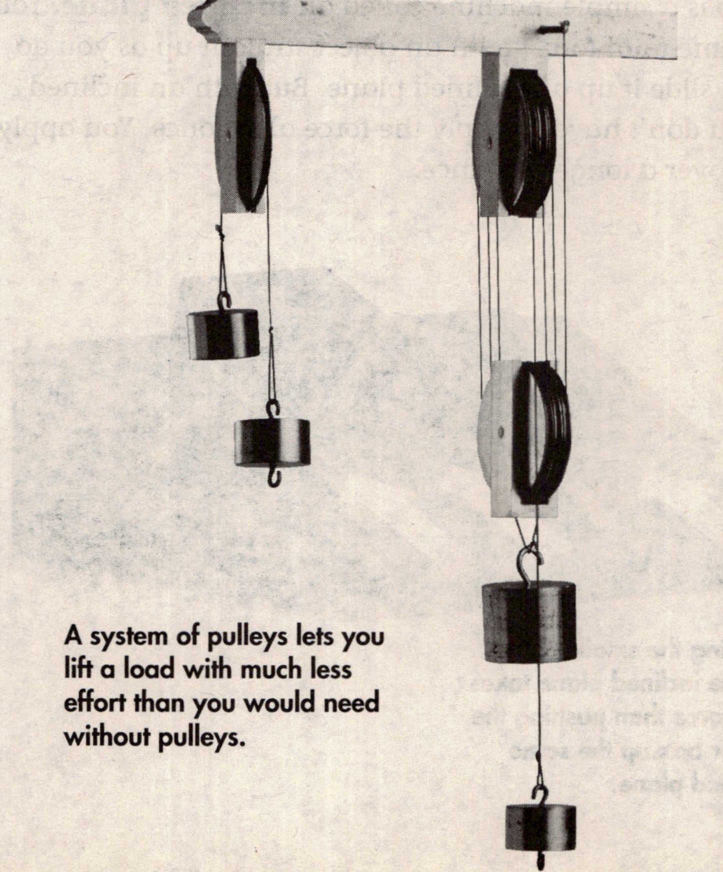

A system of pulleys lets you lift a load with much less effort than you would need without pulleys.

Space and Technology

# Earth's Cycles

by Carol Levine



| Genre | Comprehension Skill | Text Features | Science Content |
| --- | --- | --- | --- |
| Nonfiction | Cause and Effect | • Captions<br>• Diagrams<br>• Labels<br>• Glossary | Earth Cycles |

**Scott Foresman Science 4.17**

PEARSON
Scott Foresman

scottforesman.com

ISBN 0-328-13907-6

9 780328 139071

90000

## What did you learn?

1. Why do objects in the sky appear to move?

2. What is the difference between a partial eclipse and a total lunar eclipse?

3. Why is the number of daylight hours during the year different in some places?

4. **Writing** in Science  The Moon has several phases. On your own paper, explain what these phases are. Use details from the book to support your answer.

5. **Cause and Effect** What causes shadows to change?




**Illustration:** 8 Peter Bollinger
**Photographs:** Every effort has been made to secure permission and provide appropriate credit for photographic material. The publisher deeply regrets any omission and pledges to correct errors called to its attention in subsequent editions. Unless otherwise acknowledged, all photographs are the property of Scott Foresman, a division of Pearson Education. Photo locators denoted as follows: Top (T), Center (C), Bottom (B), Left (L), Right (R), Background (Bkgd).
Opener: ©Paul & Linda Marie Ambrose/Getty Images; Title Page: ©David Nunuk/Photo Researchers, Inc.; 2 ©David Parker/Photo Researchers, Inc.; 9 ©John Sanford/Photo Researchers, Inc.; 10 ©David Nunuk/Photo Researchers, Inc.; 11 ©Mark Garlick/Photo Researchers, Inc.; 12 ©Mark Garlick/Photo Researchers, Inc., ©Adrian Neal/Getty Images; 13 ©David Parker/Photo Researchers, Inc.; 14 Royal Greenwich Observatory/©DK Images; 15 Royal Greenwich Observatory/©DK Images

ISBN: 0-328-13907-6

# Glossary

| | |
|---|---|
| **axis** | an imaginary line passing from the North Pole through the center of Earth to the South Pole |
| **constellation** | a pattern of stars in an area of the sky |
| **eclipse** | the passing of an object in space between the Sun and another object, causing a shadow to be cast on the other object |
| **ellipse** | a stretched-out circle |
| **lunar eclipse** | the passing of Earth between the Moon and the Sun, causing Earth's shadow to be cast on the Moon |
| **orbit** | the path an object takes around another object |
| **revolution** | the movement of one object around another |
| **rotation** | the spinning of an object around an axis |
| **solar eclipse** | the passing of the Moon between the Sun and Earth, causing the Moon's shadow to be cast on Earth |

# Earth's Cycles

## by Carol Levine

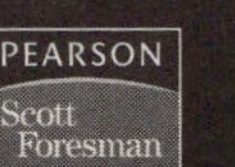

# How does Earth move?

## Earth Seems to Stand Still

Earth is moving steadily and smoothly all the time. You cannot feel it because you are moving with it! You move at the same speed as the part of Earth you are on.

How can you tell Earth is moving? One way you can tell is by looking at the sky. The Sun and stars seem to move across the sky. They seem to move because Earth is turning.

## Star Patterns

A **constellation** is a pattern of stars. Stars are often identified by the constellation they are in. Stars in the same constellation may not be close to each other.

Stars seem to move across the sky as Earth rotates. They seem to move in straight lines at the equator. They seem to move in circles at the poles. Constellations seen in the Southern Hemisphere are different from those seen in the Northern Hemisphere.

The North Star, or Polaris, appears in the sky above the North Pole. The constellation Cassiopeia is near Polaris. Its position changes during the year.

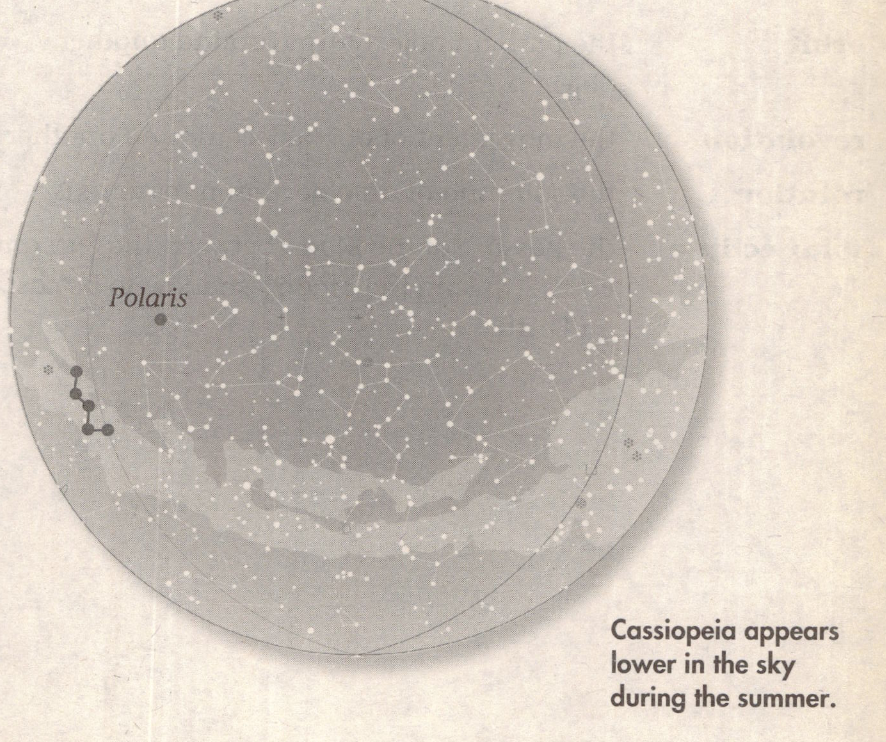


Cassiopeia appears lower in the sky during the summer.

# Stars

Scientists believe that there are 1 billion trillion stars in the universe. That number is a 1 followed by 21 zeroes! For Earth, the Sun is the nearest and most important star. Living things need its energy and light. The Sun is an ordinary star. Like all stars, the Sun is a hot ball of gas. Some stars are bigger, brighter, or hotter. Many others are smaller, dimmer, and cooler.

The bright light of the Sun keeps us from seeing other stars in the daytime. City lights and cloudy weather can make stars hard to see at night in some places. The light from stars that are very far away may seem dim. Some stars are so far away that they can only be seen with a telescope.

Another way you can tell that Earth is turning is by the change in seasons. Some places on Earth have dramatic changes in season. These changes are not as easy to notice in other places. Changes in season are caused in part by how Earth moves through space.

Scientists have learned a lot about stars since people began studying the sky thousands of years ago. Tools such as telescopes, cameras, and computers help them study Earth's movement.

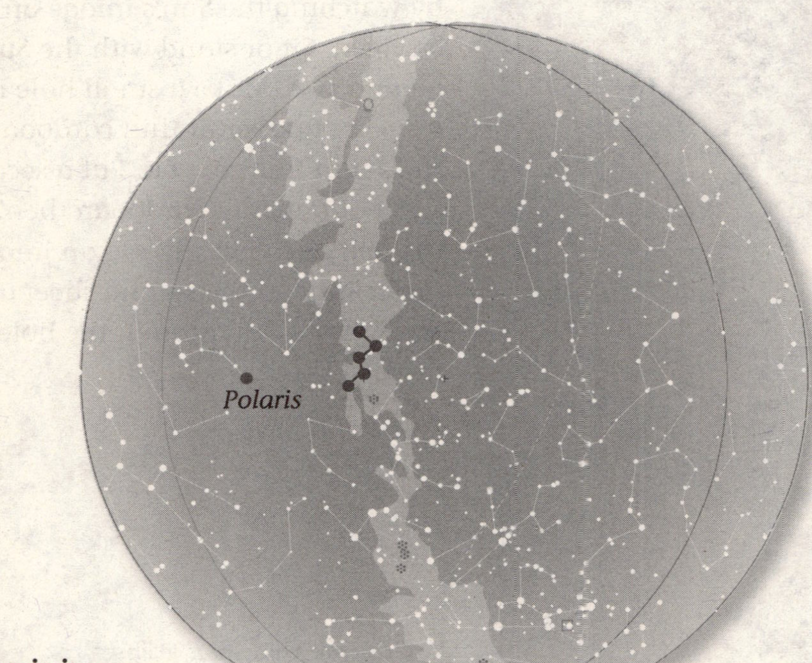

Cassiopeia is a constellation in the Northern Hemisphere. It appears high in the sky during late fall and winter.

# Earth's Rotation

A merry-go-round spins around a post in its center. Earth spins around an imaginary line that goes through its center. This line goes from the North Pole to the South Pole. It is Earth's **axis.**

The spinning of Earth around its axis is its **rotation.** One rotation of Earth is one full turn around its axis. One rotation of Earth takes almost 24 hours. Earth rotates from west to east. This makes objects in the sky appear to move from east to west.

Earth spins from west to east around its axis.

# Viewing a Solar Eclipse Safely

It is very dangerous to look directly at the Sun. It is even dangerous during an eclipse. It is not safe to look right at the Sun using binoculars, sunglasses, smoked glass, exposed film, or a telescope. The Sun can cause permanent damage to your eyes. It can even cause blindness.

You can see a solar eclipse safely by watching the Sun's image on a screen. Sit or stand with the Sun behind you. Make a small hole in a sheet of paper or thin cardboard. Hold it in front of you. Put a second sheet of paper or cardboard behind the first one. You will see an image of the eclipse on the second sheet as the sunlight passes through the hole in the first sheet.

You can watch a solar eclipse safely by projecting its image through a telescope onto a sheet of paper.

## Solar Eclipses

When the Moon passes between the Sun and Earth, it casts its shadow on Earth. This is a **solar eclipse.** The Moon's shadow covers only a part of Earth. The solar eclipse can be seen only from places on Earth where the Moon's shadow falls.

There can be solar eclipses two to five times each year. Total solar eclipses can last as long as 7.5 minutes. A solar eclipse can make the day seem as dark as night.

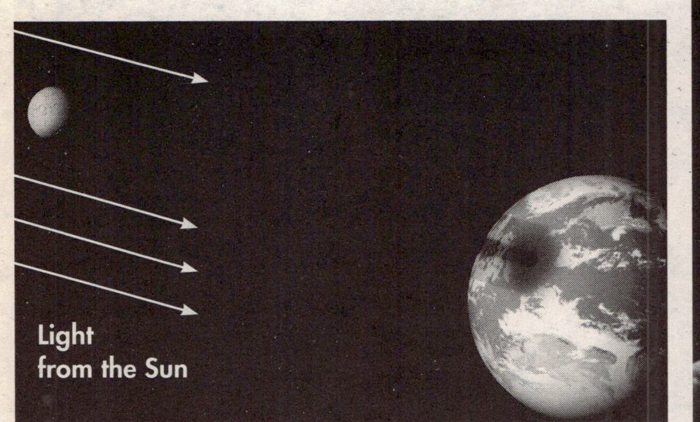


In a solar eclipse, the Moon is between Earth and the Sun. The Moon casts a shadow on Earth.

During a total solar eclipse, a bright ring of sunlight may appear around the Moon.



## Why Shadows Change

A shadow appears when light shines on an object but cannot pass through it. Earth's rotation causes the Sun to shine on objects from different angles at different times of day. Earth's rotation also causes the change from night to day and day to night.

## Daylight Hours

How do the number of daylight hours change during the year? Look at the chart below to see the data for a city in the Northern Hemisphere.

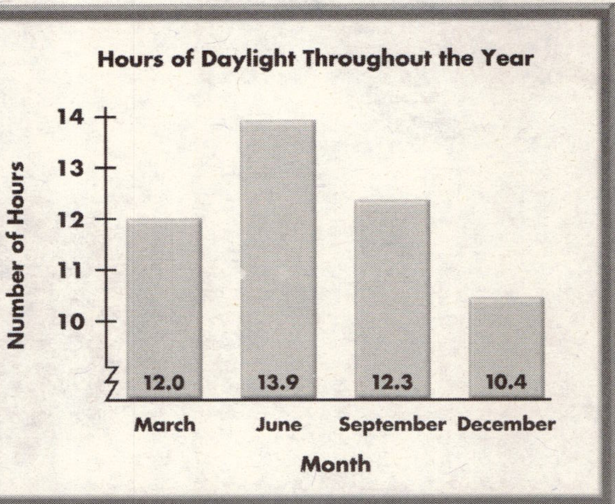

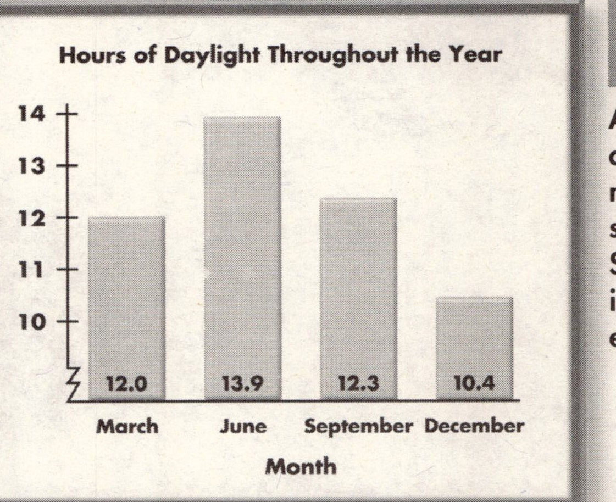


A short shadow appears around noon when the Sun seems high in the sky. Shadows are longer in the morning and evening.

## Earth's Revolution

Earth travels around the Sun as it rotates. The path Earth takes around the Sun is its **orbit.** A **revolution** is the movement of one object around another. One revolution of Earth is one complete orbit around the Sun. One revolution takes about 365 days, or one year. Earth travels about 940,000,000 kilometers during one revolution. Earth's speed is about 107,000 kilometers per hour.

The shape of Earth's orbit is an **ellipse,** or a stretched-out circle. Earth is closer to the Sun in some parts of its orbit. It is farther from the Sun in others.

Earth would fly off into space if gravity did not pull it toward the Sun. If Earth did not keep moving, the attraction between Earth and the Sun would cause them to crash.

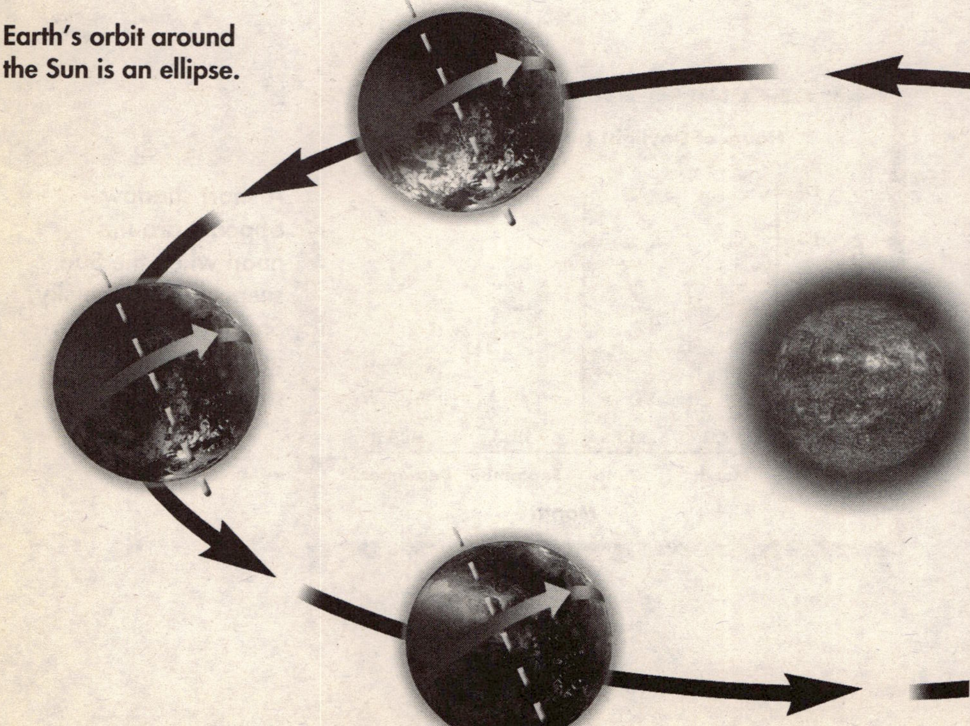

Earth's orbit around the Sun is an ellipse.

Sometimes only part of the Moon crosses Earth's shadow during an eclipse. This makes the Moon look as if something took a bite from it. This is called a partial eclipse. A total lunar eclipse happens when the entire Moon is in Earth's shadow.

A lunar eclipse may last 100 minutes. Several lunar eclipses can take place each year.

During a lunar eclipse, Earth is between the Moon and the Sun. The Moon is in Earth's shadow.

## Eclipses

An **eclipse** happens when one object in space comes between the Sun and another object and casts its shadow on the other object. This takes place when the Moon passes through Earth's shadow, and when the Moon's shadow falls on Earth.

Light from the Sun allows us to see the Moon. But during some full moons, the Moon and the Sun are on opposite sides of Earth. That means Earth is between the Sun and the Moon. The Moon will usually move above or below Earth's shadow. But a **lunar eclipse** happens when the Moon passes through Earth's shadow.



## Earth's Tilted Axis

Earth's axis is always tilted in the same direction. One end of the axis is always tilted toward the North Star. This tilt causes different places on Earth to face the Sun directly at different parts of the orbit.

When the Northern Hemisphere is tilted toward the Sun, the Southern Hemisphere is tilted away from it. The Northern Hemisphere has summer. Daylight is longer than night. More direct sunlight means temperatures are higher. At the same time, it is winter in the Southern Hemisphere. Daylight is shorter and the temperatures are lower. When the Southern Hemisphere is tilted toward the Sun, it is summer there.

In spring and fall, the number of daylight and night hours is almost the same. Temperatures are neither very hot or cold.

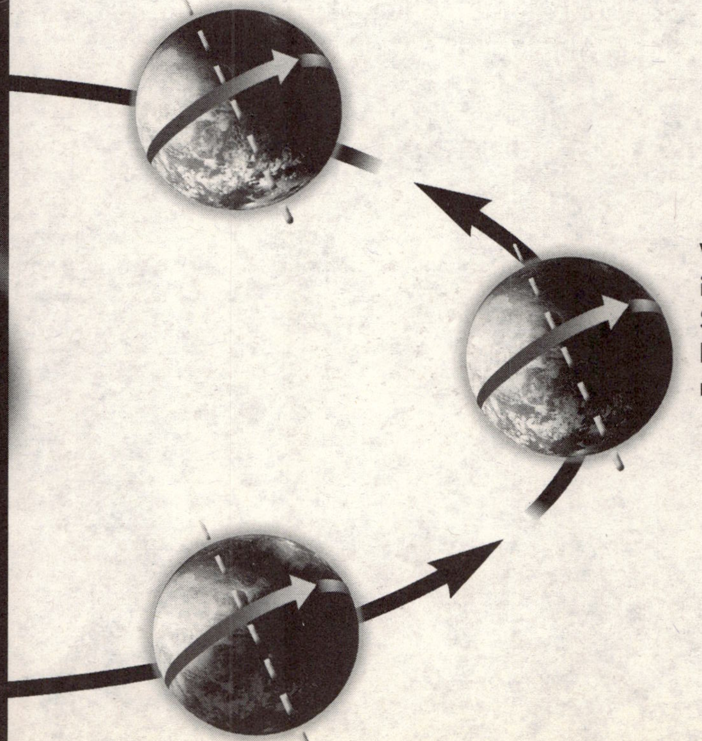

# What patterns can you see in the sky?

## Sun, Moon, and Earth

Sometimes the Moon can be seen at night. Sometimes the Moon can even be seen in the daytime. The Moon seems to shine. But it does not make its own light. Sunlight reflects off the surface of the Moon.

The Moon revolves around Earth. Its orbit is an ellipse. Gravity between Earth and the Moon keeps the Moon in its orbit. The Moon revolves around Earth in about 27 days.

The Moon also rotates around its axis. Each time it rotates one time on its axis, it also revolves one time around Earth. This causes the same side of the Moon to face Earth at all times. You can see only one side of the Moon from Earth.

## The Phases of the Moon

The shape of the Moon seems to change at different times of the month. These shapes are called the phases of the Moon.

Light from the Sun reflects off the surface of half of the Moon. When that half faces Earth, the Moon looks like a full circle of light. This is called a full Moon. When the Moon's dark, unlighted side faces Earth, the Moon cannot be seen from Earth. This is called a new Moon.

A crescent Moon is a sliver of lighted Moon. The first quarter is half of the lighted half we can see on Earth, or one quarter of the Moon. The last quarter is also half of the lighted half of the Moon. This happens after a full Moon. Soon a new Moon will begin a new set of phases.

*Crescent*

*First quarter*

*Full Moon*



*Last quarter*

*Waning crescent*

Space and Technology

# Inner and Outer Planets

by Kimberly Taylor



| Genre | Comprehension Skill | Text Features | Science Content |
| --- | --- | --- | --- |
| Nonfiction | Predict | • Captions<br>• Call Outs<br>• Text Boxes<br>• Glossary | Solar System |

Scott Foresman Science 4.18

PEARSON

Scott Foresman

DK

scottforesman.com

ISBN 0-328-13910-6

9 780328 139101

90000

## Vocabulary

astronomy

craters

galaxy

satellite

solar system

space probe

universe

## What did you learn?

1. What are some differences between inner and outer planets?

2. How were Mercury's craters made?

3. Why will astronauts' footprints remain on the Moon's surface for years?

4. **Writing** in Science  Neptune was discovered in 1846. On your own paper, describe how scientists discovered this planet. Include details from the book to support your answer.

5. **Predict** Do you think more moons of Jupiter will be discovered? Why or why not?



**Photographs:** Every effort has been made to secure permission and provide appropriate credit for photographic material. The publisher deeply regrets any omission and pledges to correct errors called to its attention in subsequent editions. Unless otherwise acknowledged, all photographs are the property of Scott Foresman, a division of Pearson Education. Photo locators denoted as follows: Top (T), Center (C), Bottom (B), Left (L), Right (R), Background (Bkgd).
Opener: ©Stocktrek/Corbis; Title Page: ©Mark Garlick/Photo Researchers, Inc.; 6 ©USGS/Photo Researchers, Inc.; 7 JPL/NASA; 8 Getty Images; 9 Getty Images; 10 JSC/NASA; 11 U.S. Geological Survey; 12 JPL/NASA; 13 (BL, R) NASA, (CR) Getty Images, (BR) JPL/NASA; 14 JPL/NASA; 15 ©Calvin Hamilton Solar Views; 16 (TL, BL) ©Mark Garlick/Photo Researchers, Inc.; 17 ©Mark Garlick/Photo Researchers, Inc.; 18 JPL/NASA; 19 ©Mark Garlick/Photo Researchers, Inc.; 20 NASA, 22 (BL) ©Mark Garlick/Photo Researchers, Inc.

ISBN: 0-328-13910-6

# Inner and Outer Planets

**by Kimberly Taylor**

## Glossary

| | |
|---|---|
| **astronomy** | the study of the Sun, the Moon, stars, and other objects in space |
| **craters** | bowl-shaped dents on the surface of planets |
| **galaxy** | a system of gases, dust, and billions of stars clustered together |
| **satellite** | an object that orbits another object in space |
| **solar system** | the Sun, the planets, their moons, and other objects that revolve around the Sun |
| **space probe** | a vehicle that carries cameras and other tools to study objects in space |
| **universe** | all of space and everything in it |

# What makes up the universe?

## The Universe and the Milky Way

The **universe** includes all of space and everything in it. Most of the universe is empty space.

A **galaxy** is a system of gases, dust, and billions of stars clustered together. The universe has millions of galaxies. We live in the Milky Way galaxy. The Milky Way has a flat spiral shape. There are billions of stars in the Milky Way. The Sun is one of these stars. It is near the edge of our galaxy.

Our solar system is only a tiny part of the gigantic universe. Earth is only a small part of the solar system. Mercury, Venus, Earth, and Mars are the four planets closest to the Sun. These inner planets are small and rocky. Jupiter, Saturn, Uranus, and Neptune are outer planets. They are gas giants with many moons. Neptune and Pluto are too far from the Sun to be seen without a powerful telescope. Astronomers have seen other objects beyond Pluto, but these objects seem too small to be planets.

## Sedna

Astronomers found Sedna in 2003. Some scientists think it is a tenth planet. Sedna is smaller than Earth's moon. But it is the largest body discovered in the solar system since Pluto. Sedna is as far as 84 billion miles from the Sun. Its temperature is –240°C. It is red in color, similar to Mars.

Scientists have seen other objects that are even farther out in the solar system than Pluto and Sedna are. But these objects are probably too small to be planets.

**Astronomy** is the study of the stars, the Sun, the Moon, and other objects in space. People have always been interested in objects in the sky. Experts think that the ancient Egyptians built the Great Pyramids to line up with the stars.

Other groups of people also studied astronomy long ago. Arabs, Chinese, Indians, Greeks, and others used astronomy to figure out the right time for planting or harvesting crops. Sailors used the Sun and the stars to find their way on the open sea.

## Our Solar System

The solar system includes the planets, their moons, the Sun, and other objects. All objects in the solar system revolve around, or orbit, the Sun. A planet is a large, ball-shaped object that moves around a star such as the Sun. A planet is smaller and cooler than a star.

The planets closest to the Sun are Mercury, Venus, Earth, and Mars. They are the inner planets. The outer planets are Jupiter, Saturn, Uranus, Neptune, and Pluto. An area with many asteroids is between the inner and outer planets. Asteroids are rocky objects that are too small to be called planets.

The Sun's gravity keeps Earth and other space objects in their orbits. The orbits of the inner planets are shaped like circles. The orbits of the outer planets are more like ovals.

## An Odd Orbit

Pluto travels around the Sun at a different angle than all the other planets do. Pluto has a tilted orbit. During part of its orbit, Pluto is closer to the Sun than Neptune is. This happened from 1979 to 1999. The next time this will happen is in 2237.

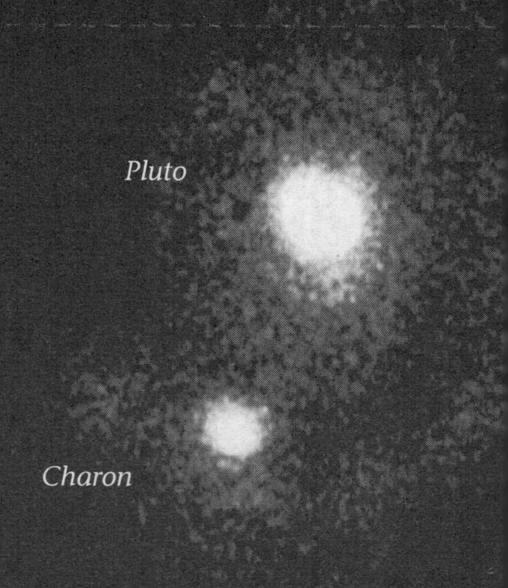

## Pluto

Clyde Tombaugh discovered Pluto, the smallest planet in the solar system, in 1930. It is even smaller than Earth's moon! Pluto is the ninth planet from the Sun. Unlike the other outer planets, it is not a gas giant. It has a solid, icy surface.

Charon is Pluto's only moon. It is smaller than Pluto. Charon and Pluto are very close together. Many astronomers believe Pluto and Charon are a double planet system. This is because they are so close together and so similar in size. They may share the same atmosphere when they are closest to the Sun.

## The Sun

The Sun is the largest object in our solar system. It is a medium-sized star. The Sun is a huge ball of glowing, hot gases. The inner parts of the Sun are much hotter than the outer parts. Energy from the Sun gives heat and light to Earth.

The Sun has magnetism, just as Earth does. The magnetic field around some parts of the Sun can be very strong. Hot gas can burst from the surface of the Sun and form loops in these areas. Sunspots are dark spots on the Sun. They appear at very strong parts of the magnetic field.

| Pluto Facts | |
| --- | --- |
| **Distance from Sun** | 5,906,000,000 km (3,670,000,000 mi) |
| **Diameter** | 2,302 km (1,430 mi) |
| **Length of day as measured in Earth time** | 6 day; spins backward |
| **Length of year as measured in Earth time** | 248 years |
| **Average surface temperature** | –223°C (–375°F) |
| **Moons** | 1 |
| **Weight of a person who is 100 lb on Earth** | 8 lb |

*The sizes and distances in this diagram are not true to scale. Also, the planets rarely line up.*

# What are the inner planets?

## Mercury

Mercury is the planet closest to the Sun. It has thousands of dents called **craters.** They were formed by meteorites crashing into Mercury's surface. A meteorite is a rock from space that hits a planet.

A **space probe** is a vehicle that uses cameras and other tools to study different objects in space. In 1974 the *Mariner 10* space probe was sent to Mercury.

## Too Hot and Too Cold

There is almost no atmosphere on Mercury. It is very hot during the day. Without an atmosphere to hold heat, Mercury is very cold at night.

**Mercury Facts**

**Distance from Sun**
57,900,000 km (35,983,000 mi)

**Diameter**
4,879 km (3,032 mi)

**Length of day as measured in Earth time**
59 days

**Length of year as measured in Earth time**
88 days

**Average surface temperature**
117°C (332°F)

**Moons**
none

**Weight of a person who is 100 lb on Earth**
38 lb

## How Neptune Was Discovered

Astronomer John Couch Adams studied objects in space, including planets. He noticed that Uranus wasn't orbiting the way he thought it should be. He felt that the odd orbit was caused by gravity of another planet. A mathematician named Urbain Leverrier also studied this idea. He predicted the position and size of the other planet. On September 23, 1846, Johann Galle pointed his telescope where the predictions said he should look. He saw Neptune!

## The Moons of Neptune

Neptune's largest moon is Triton. It has a surface temperature of about −235°C. Astronomers think that Triton formed farther from the Sun than Neptune did. They think it was captured by Neptune's gravity.

*Triton*

*Neptune*

*Neptune's ring*

# What do we know about Neptune, Pluto, and beyond?

## Neptune

Neptune is the smallest of the gas giants. It is the eighth planet from the Sun. Neptune is too far away to be seen without a telescope. Astronomers discovered Neptune in 1846.

Neptune has a very long orbit because it is so far from the Sun. One trip around the Sun takes Neptune 165 Earth years. Strong winds blow huge storms such as the Great Dark Spot across the planet.

Methane gas gives Neptune a blue color. It has bands of clouds and storms.

| Neptune Facts | |
| --- | --- |
| **Distance from Sun** | 4,498,300,000 km (2,795,000,000 mi) |
| **Diameter** | 49,528 km (30,775 mi) |
| **Length of day as measured in Earth time** | 16 hours |
| **Length of year as measured in Earth time** | 165 years |
| **Average surface temperature** | –214°C (–353°F) |
| **Moons** | at least 13 |
| **Rings** | yes |
| **Weight of a person who is 100 lb on Earth** | 110 lb |

## Venus

Venus is about the same size as Earth. It is the second planet from the Sun. Venus is very dry and hot, just as Mercury is. However, Venus has an atmosphere. This atmosphere is made of thick, swirling clouds. These clouds are very hot and poisonous. Venus has strong winds and a lot of lightning. Its clouds reflect sunlight well. At night Venus is one of the brightest objects we see in the sky.

| Venus Facts | |
| --- | --- |
| **Distance from Sun** | 108,200,000 km (67,200,000 mi) |
| **Diameter** | 12,104 km (7,521 mi) |
| **Length of day as measured in Earth time** | 243 days (spins backward) |
| **Length of year as measured in Earth time** | 225 days |
| **Average surface temperature** | 464°C (867°F) |
| **Moons** | none |
| **Weight of a person who is 100 lb on Earth** | 91 lb |

# Earth

Earth is the largest rocky planet in the solar system. It is the third planet from the Sun. It is the only planet whose surface has liquid water. In fact, water covers most of its surface.

Earth is surrounded by a layer of gas called the atmosphere. The atmosphere makes life possible. It keeps some of the Sun's harmful rays from reaching Earth. The atmosphere is mostly nitrogen, water vapor, carbon dioxide, and oxygen. Animals and plants use these gases. Earth is the only planet in the solar system known to have life on it.

## Earth Facts

| | |
| --- | --- |
| **Distance from Sun** | 149,600,000 km (93,000,000 mi) |
| **Diameter** | 12,756 km (7,926 mi) |
| **Length of day as measured in Earth time** | 24 hours |
| **Length of year as measured in Earth time** | 365 days |
| **Average surface temperature** | 15°C (59°F) |
| **Moons** | 1 |
| **Weight of a person who is 100 lb on Earth** | 100 lb |



# Rolling Through Space

Uranus spins on its side. No one is sure why it is tilted this way. Scientists think that a very large object may have hit Uranus when the solar system was forming. This bump may have knocked the planet on its side.

## The Moons of Uranus

Uranus has at least 27 moons. The moons closer to the planet were first seen through telescopes during the 1700s. They are large moons with steep ridges, craters, and deep valleys. The moons farthest from Uranus are hard to see from Earth, even with telescopes.

## Uranus

Uranus is the seventh planet from the Sun. It is the farthest planet you can see without a telescope. William Herschel discovered it in 1781. Uranus is a gas giant. It has an atmosphere of hydrogen, helium, and methane. Tiny drops of methane make a thin cloud that covers the planet. This gives Uranus its fuzzy, blue–green appearance. The temperature on Uranus is very cold.

Uranus has a ring system and many moons. The rings are dark and hard to see from Earth.

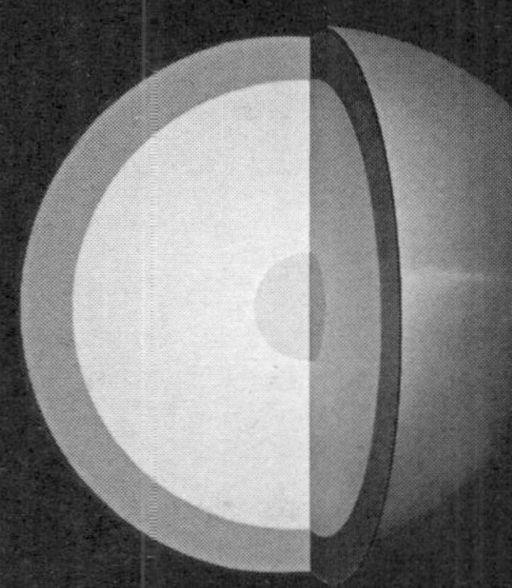

Uranus, a gas giant, has a large, liquid core.

### Uranus Facts

**Distance from Sun**
2,871,000,000 km (1,784,000,000 mi)

**Diameter**
51,118 km (31,763 mi)

**Length of day as measured in Earth time**
17 hours (spins backward)

**Length of year as measured in Earth time**
84 years

**Average surface temperature**
−216°C (−357°F)

**Moons**
at least 27

**Rings**
yes

**Weight of a person who is 100 lb on Earth**
86 lb

## The Moon

A satellite is an object that orbits another object in space. Moons are satellites of planets. They revolve around planets just as planets revolve around the Sun. A moon stays in orbit around a planet because of the force of gravity between the moon and the planet.

Earth has one moon. Earth is about four times the size of its moon. The Moon has no atmosphere. It has many craters caused by meteorites.

# Exploring the Moon

*Sputnik* was the first artificial satellite. It was launched in 1957 by the former Soviet Union. In 1959, the Soviet Union sent the first probes to the Moon. No people were on these probes.

The first person to travel in space was Russian cosmonaut Yuri Gagarin. In 1961, he circled Earth in less than two hours in the spaceship *Vostok I*. The first people to step on the Moon were Americans Neil Armstrong and Buzz Aldrin in 1969. Their footprints will stay there for years because the Moon has no wind or rain to wash them away.

## Saturn Facts

**Distance from Sun**
1,426,725,000 km (885,900,000 mi)

**Diameter**
120,536 km (74,897 mi)

**Length of day as measured in Earth time**
11 hours

**Length of year as measured in Earth time**
29.4 years

**Average surface temperature**
−178°C (−288°F)

**Moons**
at least 33

**Rings**
yes

**Weight of a person who is 100 lb on Earth** 74 lb

# Galileo's Handles

Galileo thought he was seeing a planet with handles when he saw Saturn through his telescope. The handles were actually the rings around the planet.

## Moons of Saturn

Saturn has at least 34 moons. Most of Saturn's moons are small. Titan is its largest moon. It has an atmosphere. It is larger than both Mercury and Pluto.

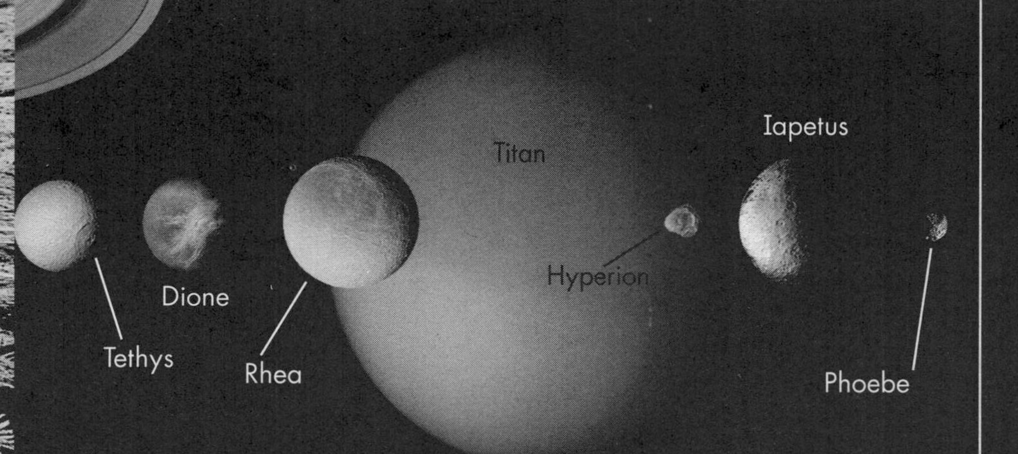

## Saturn

Saturn is also a gas giant. It is the sixth planet from the Sun. Helium and hydrogen make up most of its atmosphere. Saturn is huge, but it has only a small amount of solid matter.

The space probe *Voyager* explored the rings around Saturn. It found that the particles that make up the rings are many different sizes. Some are as small as grains of sand. Others are as large as boulders. The particles are probably made of rock, dust, and ice.

## Mars

Mars is the fourth planet from the Sun. It is covered by rocks and soil that are made of the mineral iron oxide. Iron oxide is reddish brown. Because of this, Mars is nicknamed the "Red Planet." Mars has two moons with deep craters. Phobos, one of its moons, is very close to Mars.

Winds on Mars cause dust storms that are large enough to cover the entire planet. There is not enough oxygen in the atmosphere of Mars to support life forms such as plants and animals.

Mars has volcanoes and a canyon that is bigger than Earth's Grand Canyon. Mars also has polar ice caps. Several probes have landed on Mars. They have sent data back to Earth.

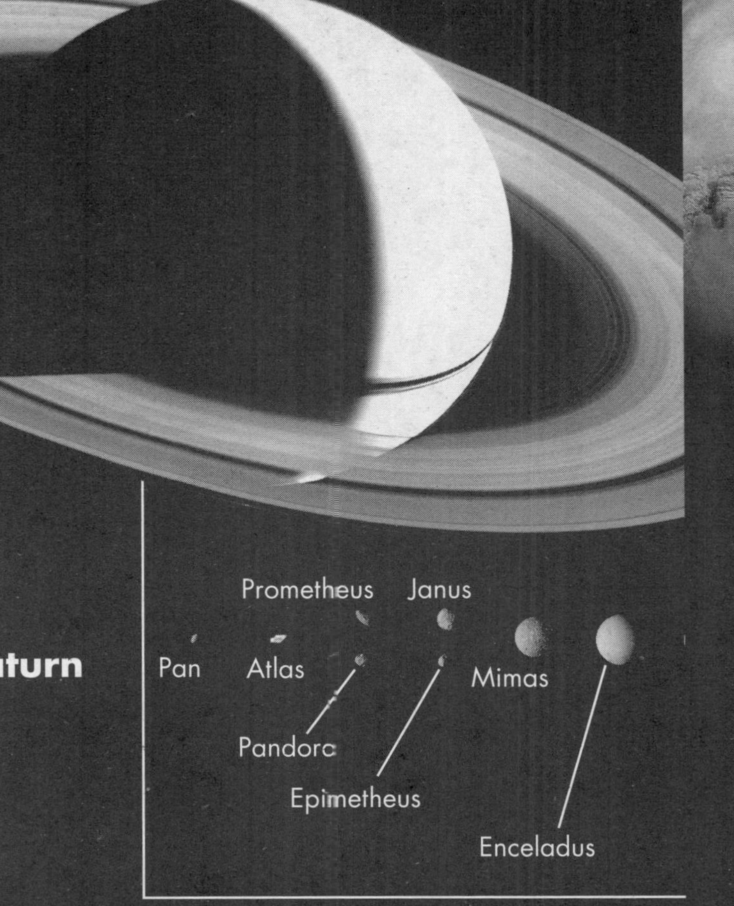



### Mars Facts

**Distance from Sun**
227,900,000 km (141,600,000 mi)

**Diameter**
6,794 km (4,222 mi)

**Length of day as measured in Earth time**
24.6 hours

**Length of year as measured in Earth time**
687 days

**Average surface temperature**
−63°C (−81°F)

**Moons**
2

**Weight of a person who is 100 lb on Earth**
38 lb

# What do we know about Jupiter, Saturn, and Uranus?

## Jupiter

Jupiter is the fifth planet from the Sun. It is the largest planet in the solar system. Jupiter is so big that all of the other planets would fit inside of it! Jupiter is a gas giant. A gas giant is a very large planet made mostly of gases. Most of Jupiter's atmosphere is hydrogen and helium. Jupiter has rings. They are too dark to be seen from Earth.

### Jupiter Facts

| | |
| --- | --- |
| **Distance from Sun** | 778,400,000 km (484,000,000 mi) |
| **Diameter** | 142,984 km (88,846 mi) |
| **Length of day as measured in Earth time** | 10 hours |
| **Length of year as measured in Earth time** | 12 years |
| **Average surface temperature** | –148°C (–234°F) |
| **Moons** | at least 63 |
| **Rings** | yes |
| **Weight of a person who is 100 lb on Earth** | 214 lb |

The Great Red Spot is a weather system in Jupiter's atmosphere. It has been active for centuries. It is more than three times the size of Earth.

## Jupiter's Moons

At least 63 moons orbit Jupiter. The four largest moons are about the same size as Earth's moon. The names of the four largest moons are Io, Europa, Ganymede, and Callisto. Io has the most active volcanoes of any body in the solar system. Europa has a frozen crust that may have a liquid ocean underneath. Ganymede is the largest moon in the solar system. It is bigger than Pluto and Mercury! Callisto has more craters than any other object in the solar system.

Space and Technology

# Effects of Technology

by Lorrie Oestreicher

| Genre | Comprehension Skill | Text Features | Science Content |
|---|---|---|---|
| Nonfiction | Main Idea and Details | • Captions<br>• Labels<br>• Call Outs<br>• Glossary | Technology |

Scott Foresman Science 4.19

## What did you learn?

1. What are some good and bad results of new technology?

2. What are three things necessary for communication to be successful?

3. How do transportation systems use computer technology?

4. **Writing** in Science Technology has led to many advancements in medicine. On your own paper, explain how doctors use technology to give better care to their patients. Use details from the book to support your answer.

5. **Main Idea and Details** What are some details that support the main idea that technology has changed the way we live?

222


**Photographs:** Every effort has been made to secure permission and provide appropriate credit for photographic material. The publisher deeply regrets any omission and pledges to correct errors called to its attention in subsequent editions. Unless otherwise acknowledged, all photographs are the property of Scott Foresman, a division of Pearson Education. Photo locators denoted as follows: Top (T), Center (C), Bottom (B), Left (L), Right (R), Background (Bkgd).

Opener: (TR) ©Royalty-Free/Corbis, (Bkgd) ©Yang Liu/Corbis; Title Page: ©Courtesy of the Museum of the Moving Image, London/DK Images; 2 ©Tibor Bognar/Corbis; 4 Getty Images; 5 Getty Images; 6 ©Stevie Grand/Photo Researchers, Inc.; 7 Simon Jauncey/Getty Images; 8 (CL) ©James King-Holmes/ Photo Researchers, Inc., (Bkgd) ©Matt Meadows/Peter Arnold, Inc.; 10 (BC) ©DK Images, (R) ©Dave King/DK Images; 11 (BL) ©Courtesy of the Museum of the Moving Image, London/DK Images, (CR) Tina Chambers/Courtesy of the National Maritime Museum, London/©DK Images, (BR) Getty Images; 12 (CL, BR, CR, CC) ©Bettmann/Corbis, (BL) ©Archive Holdings Inc./Getty Images, (BC) George H. Huey Photography, Inc.; 13 (BL) Dave King/Courtesy of the Science Museum, London/©DK Images, (CL) ©Museum of Flight/Corbis, (BC) ©Reuters/Corbis, (CR) Getty Images, (BR) ©Claro Cortes IV/Reuters/ Corbis; 14 ©Fukuhara, Inc./Corbis, Steve Gorton and Gary Ombler/©DK Images; 15 ©Tibor Bognar/ Corbis.



ISBN: 0-328-13913-0

# Effects of Technology

**by Lorrie Oestreicher**

**Glossary**

**communication**  the process of sending any kind of message from one place to another

**optical fibers**  thin tubes that allow light to pass through

**technology**  the knowledge, processes, and products that we use to help solve our problems and make our work easier

**telecommunications**  communications that are done electronically

**vehicle**  an object that carries passengers, goods, or equipment

# How does technology affect our lives?

## New Challenges

We use technology all the time in everyday life. **Technology** is the knowledge, processes, and products that we use to solve problems and make our work easier. Technology makes our lives more comfortable and healthy. It helps us get the things we need.

Technology affects all living things. Sometimes technology's effects are unplanned. These effects can be harmful to living things. Motor vehicle emissions, industrial wastes, and insecticides are some of these unplanned, harmful effects. The United States and other countries must deal with air, soil, water, and noise pollution.

New developments in technology have changed the way we live. Medical technology has improved the care doctors are able to give. Manufacturing technology has changed how products are made. Technology has changed the jobs that we do today. It has made our lives and jobs easier. Technology has improved the way people and things get from one place to another. It has increased the amount and kinds of food we grow. But, technology has also caused problems that people didn't expect. Perhaps new technology can solve these problems too.

Technology has brought us many new products. This could be the car of the future!

## The Technology of Time Measurement

Time can be measured in units such as seconds, minutes, days, and weeks. In a factory, how long do parts take to move through an assembly line? How long does it take to cross an ocean? How long does a truck take to move goods from one place to another?

Keeping track of time is important. Long ago, astronomers used the movement of the Sun to tell time. Later, people invented machines to do this. Today's clocks and watches measure time in seconds or even fractions of a second.

Many people wear watches so they know the time. The hands on a watch show the hours, the minutes, and the seconds.

Technology has changed the way we do our jobs. It has helped make work easier. Machines can produce more and do work faster than people can. Unfortunately, this can lead to people losing their jobs. Although technology can cause problems, at the same time it can also help to solve them. Some machines can do work that is too dangerous for people to do. New technology can also bring new jobs. Many of these jobs are in the electronics industry.

Technology may lead to more cities that look like this one.

## Technology and Materials

This in-line skater is using many products of technology. The materials in the equipment are not all found in nature. Many were made through technology. The in-line skates and protective gear are made from plastic, metal, rubber, and nylon. Some of these materials come mostly from natural resources. Others come from materials that have been made from natural resources.

Iron ore is a natural resource. It is used to make steel. You can find steel in the wheel bearings, screws, and axles of in-line skates. The plastic materials are made from chemicals. All of the plastic parts are shaped into the different pieces of equipment. Even clothing can be made from chemicals or recycled plastic materials.

Polyurethane comes from chemical technology. The wheels of in-line skates are often made of this material.

Helmets are light, but they have a hard outer shell. This helps protect the head from injuries.

Elevators, escalators, and conveyor belts also move people and goods. People design, build, run, and use these systems.

Today, computer technology often controls transportation systems. Computers keep systems running on time. They also keep the systems running properly. Space transportation uses computers and computer models. Scientists are able to solve problems such as weightlessness and airlessness from far away.

1914: Henry Ford's factory mass produces automobiles. More people can afford to own a car.

1959: Transcontinental jet service connects New York City and Los Angeles.

1964: High-speed electric "bullet trains" begin operating in Japan.

226

2004: In Shanghai, China, the world's first commercial maglev rail system begins operating.

## Transportation Systems

People and products move from one place to another using transportation systems. The people and goods are often carried in a **vehicle.** A vehicle may be a car, truck, train, ship, plane, or even a rocket. Vehicles travel on roadways, railways, waterways, and through airways. Today it may take just a few hours to make a trip that once took days or even weeks.

Engineers are always looking for new technology that will make vehicles safer. Seat belts, air bags, and bumpers make cars safer. But the cost of each improvement can raise the price of the vehicle.

1807: Robert Fulton builds the *Clermont*. It is the first steamboat that carries passengers—and stays in business.

1869: The transcontinental railroad across the United States links the East and the West. The railroad is completed at Promontory, Utah. The last spike is made of gold.

1903: Bicycle makers Orville and Wilbur Wright build a powered airplane. Orville flies 120 feet in 12 seconds.

## Technology Keeps Us Healthy

Technology helps produce new equipment. It also helps us stay safe and healthy. The gear worn by the in-line skater can absorb some of the impact of a fall. The helmet can help protect his head from an injury. The plastic cushions in the knee and elbow pads and in the wrist guards can help protect his arms and legs.



## Controlling Waste

When products are made, waste and pollution are also made. Some companies are trying to make products from materials that can break down and become part of nature again. Not all materials break down easily. Products that are made through technology often will not break down easily. Products such as plastic, glass, and aluminum should be recycled. Then they can be reused to make new products.

## Technology and Medicine

Medical technology has changed the tools and instruments that doctors use. These changes improve the care people receive. Doctors may now use lasers in operations instead of using sharp knives. Lasers can open up clogged arteries. They can even fix broken blood vessels.

Doctors also use **optical fibers.** These are thin tubes that let light pass through them. Cameras with optical fibers help doctors see inside the body. This helps doctors decide the best way to treat a problem.

Keyhole surgery has reduced the pain and recovery time of many surgeries. With this type of surgery, doctors make only a cut about the size of a keyhole.

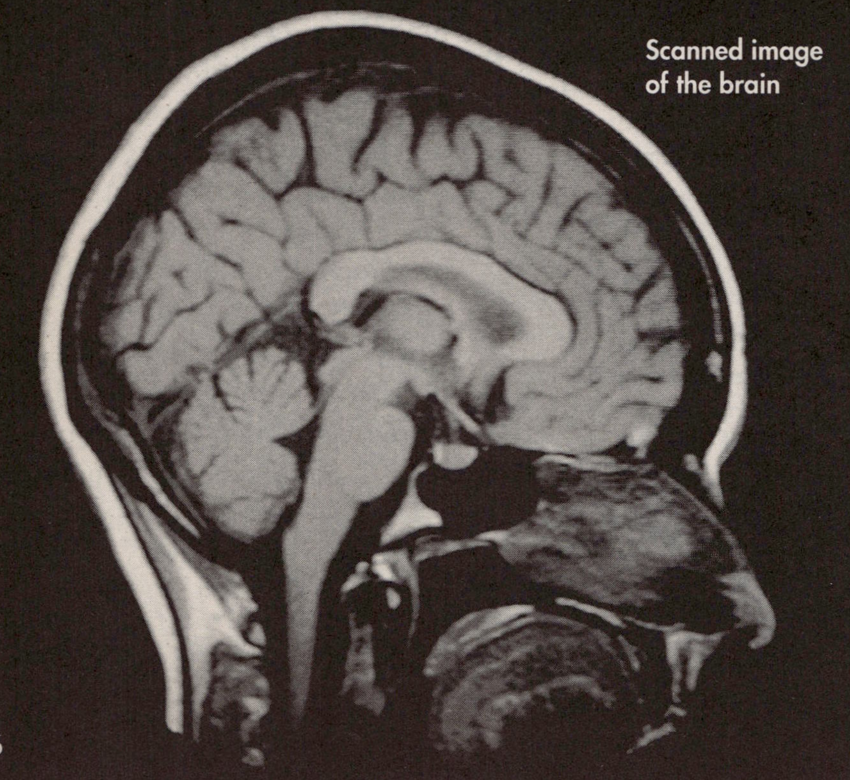

Scanned image of the brain

## Telecommunications

Electricity changed the technology of communication. With electricity, messages could be received in seconds rather than days or weeks. With new developments, people on different continents could talk to each other. Today, technology allows messages to reach hundreds of people almost instantly.

**Telecommunications** are communications that are done electronically. A signal with information is sent out through a transmitter. The signal reaches a receiver. The receiver changes the signal back to a clear message. Telephone, radio, TV, and other signals are sent from one part of the world to another by communication satellites. Information from satellites helps ships, cars, trucks, and aircraft find their way.

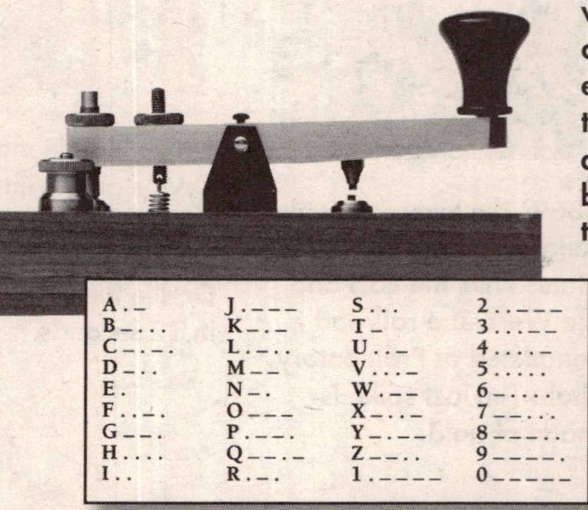

The electric telegraph was the earliest means of telecommunication. An electric current moved through a wire in short and long bursts. These bursts were the letters of the Morse code.

| | | | |
|---|---|---|---|
| A .- | J .--- | S ... | 2 ..--- |
| B -... | K -.- | T - | 3 ...-- |
| C -.-. | L .-.. | U ..- | 4 ....- |
| D -.. | M -- | V ...- | 5 ..... |
| E . | N -. | W .-- | 6 -.... |
| F ..-. | O --- | X -..- | 7 --... |
| G --. | P .--. | Y -.-- | 8 ---.. |
| H .... | Q --.- | Z --.. | 9 ----. |
| I .. | R .-. | 1 .---- | 0 ----- |

# How has technology changed communication and transportation?

## Communication

You are communicating any time you call someone, send a letter, or write an email. **Communication** is the process of sending any kind of message from one place to another. Communication helps you let others know what you need or what you are doing. Speaking and writing are two ways you can communicate.

Three things must happen in communication. You must send a message. The message must be received. Then it must be understood. Email is a form of communication. Letters send messages using ink and paper. Phones send messages using speech.

By 1455, Johannes Gutenberg had invented a system of making movable type with single letters.

The quill is the hollow part of a feather. Quills were first used as pens around A.D. 600.

## Technology and Food

To be healthy, you must make good food choices. We get our food from nature. To grow bigger and better crops, farmers use tractors, chemical fertilizers, and pesticides. By using these things, farmers can produce more. The crops they harvest provide the foods we need to be healthy. But the technology causes a problem if the pesticides and fertilizers harm the environment.

## X rays and More

Machines also help doctors know more about our bodies. The technology of the X-ray machine allows doctors to see inside our bodies. A broken bone is easier to fix once it is seen in an X ray. The X ray shows the doctor exactly where the break is and how the bone is broken.

Wilhelm Roentgen discovered X rays in 1895. At first he did not know what he had discovered. In science, the letter *X* represents the unknown. Roentgen called what he found X rays. This was the first time doctors could see inside the body without even touching it.

Dentists use X rays to help them find where a cavity may form in our teeth. X rays are also used to find tumors or help treat cancer. But too much contact with X rays can cause burns. It can even cause cancer.

Nuclear magnetic resonance, or NMR, is a technology that helps doctors find the chemical makeup of matter. Magnetic resonance imaging, or MRI, allows doctors to see things in our bodies that X rays don't show. This technology helps doctors give their patients better treatment.

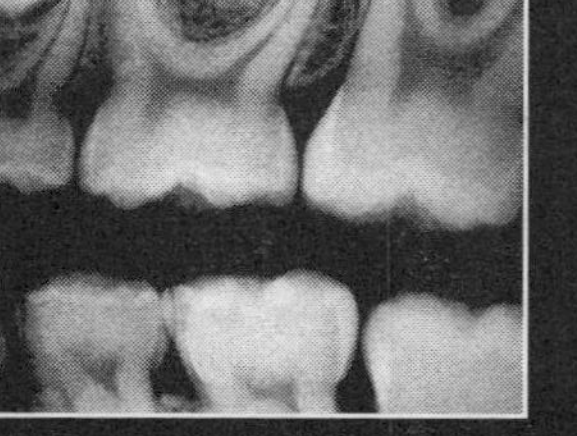

### How X Rays Work

X rays pass through skin and other organs. Bones, metal, and other objects block the rays and cast clear shadows on film. We call the shadow picture an X ray.